Supervision:
A Reappraisal

KEITH THURLEY
London School of Economics
and Political Science

and

HANS WIRDENIUS
Swedish Council for
Personnel Administration

Published in co-operation with the
Swedish Council for Personnel Administration

HEINEMANN : LONDON

William Heinemann Ltd
15 Queen St, Mayfair, London W1X 8BE

LONDON   MELBOURNE   TORONTO
JOHANNESBURG   AUCKLAND

First published 1973
434 91958 6

Printed in Great Britain by
Cox & Wyman Ltd, London, Fakenham and Reading

To Birgit and Fusae

Foreword

Much of the discussion about supervision arises from sloppy thinking. The group that has been called 'supervisors' seems to me to be just as meaningful a group as one that would come about by collecting red-haired, blue-eyed, and left-handed people out of the general population, telling them and ourselves that 'now we will look at the problems you have in common'.

The authors have realized that such is the basis of the problems that have been collected, more or less unthinkingly, under the heading 'Supervision'. They prove this by discussing how we define an elephant. I think that C. West Churchman once and for ever has clearly indicated that the usual story about the seven blind men who encountered an elephant in the jungle and defined what they thought they had come up against is a story about colossal arrogance. I quote: 'It assumes that a very logically astute wise man can always get on top of a situation, so to speak, and look at the foolishness of people who are incapable of seeing the whole.'

It is about time we realized that we have for a long period been constructing a non-existent elephant out of parts that have very little to do with each other, and naming the resulting mare's nest 'supervision'.

We should be grateful to the authors for emphasizing that a number of the problems we have been dealing with in early research have been pseudo-problems.

This makes the book difficult to accept. It goes against many commonsense opinions and against much training and tradition. It also indicates, by dissolving some of the general constructs we have been working with, that the problems to be attacked are much more numerous and separate in their nature than we ever imagined. We will have to accept that many of our approximate solutions, including those which are applied in practice, may be solutions of problems that do not exist.

I also think that the authors have proved satisfactorily that we have imagined the influence of formal supervision to be much greater than it really is. Recently we have had some research and more discussion about the impact of the non-formalized organization. Some have even ventured to apply percentage figures to the factors affecting supervisory activities in the enterprise, suggesting that only 15 per cent of all these activities are the result of the formalized organization, while the rest are due to the non-formalized organization.

This contributes to increasing the complication of the field to which the authors have applied themselves. I think this is something that we also have to be grateful for and accept. Their approach is much more realistic than has been the case with earlier analyses in this area.

We also have to take into account the necessity for foremen to be able to act flexibly, to adapt themselves to changing circumstances and to be aware that the situations and the people with whom they work keep changing constantly.

It seems to me that the moral of this is a very important one: *It is absolutely wrong to aim at reproducing today's foreman and supervisor in the traditional form.*

I think that this book is an important link in the development of our perspective on supervision. It re-states the problem in a much more complicated way than we used to formulate it. We find ourselves faced by a much greater number of separate problems to be attacked and solved separately.

I wonder whether this can be done with a type of systems thinking? The main problem here seems to be the influence of factors outside the system of the enterprise on the role of the supervisor. To my mind, one of the points we have to investigate is the degree to which the foreman is an isolated person within the enterprise viewed as a system.

This book not only tears down a flimsy superstructure of loose thinking; it also offers a choice of strategies for attacking the new problems. I think that such an eminently practical thing as the checklist in the penultimate chapter must indicate that there are ways of attacking the new problems; methods which promise results. However, such results will be rather different from the easy and generally applicable ones that we thought we had arrived at.

Stockholm　　　　　　　　　　　　　　　　　　　　Gunnar Westerlund

Preface

The writing of this book arose from collaboration between research teams at the Swedish Council for Personnel Administration and the London School of Economics and Political Science. In the early 1960s both groups were studying the nature of supervisory tasks in manufacturing industries and quite independently had arrived at a similar frame of reference and similar methods. A special feature of these methods was the emphasis on direct observation of supervisory behaviour. This led to the realization that supervisory tasks varied widely and that consequently the concept of leadership style was somewhat inadequate for supervisory analysis. It was suggested by a mutual friend and colleague, Bengt Gustavsson, that it would be useful to integrate both research approaches and produce a guide for those considering the supervisory problem.

At that time, in both countries, there was a fairly coherent set of beliefs which governed policy towards industrial supervision. These could be expressed as follows:

1. Supervisors occupy a key role between managers and workers and can critically affect relationships at the shop floor level.
2. Supervisors have various technical tasks to perform which are specific to each enterprise. They have common human relations and managerial tasks, which are discrete and can be improved by training.
3. Supervisors tend to believe in authoritarian styles of behaviour; they are unskilled in leadership practices and lack a systematic 'scientific' approach to problem solving.
4. Supervisors are largely recruited from the shop floor and are still identified with workers, rather than management.
5. Supervisors should therefore be selected for their leadership and managerial capacity and less for their technical competence.

In Sweden, the strategy favoured by the Employers Confederation (SAF) was that of providing a standardized basic managerial education for all supervisors through the Arbetsledareinstitutet (Supervisory Training Institute). A standardized method of selecting supervisors with a lavish use of psychological tests was also advocated through the PA Council's consultant staff. In Britain, the Ministry of Labour continued to sponsor Training Within Industry programmes and stimulated various committees of inquiry into the problem. Many large firms experimented with supervisory training courses, although in some case these did not stay in being for a long time. In both countries there were undercurrents of dissatisfaction with supervisory training, but in the late 1950s this led to boredom and indifference to the subject rather than fresh policies. Indeed, all parties concerned with supervision tended to share the same frame of reference.

As stated above, the data produced by both research projects suggested that supervisory behaviour varied considerably, according to the technology and market situation. The implication appeared to be that managers should make studies of their supervisory roles, appraise them, and decide their policies according to the situation.

The first draft of this book was completed in 1964 and advocated a systematic study of supervisory situations to be followed by specific policies for 'improving' supervision. This concept was naïve on two counts. It assumed a consensus of opinion would back changes once the situation was 'objectively' studied. It also assumed that the direction of changes could be easily decided once the facts were known about the nature of supervisory performance. The provision of an elaborate list of methods for data collection and a nine-point plan for designing changes did not answer the point that supervisory behaviour itself only reflected a 'compromise' position between pressures from different parties in the situation, each with their own objectives. If supervisory performance is defective, then the causes may lie far beyond supervision itself. It follows that attempts to improve performance have to be more sophisticated than training supervisors to jump through particular hoops or choosing only supervisors who can jump. It is necessary to understand the determinants of role behaviour; the type of power game being played; the ideas, beliefs, values, and goals of supervisors themselves and all members of the organization (and outside it) who are party to their daily or weekly tasks. Further than this, it is necessary to judge the approach which is most likely to yield acceptable and lasting changes. A strategy which is highly successful in one situation may be an abysmal failure in the next. To judge strategy, therefore, it is necessary to build up a classification both of strategies themselves and of the types of situations which may suit a particular one. We did not have such a typology of strategies and situations and it was necessary therefore to create one. In this way, a 'cook-book' of prescriptions for supervision was gradually transformed into a set of concepts, ideas, and methods for dealing with change at the level of the supervisory system. It was a slow task and one that took more than six years. A book devoted to production supervisors alone changed to one concerned with all types of supervision. The concepts adopted drew heavily on personal studies in the construction industry and the understanding of the complex way that site management decision-making actually works. The argument also reflects a growing interest in cross-cultural research, as a way of illuminating assumptions of belief and action. In this second period of writing, finishing in 1972, it should be noted also that the unionization of supervisors in the United Kingdom has grown rapidly and the demands for job enrichment and worker participation can now be heard on all sides. It is no longer possible, even if it were once desirable, to see the supervision problem as one purely of improving managerial efficiency and control. There are clearly a variety of goals possible for any change programme and a realistic approach has to come to terms with the question of trade-off between goals.

The final version of this book is a *reappraisal* of supervision, therefore, in several senses. To the academic researcher or student, it is suggested that the concepts and designs of much previous supervisory research are inadequate and bound to lead to inconclusive results. To the trainer or supervisory 'expert' it questions how far conventional training and selection methods are successful. To the manager, it is argued that supervision has been under-valued in the past and the 'supervisory problem' over-simplified. To supervisors themselves, it is an argument that their role has undergone major changes in many industries so that old concepts and beliefs are increasingly under challenge. A formal 'reappraisal' of supervision is becoming a necessity for all parties, as the old concepts prove to be irrelevant and misleading. It is hoped that the ideas in this book will be suitable as a basis for such a re-think, or at the very least will serve as a stimulus towards one.

It is important for us to put on record our gratitude to the PA Council and its previous and current Directors, Mr Rolf Lahnhagen and Dr Lennart Lennerlöf, who supported the idea of the collaboration between the two teams from the beginning. International collaboration in research is notoriously difficult to achieve, and the progress seen here was certainly due in no small measure to the financial help from the Council and the personal encouragement from Mr Lahnhagen and Dr Lennerlöf. Acknowledgments and thanks are due to many people who provided assistance, research opportunities, and ideas. Gunnar Westerlund, Nancy Seear, John Smith, and Pjotr Hesseling provided much encouragement. Bengt Gustavsson, Maria Pinschof, and Tony Hamblin contributed directly to many of the ideas in the book. Peter Jackson was responsible for the account of the Olsen Experiment in Chapter 10. Indirectly, of course, we are indebted to a great number of research workers, supervisors, and managers from many companies and this debt is mirrored in the notes and references.

KEITH THURLEY AND HANS WIRDENIUS

Contents

List of Figures

List of Tables

1. *The Problem of the European Foreman*

COMPLAINTS AND CRITICISMS

'Robboe the gaffer [foreman] passed along the gangway talking to a toolsetter. Robboe was a bloke of about forty who had been with the firm since he was fourteen, having signed on as an apprentice and put in a lot of time at night-school, a man who had not suffered the rigours of short-time before the war . . . and who had been in a "reserved occupation" during the war so that he had kept out of the army. He now drew about twenty [pounds] a week plus a good production bonus, a quiet man with a square face, tortured-looking eyes and brow, thin rubbery lips and one hand always in his pocket twiddling on a micrometer. Robboe kept his job because he was clever at giving you the right answers and took back-chat with a wry smile and a good face as long as you did it with a brutal couldn't-care-less attitude and didn't seem frightened of him.'

(A worker's view of his foreman from Alan Sillitoe's novel.)[1]

'Why do I get on with my foreman pretty well? He leaves us alone – that's reason enough isn't it?'

'He's a foreman who's a bit out of touch. He's wrapped up in office work and has lost all contact with the blokes. When he speaks, it's like he was a higher class than you and you're a lower class.'

'He doesn't bother you and I don't have a lot to do with him, but he thinks he's the little king over the shop. He doesn't have a lot to say to anyone – like a little god.'

(Workers' views of their foremen, recorded by research workers.)[2]

'The foremen of today are excellent when compared with those of ten years ago, but they are no good when compared with the foremen needed in ten years time.'

(A trade unionist's view in 1956.)[3]

'The foreman's task is to do what is left over by the specialists and to correct their errors so that the work group won't suffer.'

(A foreman's view of his job.)[4]

'As I like to tell my friends, an assembly line is just one damn emergency after another.'

(An American foreman's view of his job.)[5]

'We want to have foremen in our departments to whom the workers will go for advice and clarification when they meet difficulties on the job. The foreman should be able to help them out; he should know more than the workers about the production, the processes, the firm, the personnel policies and the social arrangements, in short about how problems facing the worker can be solved.'

(A manager's view.)[6]

The position of the foreman in Europe has been widely regarded as a *problem* for the last twenty-five years. A common argument can often be distinguished in speeches at management conferences or in articles by training experts. It is stated that unless management tries to modify supervisory attitudes and change supervisory practices it will be impossible to carry out any effective modernization in industry. 'The tragedy of European manufacturing is of course that it developed under conditions where strong pre-established currents determined the general pattern of the change which the formerly static society was experiencing,' states Van der Haas,[7] and this could be applied particularly to foremen. The roles of foremen were developed in many European countries at a very early stage of industrial development, and (it is often argued) their ideas on work and discipline have tended to survive into organizations where they are technically and socially out of date and irrelevant.

In detail, the complaints against traditional foremen are remarkably similar in different countries. A typical list of such complaints is given by van Herzelle.[8] One of the most common arguments found in the literature on foremen is that they are basically conservative and resistant to changes introduced by management. Several studies indicate the gap between the self-perceived objectives of foremen and those of line and functional management. Those made by Kahn and his colleagues are typical of American studies.[9] The foreman is much more tied to running a particular production system and much more likely to want to defend the *status quo*. Wilfred Brown sees supervision as directly tied to the production line. 'The essential basis of the supervisor's work arises from the need to have somebody available to do that component of the production job which the machine operator is unable to do without stopping his machine.'[10] The reasons for such conservatism are clear. If a foreman's skills and knowledge are based on his lifetime's experience in his trade or occupation and technical changes alter the basis of his particular production process, there is a constant danger that his experience will become devalued, or will appear so in the eyes of management. Solutions commonly offered to overcome such resistance to change range from attitude training programmes designed to broaden the perspective of existing supervisors, to selection schemes aimed at bringing younger, better qualified men into supervisory positions.

A second criticism of supervisory performance is the argument that supervisors display little logical systematic thinking in their approach to their work. It is argued that supervisors tend to jump to conclusions and are too prone to accept precedents from their previous experience as answers to all kinds of problems. There are two points being made here. One should distinguish the time span used for making decisions from the criteria used. The first is said to be too short and the latter is seen as arbitrary or *ad hoc*. Both contribute to the strategy of 'patching' in the face of problems. The Job Methods Course of the TWI Programme was designed to meet this need and Bruce Yuill in his text-book for supervisors, makes much of the need to use a systematic problem-solving technique.[11]

Another set of criticisms is concerned with educational defects. Supervisors are said to lack a good basic education and understanding of modern technology, particularly that related to the type of industry in which they are working. Not surprisingly, there is some evidence that this deficiency is felt most by management and supervisors in science-based industries.[12] They are also felt to lack knowledge of procedures, both company procedures and industrial procedures, for example, in the industrial relations field. This lack of detailed understanding of collective agreements between trade unions and management and the common misunderstandings of industrial relations and safety legislation are all recognized as important educational gaps.[13, 14]

Other writers on supervision are concerned with the fundamental responses and attitudes to work displayed by foremen. It is very common to hear criticisms of lack of drive or of motivation. In Swedish it is expressed by saying, 'They need more rye in their back.' Managers also complain that supervisors do not show initiative in taking up critical problems when they arise, or, alternatively, the criticism is that they show little evidence of strong leadership. They are alleged to vacillate in decisions and 'pass the buck' over tricky questions, particularly in industrial relations disputes. Supervisors themselves frequently complain that joint consultation means that shop stewards negotiate direct with management, bypassing the foremen, but this complaint may be highly ambivalent. Many of these points seem to refer to the uncertainty of the supervisor in his role and to the disappointment of management with the performance of that role.[15] In some companies, the sickness has been diagnosed as deriving from the lack of supervisory identification with management. Accordingly, the position of supervisors has been clarified so that they are accorded a definite managerial 'staff' status with a white coat and an office and a monthly salary cheque, all of which are seen as important symbols of this new position. Associated with such changes, one can link the training programmes that aim at encouraging economic and cost consciousness among supervisors.[16] It is clear that economic and cost criteria have frequently not been seen by supervisors as related to their work responsibility. This is partly due to the early development of accounts departments as a specialized management function. With increasing competitiveness and the growing sophistication of control systems, it is little surprise to find such an increased emphasis on supervisory cost consciousness.

A final and very common group of criticisms refer to the lack of human relations skills displayed by supervisors.[17] It is argued that many industrial disputes may be caused by lack of 'consideration' and human relations shown by supervisors in handling difficult subordinates. Similarly, within the management organization itself, supervisors are said to have difficulty in maintaining good relationships with functional staff or with other supervisors. Behind such arguments, of course, there lies the assertion that the attitudes and style of behaviour shown by supervision may be inappropriate for modern conditions. In McGregor's terminology, supervisors are still clinging to theory X and are afraid to turn to theory Y.[18] In spite of the many severe attacks on the Human Relations School, the arguments for encouraging supervisory social skills continue apace.[19, 20]

It is natural that criticisms of supervisory performance lead on to the diagnosis of organizational problems which could be said to result from the limitations of supervision. In this respect, personnel problems such as high labour turnover or absence and low job satisfaction are all very familiar problems laid at the door of faulty supervision. It is also argued that production problems, lack of adequate planning, the high waste rates or reject rates, and frequent delays in meeting programme schedules can also be partly due to defective supervision. These are direct measures of supervisory effectiveness. There are also indirect problems said to be caused by supervisory inadequacies, for example, frequent organizational 'wars' and conflicts between departments, industrial disputes, high costs in the production process, and, finally, accidents to the process and to employees. In Sweden, one jury of experts estimated that the difference between good and bad supervision on construction sites could make as much as a 10 per cent difference in total building costs.

In spite of the popularity of such arguments about the quality of supervision, it is rare to find any detailed published evidence to substantiate many of these criticisms of supervisors. The most widely known studies have been made at the Institute of Social Research at the University of Michigan and their approach will be discussed later in this book. It is certainly convenient for management to use supervision as a scapegoat for more general organizational problems which may be too difficult to solve. The growth of functional staff departments, such as personnel and work study departments, is both a cause and a result of the argument for changes in procedures and practices within management. The new staff experts have to convince senior management that their expertise is superior to the traditional 'know-how' of line management. Such experts have much to gain from convincing management of the inadequacies of department managers and foremen. It is perhaps not so surprising that training experts have frequently waxed eloquent on the subject of the training needs of foremen.

THE DEVELOPMENT OF THE SUPERVISORY ROLE

A comprehensive history of the development of supervisory jobs and foremanship in Europe has yet to be written. However, in order to understand some of the parameters of the task of changing supervision, it is necessary to outline certain sociological factors which have affected the position of foremen in Western Europe since industrialization. There are reasons for believing that the position of the European foreman, although varying from country to country, has certain similarities which distinguish it from supervisory roles in Russia, the U.S.A., Japan or the developing countries. Although there is as yet no work published known to the authors which compares the development of the supervisory role in various European countries, there are a growing number of individual research reports and surveys. These give much comparative information about supervisory jobs and characteristics. Some of them are listed in the notes and references (21–31). Much of this similarity arises from the pattern of industrialization in the eighteenth and nineteenth centuries in Western Europe. The pace of industrial change was such as to allow considerable continuity between the supervisory roles which existed in the pre-industrial society and those emerging in the early industrial concerns. In particular, we can trace the slow metamorphosis of the master craftsman into a craft foreman or 'meister' role. Some early factories in England advertised for craftsmen from such trades as watch-making in order to develop them as engineers and foremen.[32] Famous examples of early factories such as that of Ambrose Crowley at Swalwell in County Durham,[33] show a combination of an embryonic factory organization and an enlarged personal household.

If master craftsmen were engaged for such enterprises, it is not surprising that they carried their personal social status with them into the development of new organizational roles. In particular, the relative autonomy and independence of such a master craftsman role seems to have been preserved within the structure of the new factories. This was aided by the lack of any theory or concept of large-scale organization in England in the eighteenth century,[34] a situation contrasting strongly with that of, say, Japan in the nineteenth century.

Many supervisory roles have, of course, been created consciously by managers in new technologies. The chemical industry, for instance, and the radio and electronics industries are good examples of new types of production situations which required new types of organization.[35] It is, however, possible to discover the way that traditional roles have been taken over from other industries. In one brewery in the U.K. known to the authors, all the original process foremen had been recruited from the building labourers who built the brewery. In this case it was possible to trace the way that their early experiences in the building industry had been carried over into their interpretation of correct role behaviour which was displayed in their jobs as brewery foremen. In any society with a relatively open labour market, such cross-fertilization takes place.

One of the most important functions controlled by European foremen within the new industrial organizations of the nineteenth and twentieth centuries appears to have been the personnel function. This included control over recruitment and dismissal as well as discipline, the type of bonus and remuneration, and dealing with grievances and complaints. In the evidence given by construction employers to the Charity Organization Society in 1908 which is quoted by Bendix,[36] we can find a clear statement of the traditional relationship between foremen and men:

'You trust the foreman to find your men and he generally finds those he knows and they would be those in the district that he lives in. We have a great objection to giving work to anyone we do not know, because we have to train him. Each of us has his fad, I suppose, and we do not often give a man we do not know a job, unless we are very much pushed.'

And again:

'The foreman of each trade is held partially responsible, not only for the number of men but for the quality . . . Should a casual hand be taken on he is questioned as to his capabilities before starting. Very seldom would a labourer think of asking for employment in any other section than that to which he is accustomed. He can be judged in a few hours and then, if he is not satisfactory, one hour's notice finishes it.'

What is noticeable here is that the labourer/foreman relationship was highly dependent and in many cases a long-term relationship. The labourer moved with the foreman.[37] It is also clear that the power of the foreman over the labourer depended on his use of the 'sack' as an ultimate weapon and that it would be possible in such a system for considerable personal loyalties to grow. Labour gangs of this type could be employed as subcontractors, as in the early Boulton & Watt factory,[38] or could be taken on as direct employees. We can compare this system with the development of Japanese supervision since the Meiji Restoration. In this case, it is also true that foreman/labourer relationships were traditionally expressed in terms of dependence.[39] The transition from subcontractor to company foreman took place in Japan, however, in a situation where personal loyalties to the organization were all-important and where there was much effort invested in socializing personnel to accept the goals of a. particular enterprise.[40] This appears to have resulted in considerable changes in the type of function and work performed. In particular the personnel function was largely taken away from such supervisors. Since the Second World War, there has been much interest among management in Japan in *expanding* the personnel function of foremen.[41]

The development of supervisory roles in modern European enterprises, then, has depended on:

(a) the extent to which labour had been recruited from other occupational roles where there was already an ongoing and powerful set of norms and expectations governing their behaviour;

(b) the extent to which an organizational role for foremen had been clarified and defined within the enterprise.

In Western Europe, one can hypothesize that the foreman's role behaviour has more often been learnt directly from *other* foremen (or by observation of *other* foremen) than by direct influence from management or entrepreneurs in the companies in which they worked. Slowly this situation has been changing. We are dealing now, in a word, with traditional occupational systems that are developing gradually into bureaucratic structures.

PRESCRIPTIONS FOR CHANGE

The movement for improving the effectiveness of supervision in European enterprises started in the 1920s and 1930s with the development of personnel departments in a few progressive companies. In the 1920s, for example, it was common for such companies in the United Kingdom as Rowntree's, Peek Frean's and Cadbury's to develop labour relations and personnel departments and to start experimenting with foreman training.[42] Similarly in Sweden in 1930, one can note the beginnings of the Swedish Supervisory Training Institute, founded by the Federation of Swedish Industries and developed by Ekelöf.[43] In this period, supervisory training was much concerned with attempting to change the attitudes and behaviour of traditional foremen from an authoritarian set of responses towards a more democratic model:

'The personal atmosphere in a work room does not depend upon the director in his office, but upon the foreman close at hand. The workman's outlook upon life and industry, his loyalty to the firm, his devotion to his work, are intimately bound up with his relation to his own superior officer. I would like every foreman to have a high ideal of his functions. I would like him to think as he sees a lad just starting work "There is a human being with the most of his life before him and what he makes of it depends very largely upon me! I mean to surround him with conditions which will help him to become a fine true man!...." That is the task I would have every foreman contemplate, but it demands the characteristics of a leader of men. We cannot lead from behind. The foreman's own standard of life must be high and he must live up to it.'[44]

A second element introduced in the 1930s was the application of scientific management concepts to supervision. Taylor himself was much concerned with the problem of foremen, and this fact was noted by many European management experts. It was, however, the use of work study techniques or rationalization which was seen as especially significant in changing the effectiveness of shop management. The ideas of Gilbreth were read widely in Sweden. Companies experimented in training foremen in handling the new methods of work analysis and work simplification. In the United Kingdom, the scientific management message was largely expressed through the management consultants, especially Associated Industrial Consultants (AIC) and Urwick, Orr & Partners, and these organizations ran into considerable difficulties due to their emphasis on the Bedaux and other bonus systems, which were much resisted by trade unionists.[45]

With the public attention given to the Hawthorne experiments, we can trace a further set of ideas on 'human relations' and its fallout on supervisory theory and supervisory training. The crucial idea here was that supervisors should be trained to become effective leaders of their work groups so that workers would be encouraged to have an interest in their work. In this way, their motivation to work and personal drives would be enhanced. Between 1945 and 1955 Human Relations training swept the field in supervisory institutes and training departments throughout the world.[46, 47]

Concern with the effects of technical change and its implications for supervisory work is a much more recent phenomenon. It is probably true that the social implications of newer developments in technology are only beginning to be assessed by managers in many European countries. The effect of the computer in particular, used either in data processing or directly in controlling process plant, may well have fundamental implications for the role of supervision.[48] In the last decade, therefore, one can trace a gradual preoccupation with technical change and adaption to change. In many companies this has largely replaced the earlier concern with human relations skills and training of supervisors in work study techniques.

Recent changes in the structure and organization of management in Europe also have had fundamental implications for supervision. In particular, the development of more complex management organizations, carrying within them a veritable forest of staff departments, has raised the problem of the foreman's authority and role. As already indicated, the personnel functions of supervisors have been seen by them to be very critical for their relative social position and power. The development of personnel departments, therefore, and the resulting take-over of such personnel functions by these departments meant a very serious change in power for many foremen. In some companies it is possible to trace the conflict which was engendered on this issue between personnel departments and production foremen. Newer staff departments, such as work study, planning departments, and quality control sections also, in their turn, served to threaten the autonomy of supervision. As management has become a more self-conscious process and managers have tried to see themselves as a profession, supervision itself has often been persuaded to follow, by setting up foreman associations. The Institute of Industrial Supervisors was thus founded in Britain in 1947.

The impact of popular training programmes, such as the TWI Programme, imported from America to the United Kingdom at the close of the Second World War, should also not be underestimated. This training programme, dealing with human relations, elementary work study, methods of teaching and instruction, and later the problem of safety, has had an impact on the thinking of management and supervisors which is perhaps wider than has often been appreciated. Although the TWI courses have been widely criticized as consisting of ineffectual stimulance with little long-term effect on supervisory behaviour, nevertheless it is clear that the use of TWI made the experience of adult training familiar to many managers and supervisors for the first time. They became used to the analysis of cases, with taking problems from their own experience and discussing them round a table, and, indeed, with the whole small-group conference technique of learning. In this way, TWI was a pioneer method of supervisory training which helped to bring the supervisory problem to the notice of top management.

Another development of considerable importance was the use of more systematic methods for the selection of supervisors. Selection tests for operatives and workers were devised in most European countries in the 1920s and 1930s. In Germany, Münsterberg created a number of psycho-technical tests for a whole variety of jobs,[49] and this was paralleled in Britain by the National Institute of

Industrial Psychology, which was founded in 1926. The use of such tests for supervisors came at a later period, generally after 1940. In Sweden, Westerlund and Anderberg developed tests for the selection of supervisors for the first time in the 1940s. These tests included technical tests of mechanical comprehension as well as simple case-study judgement tests of the human relations type. In the United Kingdom, after the finish of the Second World War, several leading companies experimented with the use of individual performance tests and intelligence tests in their programmes for potential foremen. Other tests used included group performance tests, such as the leadership of discussions or the command of groups undertaking tasks.

The National Institute of Industrial Psychology's study of the foreman in 1951[50] laid heavier emphasis on the importance of systematic selection for supervisors. This message was translated into a programme for assisting companies to select their supervisors by the Swedish Supervisory Training Institute, i.e. Arbetsledareinstitutet (ALI), and carried on later by the Swedish Council for Personnel Administration. In the United Kingdom and in most other European countries, no national guidance of this type was created for assisting managers to select their supervisors. The problem of increasing the aptitudes and capabilities of their supervisors was noted, however, and in more recent years the problem of devising adequate career development for supervisors has been increasingly discussed.

The advent of a rapid increase of the number of graduates and technologists in the ranks of senior management has led many to suggest that the promotion chances for supervisors have been drastically reduced and this has had a consequent effect on supervisory morale.

One point of considerable importance in understanding the supervisory problem is the degree to which supervisors have accepted either trade union membership or a position as a formal member of the management team. In Sweden, for the last sixty years, most supervisors have accepted membership of their own special trade union.[51] This position was not found in most European countries, although there are signs, in the last five years, of a fairly rapid increase in trade union membership among supervisors in Great Britain. It could be said generally that European foremen have rarely been expected by managers to identify completely with management objectives. The position of the supervisor as the 'middle man', partly identified with workers and workers' movements, and partly identified with and related to the management organization, has been generally accepted, but in many cases this understanding did not completely prevent the type of stress situation described in much American literature. The habit of top management of informally allowing supervisory autonomy at shop level was a widespread one, however, and this has helped to ease role conflicts for supervisors torn between management and men. There are indeed numbers of cases of supervisors simultaneously occupying positions as shop stewards for their men. Nevertheless, as the use of data processing has increased and as the importance of running a totally integrated management control system has been perceived by managements, so management tolerance of autonomous supervisory control has diminished. Automation could present a major challenge to this tradition of supervisory autonomy. Another merging challenge to this tradition is the current argument in favour of the 'democratization' of the work force and, by implication, the reduction of supervisory power over workers.[52-56]

IS IT A PROBLEM?

The 'problem' of the European foreman can be seen from this brief discussion to be neither dramatic or simple. Should one therefore refer to it as a problem? In what way does it have any single coherent form? Is it a question of status or role or function or unionization?

One of the major starting points for this book was the discovery of the extent of the differences between various supervisory situations. This knowledge certainly prevents us from defining our topic in advance by asserting that the 'real' problem underlying the smaller issues is the question of authority or role, status or power. All these questions are usually important to foremen, but not universally so. In many organizations, the traditional position of foremen has only recently begun to be questioned. The warning signs of possible conflict ahead are often infrequent and muted.

There is only one sense in which we can reasonably describe the European foreman as being a problem for most organizations and countries – and that is because supervisors are largely a neglected group. In spite of the developments in literature and policy noted above, in spite of unions and institutes, training boards and selection research, it is still true that supervision ranks low on the priorities of governments, firms, managers and trade unions. The reasons for this are fairly obvious. Supervisors represent no powerful social pressure group; they are typically low-status, marginal men, often despised as social climbers. The problem of supervision is rarely a dramatic one and is usually a question of irritants and grumbles rather than a crisis issue.

The research experience of both authors has led to the conviction, however, that this neglect needs urgent rectification. If this is to be done, it seems necessary to challenge the range of ideas and concepts applied to supervision and provide a new and coherent frame of reference. Although our starting point is the European foreman, therefore, it becomes necessary to discuss supervision and supervisory theory in general terms. Much of the world literature on supervision is American and this is reflected in many of the references quoted. Most of the literature, too, deals with production first-line supervisors who are so often promoted from blue collar employees. The frame of reference developed, however, is a general one and could be used in all supervisory situations, in offices, shops, construction sites, and service organizations. There is little literature to draw on for these applications and the book remains highly biased to the manufacturing situation. The concern expressed about the supervisory role is largely a concern about decaying role systems in European manufacturing and construction industries. In this sense, the analysis is a specific one relating in many cases only to Sweden and the United Kingdom. It is hoped, however, that researchers, managers and specialists in other parts of the world will be able to draw from the approach in order to analyse their own supervisory problems. It is also hoped that studies of, and policies dealing with, office and other non-manufacturing situations will also be stimulated so that managers and supervisors in those situations can make their own applications of the general approach.

Notes and References

1 SILLITOE, A. (1958). *Saturday night and sunday morning*, pp. 38–9. W. H. Allen, London.

2 GOLDTHORPE, J. H., LOCKWOOD, D., BECHHOFER, F. & PLATT, J. (1968). *The affluent worker: industrial attitudes and behaviour*, Chap. 3. Cambridge University Press.

3 GRABE, S. & SILBERER, P. (1956). *Selection and training of foremen in Europe*, p. 43. Project No. 234, OEEC (EPA), Paris.

4 GRABE, S. op. cit., p. 6.

5 WALKER, C. R., GUEST, R. H. & TURNER, A. N. (1956). *The foreman on the assembly line*, p. 79. Harvard University Press, Cambridge, Mass.

6 GRABE, S. op. cit., p. 42.

7 VAN DER HAAS, H. (1967). *The enterprise in transition*, p. 23. Tavistock, London.

8 VAN HERZELLE, E. (1961). Le personnel et cadre inférieur industrie. *Productivity Review*, Vol. 15, No. 8 (August), pp. 484–8. Fédération des Industries Belges, Brussels.

9 KAHN, R. L. (1964). *Organizational stress. Studies in role conflict and ambiguity*. John Wiley, New York.

10 BROWN, W. (1960). *Exploration in management*, p. 190. Heinemann, London.

11 YUILL, B. (1968). *Supervision. Principles and techniques*, Chap. 4. George Allen & Unwin, London.

12 Unpublished graduate report (1964). London School of Economics & Political Science. This revealed that foremen in one U.K. process plant felt that their lack of scientific sophistication was their greatest training need. This is paralleled by foremen in an ammonium sulphate plant in a Japanese company who were using on-the-job study sessions on chemical technology. (*See* THURLEY, K. E. (1967). Industrial Training in Japan. *Industrial Training International*, Vol. 2, No. 3 (March), pp. 90–4.)

13 MORTIMER, J. E. (1968). *Industrial relations*. Heinemann, London, for the Institute of Supervisory Management.

14 WHINCUP, M. H. (1968). *Industrial law*. Heinemann, London, for the Institute of Supervisory Management.

15 ROETHLISBERGER, F. J. (1945). The foreman: master and victim of double talk. *Harvard Business Review*, Vol. 23, pp. 283–98.

16 BETTS, P. W. (1968). *Supervisory studies*. Macdonald & Evans, London. Chapters 27–30 cover the financial information deemed by the author to be

necessary for the N.E.B.S.S. syllabuses of the United Kingdom. This is a scheme for part-time supervisory studies in technical colleges and firms.

17 Hoslett, S. D. (1951). *Human factors in management.* Harper Bros., New York. This is a very typical human relations training book.

18 McGregor, D. M. (1961). *The human side of enterprise.* McGraw-Hill, New York.

19 Yuill, B. op. cit., Part III.

20 Barnes, R. J. (1968). *Principles and practice of supervision.* Heinemann, London, for the Institute of Supervisory Management.

21 Van Ginneken, P. J. *et al.* (1959). *Bazen in de Industrie.* Netherlands Productivity Centre, the Hague.

22 Meigniez, R. & Nodiot, S. (1966). *Evaluation des résultats d'une formation d' agents de maîtrise.* Jure. AFAP, Paris.

23 Kile, S. M. (1966). *Evaluering av arbeidsledertrening.* Universitetsforlaget, Bergen.

24 Syrek, M. (1964). Rola mistrza we wzroscie kultury i wydajnosci prazy w hutnictwie zelaza. *Wiadomosci Hutnicze,* Vol. 15, No. 3 (March), pp. 82–92. Katowice. (Roles of foremen in metal industry.)

25 The Swedish Council for Personnel Administration and SALF (Swedish Supervisors' Union) (1963). *Arbetsledarnas rekrytering och utbildning.* (Survey of foremen.)

26 Warr, P. & Bird, M. (1966). *Foremen training in the steel industry.* Iron and Steel Training Board, London.

27 Eldridge, J. E. T. & Jones, F. C. (1961). *The selection and training of supervisors in the Black Country.* Staffordshire College of Commerce.

28 Arlt, F. (1961). Industriemeister. *Berufspädagogische Beiträge der Berufspädagogischen Zeitschrift.* BPZ, Braunschweig. Vol. 10, No. 14, p. 24.

29 Koluskin, V. (1963). Master-organizator proizvodstva, vospitatel. *Kommunist,* Vol. 40, No. 17 (November), pp. 97–105. Moscow.

30 Rainio, K. (1955). *Leadership qualities. A theoretical enquiry and experimental study of foremen.* Suomolarsen Academiae, Helsinki.

31 Hamblin, A. C., Thurley, K. E. & Voon, D. (1963). *Essential facts on the British foreman.* Institute of Industrial Supervisors.

32 Fitton, R. S. & Wadsworth, A. P. (1958). *The Strutts and the Arkwrights, 1758–1830: a study of the early factory system,* p. 65. Manchester.

33 Lassett, P. (1965). *The world we have lost,* p. 155. Methuen, London.

34 Pollard, S. (1965). *The genesis of modern management,* Chap. 7. Edward Arnold, London.

35 Burns, T. & Stalker, G. M. (1961). *The Management of innovation.* Tavistock, London.

36 Bendix, R. (1956). *Work and authority in industry,* pp. 55–6. Wiley, New York and London.

37 Paulsson, G. (1967). *The work situation of the chargehands in Stockholm.* Unpublished paper delivered at Anglo-Swedish Conference of Building Research, Cambridge.

38 ROLL, E. (1930). *An early experiment in industrial organisation. Being a history of the firm of Boulton & Watt, 1775–1805*, p. 19. Longmans, Green, London.

39 BENNETT, J. W. & ISHINO, I. (1963). *Paternalism in the Japanese economy. Anthropological studies of oyabun-kobun patterns.* University of Minnesota Press, Minneapolis.

40 ABEGGLEN, J. (1957). *The Japanese factory.* Free Press, Glencoe, Illinois.

41 OKAMOTO, H. & MORI, G. (1964). Nihon no Genba Kantoksha (Workshop supervision in Japan). *Sangyo Kunren Shriyo*, No. 57 (October).

42 *Report on lecture conferences organised for works directors, managers, foremen and forewomen.* Balliol College, Oxford (1920).

43 EKELÖF, G. (1953). *Att vara arbetsledare.* Sveriges Industriförbund, Stockholm.

44 CHILD, J. (1969). *British management thought.* George Allen & Unwin, London.

45 ROWNTREE, B. S. (1920). *Training for industrial administration*, p. 11. Lecture conference for works directors at University College, Durham.

46 ARENSBERG, C. M. (1957). *Research in industrial human relations: a critical appraisal.* Harper, New York.

47 GOLDTHORPE, J. H. (1961). La conception des conflits du travail dans l'enseignement des relations humaines. *Sociologie du Travail*, No. 3.

48 THURLEY, K. E. (1970). Implications of the use of electronic computers for future roles and behaviour of industrial and construction supervisors. *Computer und Angestellte*, Vol. 2, International Edition. (Ed. G. FRIEDRICHS. Verlagsanstalt (Europäische) Frankfurt am Main.) Also reprinted in English as: Computers and Supervisors (1969). *Productivity*, Vol. 10, No. 1 (Summer). National Productivity Council, India.

49 MÜNSTERBERG, H. (1913). *Psychology and industrial efficiency.* Cambridge University Press and Houghton Mifflin, Boston.

50 National Institute of Industrial Psychology (1951). *The foreman.* London.

51 *SALF 60 år. En bildkrönika kring Sveriges Arbetsledareförbund* (1965). (A history of the Swedish Supervisors' Union.)

52 BROOM, L. & SMITH, J. H. (1963). Bridging occupations. *British Journal of Sociology*, Vol. 14, pp. 321–34.

53 EMERY, F. E. & THORSRUD, E. (1969). *Form and content in industrial democracy; a study of workers' representation at board level.* Tavistock, London.

54 FRIEDMANN, G. (1955). *Industrial society.* Free Press, Glencoe, Illinois. *See* Part III, Chap. III, for discussion of European experiments in work-place democracy.

55 RICE, A. K. (1958). *Productivity and social organisation. The Ahmedebad experiment: industrial innovation, work organisation and management.* Tavistock, London.

56 THORSRUD, E. & EMERY, F. E. (1969). *Mot en ny bedriftsorganisasjon.* Tanum, Oslo.

2. *The Planning of Change*

THE 'IMPROVEMENT OF SUPERVISION'

To talk of neglect is to raise the question of a new deal for foremen. We have already noted the numbers of criticisms of supervisory performance and the various arguments for training needs and selection requirements. The erosion of traditional beliefs about foremen and the jobs is also clear enough. What should be done? What lines of action are open to us? Can one lay down a basic policy for the 'improvement' of the position of supervisors?

The policy choices open relate to three main questions:

1. Should we rely on the evolution of a new set of circumstances or are specific planned initiatives desirable?
2. Should we attempt a radical restructuring or a series of piecemeal changes?
3. Should we invest in selected aspects of social improvement (for example, training programmes) or are more general and varied approaches required?

The debating of these questions inevitably runs throughout much of our whole discussion in this book. It is necessary, however, to state the main assumptions on which the analysis and argument are based.

The first of these is the view that it is better to intervene than to allow drift. If nothing is done about the questions of supervisory role, performance and satisfaction, it can be fairly assumed that a number of dangers, at present latent, will become clear risks. There is the possibility of a growing unwillingness among workers (and perhaps among graduates) to undertake supervisory roles. There is the possibility of head-on conflict developing between shopfloor workers and an increasingly technocratic management trying to extend its control systems. There is the possibility of a growing Ludditism on the shop floor, with opposition to managerial plans for change led, perhaps secretly, by supervisors. There is the other possibility that supervision will erupt into militant union action, blocking and paralysing attempts at change. These are not prophecies and are not intended as mere spine-chilling statements. It is simply that these risks exist and that reliance on *laissez-faire* and 'natural evolution' policies would increase them.

Our second assumption is that social science knowledge is still relatively primitive and inadequate for the purpose of making a universal design of a solution for a specific set of problems. We know little enough about the mainsprings of human action, and it is no service to social science or social scientists to exaggerate the extent of this knowledge. The number of variables which are relevant to any social situation is indeed enormous, and it is clear that the degree of relevance and the mix of variables are likely to be unique to that situation. At the same time most of our conceptual models are two- or three-dimensional in character. There is also little chance of really being able to control experiments which can conclusively test hypotheses. Equally important, we know that we are dealing with groups which possess varying perceptions of interests and goals. They may or may not agree as to whether any set of proposals are 'improvements'. It follows that radical change may be desirable in some situations, but that we dare not apply a single set of changes as a universal solution. It is also obvious that a general solution would be irrelevant in some situations and positively harmful in others. A realistic approach has to be a heuristic one, with a range of different solutions being tested out over a long period of time.

Thirdly, it is accepted that there is an important distinction between conceptual and semantic differences which are necessary for logical thought and the reality of social interaction with which we have to deal. The latter is made up of a complex web of acts, perceptions and effects. These effects are sometimes planned, but often unexpected and unrecognized. Changes planned in one aspect of work arrangements will affect others. Conversely, the influence of 'environmental' factors frequently prevents the realization of planned objectives. We can conclude from this that an approach on a broad front may have more chance of success than one on a selected front. There is one important precondition for this conclusion. It is necessary to be able to predict interactions to some degree, if a 'broad front' policy is to succeed. This leads us inevitably to the need to make some type of predictive model, however simple, for each particular social situation.

These three assumptions:

the necessity to plan change;
the necessity to test out a variety of solutions in a range of situations;
the necessity to create predictive models and to plan synchronized changes over a variety of aspects of behaviour

are the starting points for designing strategies for 'improving' supervision. We can now turn to the main elements of that design.

THE FRAME OF REFERENCE USED

Our approach to the 'improvement' of supervision has grown out of more than fifteen years' mutual research experience in mostly European work situations. Undoubtedly, this means that the perspective given here is biased by such familiarity with European foreman systems. The limitations of most supervisory research, and of the practical personnel policies based on it, has been the poverty of the frame of reference used to guide the research and the resultant actions. Many of the studies and arguments developed in the U.S.A., for instance, which has contributed to such a large part of the literature on supervision, have been based on the concept of the individual supervisor and have centred on ideas of individual leadership and supervisory style. The relationship between the

B

supervisor and the work group, comprising his own subordinates, has been the central issue discussed. We believe this frame of reference to be quite inadequate for both research and practical purposes. It takes little account of the many factors, technical and sociological, which can affect the significance of various types of supervisory style in particular situations.

Our problem is to outline an adequate *general* frame of reference and, at the same time, highlight the importance of the unique particular situations in which supervisors find themselves. The existence of a variety of traditional foreman role systems in Western Europe has made us more sensitive to this question than would be the case in societies where supervision is largely created by the managements concerned as a method of dealing with immediate problems. Even where managers are faced with a brand-new technological situation, however, there is always the possibility that the staff recruited to man the organization will bring with them ideas, beliefs, values and concepts about their job from their previous social and work situation. It is therefore always impossible in reality to start to solve an organizational problem with *no* historical legacy. This is one reason why one cannot solve such problems purely from the application of 'principles'. To discuss ways of improving supervision does *not*, therefore, entail the distillation of a basic programme which can be applied to any problem. In the meaning developed in this book, it involves three things:

1. The outline of a *theory of change* and of *various routes to change*, so that various strategies can be compared.
2. The use of a *comprehensive frame of reference* to enable manager, consultant and researcher to develop their own models of their own situations, so that appropriate action can be designed.
3. The clarification of the various *possible objectives of change*, so that criteria can be defined to measure direction and achievement.

The use of the terms 'improvement' and 'objectives of change' raises the question 'For whom?'. The older term 'effectiveness of supervision' gave a fairly straightforward answer to this. It was clearly implied in the literature on supervisory effectiveness (*see* Chapter 4) that a move towards supervisory effectiveness was a move that demonstrated the way in which supervisors were, with their work groups, achieving organizational objectives more fully.[1] This could be fairly described as a managerial viewpoint. The quotations at the beginning of Chapter 1 show that the problem is not so simply answered. Workers may perceive that 'improved' supervision means less supervision, less control from above. Supervisors may think, quite reasonably, that improved supervision means a job which entails less stress for them and one which gives them greater job satisfaction. Supervisory unions may take the view that improvement lies with raising the status and rewards of supervisors as a group. It could also mean changing the role from a 'closing' occupation to a 'bridging' occupation[2] so that development for other jobs is a top priority in work decisions. Those supporters of the policy of work-group autonomy[3, 4, 5] could argue that improvement leads to an integration of work-group and supervisory roles. There are clearly many possible opposing objectives of change and many definitions of 'improvement'.

There is, of course, little cause for surprise in this, as foreman roles are notorious for being squarely in the middle of conflict situations. Any approach to 'improvement of supervision' has to start by proclaiming its agnosticism on the question of the ends of the improvement. One further assumption of the authors should be made explicit here, namely, that it is possible and desirable for the various parties in a supervisory situation, even though they are in some degree of conflict, to define certain goals for improvement in that place and at that time. The act of definition will clearly involve compromise and a balancing of goals between management, supervisors, workers and other parties which may be only a temporary solution. Nevertheless, such compromise is a normal part of the process of social interaction.

It follows that the underlying objective of this book is to facilitate this process of compromise by conceptualizing the problem in a relatively new way, bringing out the potentialities for change. It is unlikely that the result will be a brand-new design for the supervisory role system. More likely, changes will involve developments which are already partly perceived by the actors in the situation. Existing trends might be speeded up and new efforts might be stimulated to solve problems which are already recognized. New problems may well be created by such actions. Change will never be eliminated and the search for improvement is a continuous one.

A MODEL OF CHANGE

Our first need is for a simple concept of the process of change itself. Bearing in mind that the actual phenomenon is anything but simple in reality,[6] we can construct a model as in Figure 2.1, which at least enables us to distinguish steps or sub-problems of change. There are five such sub-problems:

1. The analysis and diagnosis of the nature of the situation;
2. the setting of objectives;
3. the design of changes;
4. the carrying through of changes;
5. the evaluation of the results of changes (and the dissemination of such results).

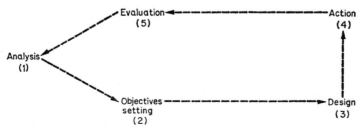

FIGURE 2.1   Steps or sub-problems of a change process

The diagram is shown as a possible learning cycle in which evaluation goes on to another cycle. The logical sequence for moving through the process of change is shown by the numbering. We shall see later that there may be many actual sequences or strategies, but for our purpose now the logical sequence is a useful model.

SIX ROUTES OF CHANGE

Next, we can distinguish six main 'routes' of change which are relevant to supervisors. To start with, it is obvious that we can concentrate on the man or the job. If we take the man, there are broadly three possible alternative approaches. The man can be *replaced* by someone with different capacities; he can be *trained* to adopt new practices of work behaviour; he can be placed in a new environment or challenged in some way so that he develops his understanding and judgement. This type of general influence, designed to promote a personal growth pattern, we can call the *educational* route.

As to the job, there are also three possibilities. The *technical environment* (the layout of the plant, the sequence and type of operations, the type of plant, etc.) can be redesigned so as to alter the number and nature of the problems thrown up by the process supervised. The *social climate* or the pattern of beliefs and practices of all those in contact with our foreman can be modified, perhaps by some type of group training. Finally, we can try to modify the organization structure itself by introducing or withdrawing roles, status levels, formal procedures, methods of communication. This we can call *'organizational change'*.

Figure 2.2 shows our six routes of change.

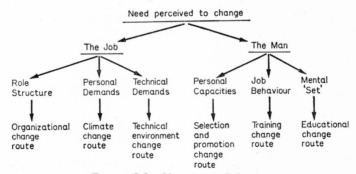

FIGURE 2.2   Six routes of change

Two points should be noted here. First, we need to distinguish this logical classification from *actual* change routes which may overlap between the various arrows. This fact does not destroy the value of making such distinctions. Secondly, we can apply Figure 2.1 to each route in turn. This gives us a matrix of thirty cells which provides a crude 'map' of areas of change relevant to supervision (Figure 2.3).

	Organization	Climate	Technical	Selection	Training	Education
Analysis						
Objectives						
Design						
Action						
Evaluation						

FIGURE 2.3   Areas of change

TYPES OF VARIABLES RELEVANT FOR ANALYSIS

It is useful at this point to illustrate the types of variables with which we have to be concerned in any analysis of supervision. There are five types in all, those describing:

aspects of the work situation of supervisors;
individual characteristics of supervisors;
supervisory work actions;
the effects of actions on supervisors;
the effects of actions on the work situation.

Figure 2.4 shows a simple 'map' of these five areas of variables. The map

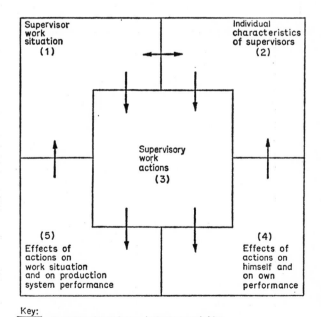

Key:
Denotes dependence between variables
and direction of effect

FIGURE 2.4   Main areas of variables in a supervisory system and their
inter-dependence

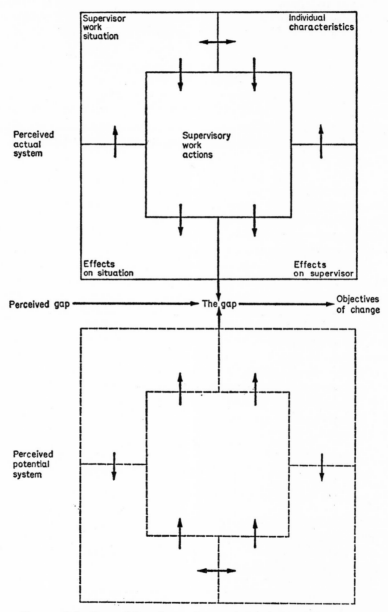

FIGURE 2.5   Potential and actual areas (of a supervisory system)

locates clusters of variables in different areas of a model. The term 'model' must refer to a simplification of the possible relationships between such variables. It is clear that variables may be both interrelated and interdependent within each area on the 'map', and between areas. Our map, therefore, is merely a type of geometrical classification at this stage and no values or hypotheses about the exact nature of the interdependence are included. Figure 2.4 does, however, show some suggested directions of casual interactions between variables. In the central area we are concerned with aspects of supervisory work behaviour (or work actions). That term may seem to be straightforward. However, on examination, it will be seen that 'work action' can mean a number of different things according to the level of analysis and the interpretation of the data actually being examined. These levels of analysis will be explained further in Chapter 3.

THE SETTING OF OBJECTIVES

The final component of our main model which needs some comment here is the question of 'objective setting'. We have already made the point that the various parties in the supervisory situation may have differing objectives and differing views of the supervisory role. Many managers, supervisors and workers may be more interested in deciding the way that supervisors *ought* to behave, or in discussing what they *could* do, than in the realities of the actual performance. We can see that all our areas of variables could be viewed as *potential* behaviour, characteristics or performance, as well as descriptions of reality. If the 'actors' in any situation see a large gap between the potential and the actual, they are deciding the objectives of change. Without such a perceived 'gap', there is no motivation for change. A clarification of the differences between actual and potential leads towards a definition of objectives.

We can show this in diagrammatic form by sketching in the 'potential' areas as 'mirror' images of the 'actual' areas. The gap can be shown visually by this method. It will be perceived differently according to the perspective of the perceiver (Figure 2.5).

A MODEL FOR CHANGING SUPERVISION

Putting together the four components of our argument discussed above:

the stages of the change process (Figure 2.1);
the routes of change (Figure 2.2);
the areas of variables describing a supervisory 'system' (Figure 2.4);
the setting of objectives (Figure 2.5)

we arrive at our main model which is shown in Figure 2.6. This shows six routes of change with each stage indicated, as six possible 'learning cycles'.

(a) *The selection and promotion route* implies changing individuals so that new characteristics are introduced. New-style foremen are selected, either

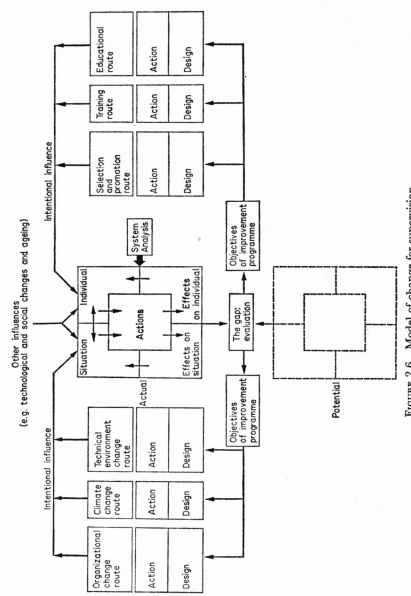

FIGURE 2.6   Model of change for supervision

to replace older foremen on retirement, or perhaps as a systematic policy, as occurs in some American companies, where new foremen are introduced regularly after a five-year period. If a programme for supervisory development and promotion exists, then there is some possibility of planning a regular change in the individual characteristics of the supervisory work force by this method. In this route, a complicated procedure may be necessary for the design of selection procedures, taking decisions on the most appropriate criteria, and deciding methods for validating procedures.

(b) The second route is labelled *training*, which includes all influences on the individual supervisor intended to remodel his work behaviour. Training includes an input of knowledge, new skills or new attitudes, and is characterized by the objective of changing behaviour in a way which is relevant to his present or future job and its requirements. This route has many stages. Problems here are the design of the training, control over the effectiveness of the training situation and relating this to the work situation.

(c) *The education route* refers to the influences which may be brought to bear on individual supervisors to change their thinking and behaviour in a general way, unrelated to the particular work situation in which they are situated. It implies, therefore, any general development experience which might be arranged and includes voluntary activities, for example, in supervisor clubs.

(d) *The technical environment change route* on the left-hand side refers to any attempt to redesign the production situation in order to produce a more effective supervisory control system. In one example, a shoe factory introduced a power conveyor into a 'closing' room (where machinists made the upper parts of ladies' shoes). This altered the whole nature of the production system and concentrated decisions on a semi-supervisor who operated a console at one end of the conveyor. The plant was withdrawn after a trial period as the supervisor was unable to cope with the decisions required by the system. A modified conveyor was then used.

(e) *The climate change route* includes all influences which are designed to change the social climate within which supervisors and the supervisory system has to exist. Mainly, therefore, this includes the expectations and norms of managers and functional staff and workers and their beliefs as to what supervisors ought to be doing. Changes here might imply a reappraisal by management of their expectations as to supervisor behaviour, greater understanding of supervisory problems, attempts to discuss with supervisors in supervisory committees, and types of consultation. Therefore, any kind of management training belongs to this route. The term 'climate' is taken here from Fleishman.[7]

(f) *The organizational change route* on the extreme left implies more systematic attempts to change organizational design by specifying new types of supervisory role, by increasing the numbers of supervisors, attaching assistants or instructors to the supervisory team, or by making alterations in the organization of the staff departments or management departments around the supervisory system. It could also signify changes in styles of organization, e.g. away from more formalistic types of roles to a more organic type of situation. If a company produces a supervisory handbook, or after job analysis produces job specifications and role descriptions, then this could be seen as an organizational change and included under this route.

Our model is the basic tool for the discussion of change strategies applied to supervisory situations. It needs to be emphasized again that it is only a *conceptual* tool and is of value only in so far as it aids discussion. We have merely made certain distinctions between stages, problems, routes, etc., which provide a short-hand for discussion purposes. It also suggests the need to see the interdependence between the various ways of approaching change. One problem in many 'progressive' companies undoubtedly is that new techniques and functions are developed by specialist staff departments who become identified with that approach to the exclusion of all others. Supervisory training, in particular, looms so large in the supervisory world, that its adherents frequently forget that there may be many situations in which training is not the best route of change. On the contrary, it might be the worst way to try to bring about any real change.

Notes and References

1 GEORGOPOULOS, B. S. & TANNENBAUM, A. S. (1957). A study of organizational effectiveness. *American Sociological Review*, Vol. 22, pp. 534–40.

2 BROOM, L. & SMITH, J. H. (1963). Bridging occupations. *British Journal of Sociology*, Vol. 14, pp. 321–34.

3 FRIEDMANN, G. (1955). *Industrial society*. Free Press of Glencoe. (See Part III, Chapter III, for discussion of European experiments in work-place democracy.)

4 RICE, A. K. (1958). *Productivity and social organisation. The Ahmedebad experiment: industrial innovation, work organisation and management.* Tavistock, London.

5 EMERY, F. E. & THORSRUD, E. (1969). *Form and content in industrial democracy: a study of workers' representation at board level.* Tavistock, London.

6 SCHON, D. (1970). What can we know about social change? Reith Lectures No. 6. *The Listener*, Vol. 84, No. 2178 (24 December), pp. 874–6. BBC Publications, London.

7 FLEISHMAN, E. A. (1953). Leadership climate, human relations training and supervisory behavior. *Personnel Psychology*, Vol. 6, pp. 205–22.

3. *Analysis I: Basic Concepts*

HOW DO WE DEFINE AN ELEPHANT?

To the practical man the discussion of definitions is a tiresome business and frequently an unfruitful one. Why worry about it? The only purpose would seem to be to help us clarify the parameters of our problem. We do, however, need to use a number of basic concepts in our discussion and these need some consistent meaning to be attached to them. Let us take the case of the word 'supervisor' or 'foreman'. Here, there have indeed been many attempts at definition, very few of which appear to be of general use. The problem is that 'supervision' is a term with a popular meaning (in different languages), but it is also a term which writers attempt to use more precisely by introducing a special interpretation of it. We can take, for instance, these definitions:

'A supervisor is a person in constant control of a definite section of a labour force in an undertaking, exercising it either directly or through subordinates and responsible for this to a higher level of management.'[1]

'Throughout the report the word "foremen" is used to mean the men and women in industry who are in charge of a production or maintenance unit and who are in immediate daily contact with the operatives whose work they direct and control.'[2]

'Supervisor (arbetsledare) is the person who has received the commission to carry out the intentions of top management through direct leadership of a work group in the company organizationally subordinate to him. Thereby he has taken over the responsibility for carrying out these intentions as concerns this organizational unit. He is supposed to do work of the same kind as his subordinates only in emergencies or for training purposes.'[3]

It is very difficult in these definitions to avoid using phrases such as 'control of a definite section of a labour force' or 'in charge of a production or maintenance unit', which are of little concrete meaning.

There are at least three possible theoretical ways of distinguishing supervisors from other employees in an organization. They can be distinguished by their job titles, by the managerial status and authority accorded to them, or by the tasks they carry out. It is not very satisfactory to mark out a supervisor by his job title. Most industries have traditional titles which they use for particular jobs and these terms are not interchangeable between industries. They often refer to quite different kinds of responsibilities and tasks. For instance, in a Swedish study[4] among others the following examples are mentioned: verkmästare, förman, maskinmästare, inspektor, vägmästare, driftsingenjör, arbetschef, övermontör. In the 1951 inquiry of the National Institute of Industrial Psychology, at least 200 different job titles were found among men and women regarded as supervisors.[5]

If we say that supervisors are employees with a distinct managerial status, we mean that it is recognized that they have some degree of authority over others and some type of higher status than the operatives or workers on the shop floor. It is also often unofficially recognized in many organizations that supervisors are in an in-between position, being neither full members of the management nor workers. This fact has been pointed out by numerous writers, for instance by Roethlisberger[6] in his famous article. There is a clue here, therefore, to the nature of the supervisory role.

Managerial status taken by itself, however, is not a good criterion for distinguishing supervisors from managers or workers. The reason for this is that such perceived status may be extremely ambiguous. Status as a supervisor may seem to imply some sort of managerial authority. Yet formal authority and status recognized by management may not coincide with informal status and authority recognized by workers or junior or staff managers. It is very common indeed to find individuals with such an ambiguous and ill-defined authority situation who are giving orders or leading groups without any clearly prescribed managerial authority to do so. It may be that their influence over workers depends on *not* having formal supervisory authority.

THE SUPERVISORY JOB

It may seem easier to define supervision as being composed of a number of common 'supervisory tasks'. In particular, in many studies, supervision has been identified with 'man management' or leadership tasks and the actual process of getting workers to do what the management wish them to do. Unfortunately, many of the studies of supervisors' jobs which have been carried out in the past twenty years, particularly in Sweden and the United Kingdom, have shown that such 'man management' tasks usually are a rather small proportion of the total tasks carried out.[7, 8] Not only are these human relations tasks in many cases a small percentage of the total time spent at work, but there are great variations between industries and firms and even between departments and shifts as to the nature of these tasks. It is very difficult to identify any task common to all supervisors. A person called a 'supervisor' could apparently be doing anything in his job from clerical work, inspection of raw materials, giving instructions to operatives, pushing trucks around, to feeding conveyor belts, physically opening valves, showing visitors around the section, mending machines, sweeping up, settling a dispute with a shop steward – in fact any number of a hundred or more managerial or technical tasks. In these studies the pattern of tasks seems to vary with the 'level' of supervisor and with the industry concerned. In this sense, a supervisor's job appears to be a type of empty box, to be filled with activities and tasks according to the particular situation.

THE SUPERVISORY ROLE

There seems, therefore, to be no simple way of defining a supervisor's job which fits all industries and all situations. This problem is, however, more a difficulty for the theorist than a practical problem for managers. In any particular company, managers and workers can usually identify and explain who their supervisors are. This is easy if job titles and specifications have been formalized, but it is also possible in most cases for supervisors whose position rests on informal understanding. Workers and managers 'recognize' supervisors by perceiving behaviour and interpreting it as being connected with a supervisory role. The connotations attached to a supervisory role depend on the culture of the society in which the organization exists. There are differences in the general social meaning of a supervisory role between Europe, Japan and the United States and even for instance, between Sweden and the United Kingdom (see Chapter 1).

The term 'work role' refers to the part played by 'actors' within an organization. Each role has a stereotype of certain combinations of behaviour patterns attached to it and expected of the person occupying the role. Participants in an organization may or may not agree about these expectations. They may refer to the behaviour itself or to the supposed norms governing the behaviour. Supervisors, therefore, occupy roles which imply expectations of behaviour from workers, superiors, functional management and other supervisors (not to mention their wives and others outside the occupational group). Role behaviour is, itself, partly created by the supervisors themselves to conform with their own ideas and beliefs about supervision and is partly 'sent' to them by the expectations of others.

SYSTEM OF SUPERVISION

A 'system of supervision' is a set of interacting supervisory roles. The use of the term 'system' is dangerous due to its ambiguity but a good substitute is hard to find. In this context, it does not imply complete autonomy or refer merely to norms or procedures. It is a social system consisting of people who are engaged in the continuing control of a 'production system'. This does not, of course, mean that all supervisors are production supervisors; they might be concerned with other functions. In large or complex systems there are supervisors on several different status levels. Many of the studies of supervision in the past have avoided discussion of this problem by referring only to the so-called 'first-line supervisor'. In many systems of supervision, however, there may be anything up to four or six levels – as measured by status – of people who are perceived to be carrying out supervisory roles. It is useful, however, for our purposes to distinguish three basic types of supervisory role:

1. The 'pure' type of supervisor role, wholly concerned with direct control of a production system in daily work and formally recognized as 'supervisory'

by management, and informally recognized as such by those supervised, his colleagues, etc. (as measured by their expectations).

2. The 'mixed' type of supervisory/managerial role, where the status may be *formally* that of a supervisor but the work content is such that the person concerned is dealing most of the time with specialized tasks and not with the overall control of a production system. Another case is the contrary, where a manager does not trust his supervisors and insists on exercising direct supervision himself.

3. The 'mixed' type of supervisor/worker role, where the person concerned again may, for instance, have a formal role status as a supervisor but no actual recognized authority in practice. A worker may also possess informal 'authority' but have no formal role position as a supervisor.[9]

Examples of the first type of role could include traditional roles, such as the 'Meister' or craft foreman, the building site agent, or, in modern technology, a production foreman on a car assembly line. There are many examples to be found of the second and third types of role in large manufacturing organizations. Technical assistants, for instance, may be used as assistants to line foremen, as in many Japanese companies, but their position within the supervisory system is often extremely unclear. They may also be key process operators or relief operators who assist and work with the formal supervisors in the task of controlling the production system but who do not see themselves as supervisors. It may be very difficult, therefore, to distinguish the exact boundaries of the supervisory system.

The only practical answer to this problem is to say that where *the system of roles is formally and informally recognized as dealing with a discrete area of control responsibility and where the supervisors themselves are actually working together on common problems, then it is not misleading to refer to a distinct supervisory system.* Sometimes, therefore, there may be no supervisory system existing, in the sense defined. Supervisors may be entirely isolated, or they may be integrated with other management control systems, as could be the case in a hospital or a large retail organization. Much depends on the organizational history of each case examined. To repeat, the existence of a supervisory system is contingent on both recognition and social interaction.

The shape, size and importance of each supervisory system depend not only on the problems and difficulties to be overcome in a particular trade but also on previous managerial decisions on manning, promotions, salary levels, status distinctions, etc. Each supervisory system can be described in terms of the types of roles and sets of roles within it; the norms and values of the members; the informal power, relationships and groupings within it; and the type and efficiency of communications within each system.

Supervisory systems vary enormously in the functions performed, but they could be classified by:

1. The degree to which procedures, methods, targets are prescribed by senior management or decided within the system.

2. The degree to which supervisors are meeting unexpected difficulties and demands.

3. The degree to which the tasks carried out and problems met in their daily work are new to them.

If we relate the second and third types to the degree to which supervisory situations and tasks are programmed, using the term as defined by Simon,[10] we could classify some types of supervisory system as in Figure 3.1.

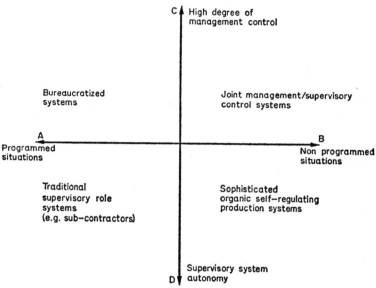

FIGURE 3.1   Types of supervisory system

We will see later the importance of these dimensions in the world of supervision.

In our previous discussion in the last chapter, the variables comprising a given supervisory system were classified into five areas or types. We need now to examine the meaning of these areas, and the variables themselves, which may be of crucial importance for the task of analysis.

SUPERVISORY WORK ACTIONS

The central position of the work actions box in Figure 2.4 is a useful corrective to any tendency towards undue abstraction caused by the 'systems' concept. We are indeed, in any attempt to change supervision, bound to take cognizance of *both* the facts of actual behaviour as well as the possible influences on that behaviour from individual, social, technical and economic factors. Work actions are supervisory acts within the pressures and turmoil of the work environment, acts with intended and unintended consequences. They can be analysed according to the *level* of interpretation of the 'actors' themselves or any given observer (Table 3.1).

This Table gives a suggested classification of levels of work action or behaviour and examples of items of behaviour at each level.

At level 5, information would be collected and used for analysis of work in ergonomic terms. There are several aspects of supervisory work behaviour for instance, the pace and amount of walking, reactions to field displays in control equipment and the reaction to the amount of noise, which are all open to ergonomic analysis. This discussion cannot be elaborated upon further in this text.[11] The amount of research on the physiological components of supervisory work is so far, extremely limited.

TABLE 3.1

Levels of supervisory action (with types of behaviour)

Levels of analysis of work action	Name of sequences of work behaviour	Example of action
1. Role	Style or strategies followed	Putting pressure on functional departments in order to get better service
2. Functions	Functions performed and tactical behaviour in solving problems	Personally inspecting machine in order to check how far maintenance is responsible for breakdown
3. Tasks	Prescribed tasks carried out and disturbance-handling behaviour	Checking controls on a particular machine after a breakdown
4. Activities	Habitual actions or procedures followed	Operating machine
5. Physical actions	Reflex actions	Moving muscles in arms and hands

At level 4, one can discuss behaviour in purely 'overt' terms. This means, for instance, that one is describing a supervisor walking, climbing ladders, writing letters, operating a machine, answering the telephone, etc. This would be a fairly objective description and does not include much interpretation as to the meaning of such behaviour.

The third level can be seen as the description of this behaviour in terms of tasks (or activities performed for specific ends). An example here would be the classification of behaviour in terms of clerical work or communication or inspection and other types of tasks.

These tasks can be grouped into broad functions on level 2, which can be defined by the purpose or aims of the organization within which the activity is taking place. For example, a clerical activity can be seen on this second level to be significant, as it is related to a remuneration problem.

On level 1, the description of behaviour is concerned with the style or the strategies followed.

The example given in Table 3.1 emphasizes the way in which the meaning of a particular item of supervisory work behaviour, i.e. the operation of a machine, takes on new significance when interpreted at each level. With a higher level, a larger 'unit' of work behaviour is required. At level 4, for instance, a snap-reading observation lasting only a second might be significant, whereas at level 1, knowledge of the sequence of behaviour over hours and days is necessary in order to make a correct interpretation. The higher the level, the more additional information is required in order to make sense of the piece of behaviour described.

At each level, any description of supervisory behaviour is necessarily *selective* and is certain to miss out aspects of behaviour on other levels. For instance, to classify an activity or behaviour as 'walking' is to give a description only on the fourth level, and this omits the direction of where the person is walking to and the reasons for it, and also does not mention (at a lower level) the physiological description which could be made of the movements which constitute that particular activity of walking. Descriptions, therefore, and classifications of behaviour can never be complete or comprehensive in themselves and have to be seen as being derived from a set of defined viewpoints or 'frames of reference'.

We can take an example of this from supervisory behaviour, a very simple one, an incident in the daily life of a supervisor. Let us say that the supervisor is giving a piece of paper to another member of the staff. At the overt level this would be classified as giving or handing paper from A to B. This does not include, therefore, any information as to what the person is saying as he gives this paper to the other person, the way he says it, to whom he gives it, what is on the paper, why he is giving it, whether he ever gave it to the man before, and finally whether he normally gives this paper at this time to that person.

The term 'supervisory work actions', therefore, is a very complex one and can only be understood accurately when we know at what level the term is being used. For this particular book, supervisory action refers only to *work* behaviour and will exclude trivial behaviour on the job which is irrelevant to the work or role concerned. This means that when the term is being used, it must be further defined according to the specific 'dimension' of interest. For instance, we may talk about supervisory work behaviour and then list the specific level and reference points after this. The most accessible level is undoubtedly the third. The first and second can often be discussed in terms of an initial study on level 3.

By the term 'work action analysis', therefore, is meant a systematic study of supervisory behaviour at work. Just as supervisory behaviour itself can be interpreted in different ways and on different levels, so the methods of analysing work are related to different frames of reference and can result in different kinds of studies for different purposes. We may be analysing behaviour with the ultimate aim of improving organization or perhaps of changing selection criteria or training programmes. We may be engaged in testing a research hypothesis. Whatever it is, actions include the elements of behaviour and the interpretations and feelings of the actors. In a case study, information on these matters is necessary for adequate judgement about the effect of any given set of changes. The analysis of supervisory work actions is central to the building of any predictive model.

This might be challenged, however. The critic might argue that one could carry out an assessment of supervision without a lengthy and perhaps tedious analysis and description of the pattern of work activities. Surely it should be possible to make predictions and discover meaningful correlations between individual characteristics and effects without knowing about work actions in detail? The answer to this argument is that, *if* one had a very extensive knowledge of the variables comprising important individual characteristics and the work situation, it might be possible to predict behaviour patterns, provided the environment one was dealing with was relatively predictable. An example here would be an automatic process plant where the man-machine system was operated by workers with limited opportunities for any deviations from the programmed tasks. In the normal industrial situation, however, it would be very difficult to create a simple model of supervisory system and behaviour patterns and to make accurate predictions from the knowledge of background variables alone. In the cases of manufacturing and construction industry which have been examined by the authors, the numbers of interacting variables are in fact enormous, possibly infinite, in the boxes which have so far been labelled in the model in Figure 2.4. This is one important reason why there are, in reality, tremendous variations in work patterns among supervisory systems if we compare them company by company, industry by industry, country by country.

Many researchers, managers and consultants have indeed been operating with models of supervisory behaviour which are gravely inaccurate. The inaccuracy arises in the research worker's case because academics have tried to suggest hypotheses and test relationships between selected criteria and related variables (such as types of organization, leadership style and so forth) with little personal and intimate knowledge of the way foremen are in reality behaving in attempting to grapple with their problems. This could be compared with the use of the cybernetic black box analogy in that the research workers were aware of inputs and outputs but not aware of what was going on inside the box. Many of the studies commented on in Chapter 4 can be seen in this light.

Managers also have operated with ideas about supervisory behaviour that are likewise highly oversimplified. Many managers, of course, have had experience of shop-floor supervision in the past and this has made them confident that they understand the position of the foreman. Many changes have often taken place, however, since such experience, and it could be argued that experience at one time on the shop floor is no guarantee that one understands the current situation. The alternative career route for managers, that is, promotion from technologist or engineer, can lead to the possession of stereotypes by managers about supervisory behaviour of a quite different nature. These may be associated with the feeling that supervisors are operating with out-of-date ideas, are in many cases resisting change, and, in any event, are only blindly carrying out the work which was delegated from higher management. There are some reasons, therefore, for suspecting that middle and top management have a less than accurate view of the supervisory situation.

Two further reasons reinforce this point. The habit of being accustomed to relative autonomy has stimulated resistance by supervisors to the increasing attempts by functional management staff to extend their control systems over the shop floor. Supervisors have been often aware that information reported upwards to management would diminish their discretion and their room for manœuvre in tight corners. In most of the studies made by the authors, some type of 'conspiracy of silence' could be argued to exist, in which supervisors made sure that management were not aware of many aspects of shop-floor problems. A second point is related to the nature of supervisory work. Most models of supervisory jobs up to the present have attempted to describe them in terms of responsibilities and functions. We see in Table 3.2 an extract of a job description for a group of supervisors.[12] Table 3.3 shows part of a general job description for foremen, outlined by the Swedish Supervisory Training Institute.[13]

This type of job description or job specification in itself tends to give a distorted image of supervisory work. There is little account taken here of the daily pressures on the supervisors, and the description itself is a static one, giving no real

TABLE 3.2

Level of authority in various functions of a group of first-line supervisors as perceived by superiors
(from Lennerlöf, 1966)

Task	Authority level Arithmetic mean of group
Order machines within the company	3·31
Have repairs made to machines and other equipment	4·27
Introduce new working methods	3·35
Fix delivery times	2·38
Reject imperfect products	3·58
Supervise and improve the quality of the worker's work	4·74
Order overtime to be worked	4·73
Prepare and carry out instruction in new duties	3·54
Supervise safety regulations and take steps when they are ignored	4·63
Recruit permanent staff	2·56
Lay off workers	1·23
Fix price rates for a certain job	4·15
Give advances on wages	0·21
Give oral warning	3·59

Authority scale: 0 = The activity is dealt with by someone else
               1 = The supervisor does not affect the decision but only acts after given orders
               2 = The decision is made by someone else but the supervisor affects the decision
               3 = The supervisor and someone else make the decision together
               4 = The supervisor makes the decision himself but someone else influences the decision-making
               5 = The supervisor makes the decision entirely on his own

TABLE 3.3

General description of a supervisor's responsibilities for profitability, personnel matters and technical problems

Make use of and develop job knowledge of employees.
Contribute to the application and development of rational work methods.
Follow-up and analyse work results.
Take part in the recruitment of new personnel suitable for the job and the work group.
Instruct employees working in the department in an appropriate way.
Strive to adapt job tasks to the ability of each individual.
Know laws and actual contracts, and answer for the observance of them.
Watch that the workplace answers to actual requirements concerning protection, safety and health, and develop co-workers' understanding of protection and safety instructions enjoined upon, so that they are observed. Make use of and suitably place employees with limited psychical and physical resources.
Develop rational work methods and working conditions.
Co-operate loyally with specialists in development matters.
Make use of and develop the qualifications of his subordinates.
Inform his subordinates of forthcoming changes of work methods, products and of the organization.
Make clear to subordinates the economic conditions and results of the organizational unit.
Inform superiors of working climate and morale of the organizational unit.

flavour of the dynamics of such a job. A specification by management that safety should be an important priority and function of supervision, for example, may be assented to by the supervisors concerned but does not result, in reality, in much time spent on safety inspection. Why is this so? The supervisor will tell the investigator that this is because he has no time to carry out such safety inspection. The manager may say that he should *make* time. In reality it means that the supervisor has a scale of priorities; and safety problems, particularly routine safety activities, tend to come lower on that scale than dealing with breakdowns, for instance, or with crises of one type or another. Things going wrong, disturbances, problems arising that were not predicted are, in fact, among the core of the most important functions and activities in the supervisory job.[14] This point has been emphasized again and again in case studies of supervisory work; and in these cases it has been clear that many of the senior and middle managements have totally underestimated the proportion of time spent in dealing with such disturbances. They certainly misunderstood the type of responsibility which appears to be necessary in dealing with contingencies. In many cases they might, if questioned, resent the supervisors' initiatives and argue that such problems should have been passed to them.

For these reasons, therefore, it is necessary to look at work behaviour in a systematic and more objective way than can be deduced from merely asking supervisors or managers to explain their work. We describe methods of examining supervisory work behaviour later in this book. One method is using an observer diary to make a continuous record of the supervisors at work. If such a method is used, one gets a set of activities over the day dividing it into various incidents. The example in Table 3.4 is taken from a famous study of foremen on an assembly line.[15]

TABLE 3.4

Observation record of foreman Pat on the Jungle Line

2:15 p.m.   Pat checks with scheduler S. Looks at hourly report of number of cars coming through body shop.

2:16 p.m.   Walks over to R (repair man) on pickup line and checks to see if earlier repair trouble was corrected.

2:17 p.m.   Calls over inspection foreman to show him a hole missing in a piece. Inspection foreman acknowledges and will notify the trim department.

2:19 p.m.   Pat tells repair man to locate the hole by eye until it comes through all right. Pat has a drink of water.

2:20 p.m.   Pat walks over to station 5 and asks his utility man how many men he still has to relieve. (In the morning and in the afternoon, the utility man relieves each of the fourteen men for a period of 8 to 10 minutes.)

Pat moves along the line – stations 5, 6, 7 – checking visually on the quality of work.

2:21 p.m.   Checks a loose nut on a fixture at station 7. Speaks with operator.

2:22 p.m.   Man at station 3 calls for materials. Pat tells man at sub-assembly bench E to make up more material.

2:23 p.m.   Walks over to MH (stock man). Tells stock man the line is getting low on hinges. They discuss the number short and agree there are enough for tomorrow.

2:25 p.m.   Walks from MH to station 1 and makes visual check on the car body to check on the hole discussed earlier at the pickup line.

2:26 p.m.   Pat sees foreman from preceding section and tells him about the missing hole. A hand signal from welder at W.

Source: Walker, Guest, and Turner, ref. 15

Such activities show a variety of actions. If we analyse these actions and ask why they took place, we might find some that are tasks or behaviour prescribed by management. In a study of foremen carried out in the United Kingdom, a sample of liquid from the process was taken every hour, on the hour, throughout the day. This type of exactly prescribed behaviour for foremen is, however, very rare. The behaviour in the work diary may be a reflection of the beliefs of the foremen; it may reflect their own personal stereotypes about how to deal with certain issues; it may reflect ideals. It may show some significant pattern over the short or long term. In the short term, it is possible to see much of the behaviour, however, as responses to stimuli rather than reflections of personal stereotypes. A foreman noticing a machine variation or a dangerous hazard and taking action to deal with this should be an example of a response to an outside stimulus. The stimuli might also come from a grievance taken up with the foreman by a shop-steward or worker. These actions can, therefore, be thought of as responses to deviations from the expectations the supervisors have of normal work practices. These responses could range from semi-conscious reactions to deliberate planning.

The time spent on dealing with disturbances varies very considerably from one type of production system to another. It varies clearly with the amount of time, energy and resources management are putting into preventive work, such as the planning of production by specialized departments. What is undoubtedly true, however, is that in nearly all supervisory jobs examined by the authors, disturbances of some type or other represented some of the most critical areas in their job.[16, 17] The disturbance or activities connected with it will appear in a diary as a type of incident, and the 'incident' has been the unit of measurement of most researchers who have attempted to measure managerial and supervisory work by this method. The incident may be defined by the contact, by the length of time spent on the particular problem or with the particular person, and the use of the term varies from author to author.

The examination of a record of such incidents for supervisors, at first sight may appear to shed little light on the meaning of such supervisory actions. Many of the incidents appear to be isolated and have no connection with each other. It is only after a greater understanding of the work situation and the type of problems which the supervisor was facing and after assessing the relationships in the department in detail that it is possible to link and relate incidents with each other. In reality, one incident may be highly significant, if seen as part of a pattern of activities undertaken by a supervisor in trying to solve a particular long-term problem. It is possible to use this concept to describe supervisory work as a collection of problems and disturbances which the supervisor in a sense is carrying around with him.[18] Some of these problems, like the examples of disturbances quoted above, may be 'thrown' at the supervisor with no choice on his part. Other problems he might decide to take up on his own initiative. In this latter case, there is the question of how far the supervisor recognizes that a problem exists. Secondly, he has to decide whether it is a significant matter which demands action.[19]

In this way, analysis of supervisory work actions *starts* with the actual behaviour, but goes on to try to unravel the reasons for actions taken and not taken. This inevitably leads to an historical or case-study approach.

INDIVIDUAL CHARACTERISTICS OF SUPERVISORS

In the right-hand corner of Figure 2.4 the area labelled 'Individual characteristics' refers to any biographical attributes, personality traits, intellectual capabilities, acquired skills and knowledge, as well as the motivation and drives which lie behind the structure of the personality. It includes the level and type of job satisfaction felt by the supervisors in question. It includes their capacity and willingness to adjust to new situations and their mental sets.

Figure 3.2 shows examples of some of the more important types of individual characteristics which are likely to be useful in helping to explain supervisory work behaviour. It is merely a check list. The variables listed here range from those derived from a person's social environment (at the top half of the Figure) to those derived from individual psychological and physiological capacity (at the bottom right). These characteristics, therefore, refer to *all* the factors brought into the work situation by the individual concerned when he joins a 'supervisory system'.

FIGURE 3.2   Examples of important types of individual characteristics of supervisors

1. Age and sex (roles in society)
2. Type of family background
3. Social background and occupational history
4. Education and general knowledge
5. Technical knowledge
6. Skills
7. Opinions, attitudes, perceptions and expectations on work roles
8. Personal requirements for work satisfaction
9. Ideology and values

10. Intellectual capacity
11. Personality traits
12. Interests
13. Drives and motivation
14. Physiological capacity and health

THE SUPERVISORY WORK SITUATION

The term 'supervisory work situation' is a shorthand phrase to cover all the influences on supervisory behaviour which are derived from the work situation in its social, economic and technical contexts. Figure 3.3 shows examples of a number of such influences. These include the economic and market situation of

FIGURE 3.3   Examples of important types of situational variables

15. Constraints and pressures from the local community and the state
14. Level of demand for company's products and rate of growth
13. Situation of local labour market
12. Type of trade union organization and relative power
11. Values and norms held by other supervisors in the company
10. Behaviour of superiors and their norms and expectations of supervisory behaviour
9. Type of management administrative system
8. Rewards and sanctions for supervisors
7. Number and type of supervisory tasks prescribed
6 Type of supervisory system and work organization
5. Rate of change in the production system
4. Type of industry, type of production system and occurrence of disturbances
3. Rewards and sanctions for workers
2. Behaviour of workers and their norms and expectations of supervisory behaviour
1. Number and type of subordinates

an organization, the precise technical situation, the general production situation, and the sociological situation. The latter may be very complex, as it is derived from the numerous social systems related to the supervisory system itself. It includes all the face-to-face groups with which the supervisor is involved, i.e. on the shop floor, among work colleagues, and among the management. It includes the formal organization structure within which the supervisor must exist. The norms and general 'culture' guiding the supervisor in his company are also important background factors.

Although it is useful to bracket these situational factors together, this does not imply that they are of equal importance or that they affect the supervisory work behaviour in the same way. The reader will note that some of the factors listed are likely to have an immediate and direct influence on supervisory behaviour, whereas others are indirect factors acting through intermediate variables. It is also true that these factors show a different effect on supervisory work behaviour according to the level of behaviour selected for examination. They are clearly, in many cases, interdependent, and yet they may lead to a conflict situation in that the demands of the work environment may be in opposition to family or other roles with their concomitant expectations of behaviour. The factors range from those in the immediate production situation in the bottom to those in the economic and social environment of the enterprise in the top of the area.

EFFECTS OF SUPERVISORY WORK ACTIONS

Figure 3.4 shows some examples of important types of effects from supervisory work behaviour, which are often used as criteria of supervisor performance.

FIGURE 3.4 Examples of important types of effects from supervisory work behaviour on the performance of the local production system

S.W. corner of Figure 2.4

Extent to which production
targets are completed
Extent to which quality
standards are met
Extent of machine utilization
(frequency of machine
breakdowns)
Extent of material and
component utilization

Extent of personnel utilization
Relative level of personnel indices
Level of worker job satisfaction, attitudes and reactions of superiors and peers
Rate of introduction of innovations

One of the central issues in improving supervision is the search for methods by which the relative effectiveness of various types and styles of supervisory behaviour can be determined. This problem requires the establishment of criteria for the assessment of supervisory performance and for measuring the effect that the supervisor behaviour *appears* to have (or is perceived to have).

The typical supervisory situation, however, makes the measurement of his job performance a difficult matter. In the first place, a supervisor's actions are often concerned with the process of organizing and allocating work, encouraging and motivating others, planning the work of subordinates, handling disturbances and so on, rather than directly completing operations himself. In other words, the success or failure of a large part of a supervisor's efforts may depend on his success in persuading or training others to produce satisfactory work. The failure of his subordinates to meet production targets, for instance, could be due to poor supervision, but equally it may be the result of factors beyond the supervisor's control. The criteria are not 'clean' criteria.

It is very difficult, therefore, to use criteria of operative performance, let alone indices of labour turnover, accidents, etc., as relevant measures of the relative quality of supervision. On the other hand, it is clear that supervisor behaviour *may* have a critical effect on operative job satisfaction and performance. As Herzberg and his colleagues[20] argue, supervisory behaviour may not be a direct motivator for workers, but may be one of the 'hygiene' factors without which a satisfactory level of motivation is impossible to attain.

A further difficulty is introduced by the fact that much of the effort of supervisors in larger and more complex technologies, is absorbed by relationships with other supervisors and with various specialist members of management. This leads to two problems for measuring supervisor performance:

(*a*) The performance of his own subordinates under the formal individual command of the supervisor may be a relatively small concern of the supervisor within his total job. Of more importance may be the common problems affecting all the supervisors within a given production system, and his relative contribution towards the solution of such common problems may be difficult to discern.

(*b*) A supervisor may cause by his behaviour direct repercussions on the behaviour and judgements of other managers, and yet these effects may not be intentional and may be, again, very difficult to trace.

One solution appears to be to attempt to measure selected indices of performance of a particular production system as a whole and to try to relate these to the behaviour of supervisors *taken together as a 'system'*. The size of the production system chosen would depend on the type of technology and the degree of integration of processes.

It is fairly easy to see from this discussion that a supervisor's work behaviour may also have an effect on the performance of the whole organization (factory, construction site, etc.). This can be through the intervening effect of changes which he causes in his local production situation reacting on the performance of other departments. This would be a type of 'multiplier' effect. Another possibility is that supervisors may have a direct effect on factory policy, relationships or performance through their personal contacts with other departments and senior management.

Figure 3.5, therefore, is a reminder of the possible effects of supervision on total organizational performance. The likelihood of measuring such effects accurately is much less probable than in the case of the 'local' production system mentioned above.

FIGURE 3.5   Examples of important types of effects from supervisory work
behaviour on the performance of the total organization

S.W. corner of Figure 2.4

Extent to which
orders are completed
on time
Extent to which
customers' require-
ments for quality
of product are met
Extent to which
current costs are
controlled at a
competitive level
Relative size of profit per unit of
output
Extent to which the organization
can adapt its procedures and products
to new situations
Extent to which satisfactory working
relationships are maintained

Supervisory actions, however, and their effects on organizational performance *can* also have further repercussions on extra-organizational factors, or on the supervisors themselves. We show some examples of the former case in Figure 3.6.

FIGURE 3.6   Examples of types of effects on factors outside the organization

S.W. corner of Figure 2.4

Trade union strategy
and action
Government or private
organizations' educational
and training policies
for supervisors
Relations with customers and clients

The point at issue here is that although the work role and its effects can normally be seen as a discrete field of 'action', there are occasions when *one* work action could have wider implications. Examples would include the intemperate sacking of a steward by a foreman or a mistake made in a vital quality check on a product. In the latter case, Figure 3.6 shows some critical areas which may be affected by such actions.

Examples of possible effects on themselves are shown in Figure 3.7.

FIGURE 3.7 Examples of types of effects on supervisors themselves

S.E. corner of Figure 2.4

Supervisor's own personal job satisfaction Supervisor's capacity for adaption

Supervisor's sense of meaning in work.
Supervisor's acquisition of skills and knowledge

THE MODEL OF THE SUPERVISORY SYSTEM

Turning back to Figure 2.4 it will be recalled that interrelationships between variables in areas described above are expressed by arrows across the boundaries of the areas. In reality, the interrelationships between variables are too many to show accurately on any diagram of this sort. The arrows merely indicate the broad direction of possible interrelationship. The whole model can be seen as a type of input and output system, but it is an oversimplification to regard certain variables as 'causing' effects unilaterally. In most cases, one set of conditions will co-exist with another set of conditions, because they support each other. An example would be a production shop where the workers were highly productive and motivated and in which the supervisors could afford to practise a more permissive type of supervision, which itself tends to support workers in their attitudes. This type of vicious or virtuous circle can, however, change over time. For this reason, the effect of changing conditions over time would be indicated by making a set of models for various points in time. The 'effects' of actions at point one could clearly be included in the work situation, and individual characteristic variables at point two, as helping to determine behaviour at this second point in time. It is also important to note that our model does not presuppose any functional interdependence between the factors mentioned as *necessarily* existing. It does not exclude possible conflict within the various systems mentioned.

Notes and References

1 Ministry of Labour Committee of Training of Supervisors (1954). HMSO, London.
2 GRABE, S. & SILBERER, P. (1956). *Selecion and training of foremen in Europe.* European Productivity Agency, Paris.

3 *Arbetsledarens ställning och ansvar* (1964). Arbetsledareinstitutet, Lidingö (mimeographed).

4 *Arbetsledarnas rekrytering och utbildning* (1963). Swedish Council for Personnel Administration & Swedish Supervisors Union, Stockholm (mimeographed).

5 *The foreman. A study of supervision in British industry* (1951). The National Institute of Industrial Psychology, London (*see* appendix).

6 ROETHLISBERGER, F. J. (1945). The foreman: master and victim of double talk. *Harvard Business Review*, Vol. 23, pp. 283–98.

7 THURLEY, K. E. & HAMBLIN, A. C. (1963). *The supervisor and his job.* DSIR, HMSO, London.

8 WIRDENIUS, H. (1961). *Förmän i arbete.* Swedish Council for Personnel Administration, Stockholm.

9 STRAUSS, G. (1957). The changing role of the working supervisor. *Journal of Business of the University of Chicago*, Vol. 30 (July), pp. 202–11.

10 SIMON, H. A. (1962). *The new science of management decision.* Harper and Row, New York.

11 METZ, B. (1960). *Fitting the job to the worker.* Project No. 6/07 E, OEEC, Paris.

12 LENNERLÖF, L. (1966). *Dimensions of supervision.* The Swedish Council for Personnel Administration, Stockholm.

13 *Arbetsledarens ställning och ansvar* (1964). Arbetsledareinstitutet, Lidingö (mimeographed).

14 HERBERT, A., MARTVALL, K. & WIRDENIUS, H. (1967). *Perceptions and behaviour of site agents when encountering disturbances in the production process.* Unpublished paper at Anglo–Swedish Research Meeting, Cambridge.

15 WALKER, C. R., GUEST, R. H. & TURNER, A. N. (1956). *The foreman on the assembly line*, pp. 159–60. Harvard University Press, Cambridge, Mass.

16 THURLEY, K. E. & HAMBLIN, A. C. (1963). op. cit.

17 DOCHERTY, P. H. G. (1971). *A study of perceived contingencies in a Swedish building company.* University of London (Ph.D. thesis).

18 MARPLES, D. L. (1967). Studies of managers – a fresh start. *Journal of Management Studies*, Vol. 4, No. 3, pp. 282–99.

19 DEEKS, J., MAJID, S. A., PINSCHOF, M. & THURLEY, K. E. (1967). *Problem solving behaviour in construction project management.* Unpublished paper given to Anglo–Swedish Conference on 'Human factors in the construction process', September 1967. (On construction sites the evidence in the U.K. appears to be that in many cases supervisors decide against action unless absolutely necessary.)

20 HERZBERG, F., MAUSNER, B. & SNYDERMAN, B. (1959). *Motivation to work.* Wiley, New York.

4. *Analysis II: Theory*

STUDIES OF SUPERVISORY EFFECTIVENESS

The problem of measuring the effectiveness of supervisory performance has exercised the attention of researchers now for the last three decades. There are, however, rather few comprehensive studies in this field, probably because of a general lack of understanding of the complexities of the problem. Basically, in order to measure the effectiveness of any supervisory performance and to attempt to explain that performance, it is necessary to provide adequate data for measuring the factors which are supposed to contribute to that performance.

If we turn back to Figure 2.4, it can be seen that, in these terms, all factors arising from the supervisory work situation, or from the individual characteristics of the supervisor himself, might be included, as well as detailed information on supervisory work behaviour itself. The effects of supervisory work behaviour might be measured in the local situation, i.e. in the local production system or in a more general sense within the organization (organizational effects). There are many types of study design possible with different combinations of variables, but it can be said as a general principle of such research that it is necessary to have information on criteria of performance, at either the local or organizational level, and information on work behaviour, individual characteristics, and the work situation. The average study, therefore, relies heavily on statistical correlations between at least two sets of variables, performance variables and some descriptive variables.

Table 4.1 gives examples of some of the more fundamental studies in this field. They are described in terms of their hypotheses, the types of variables measured, and the research methods used. Some of the main results are noted, and, at the right-hand side, some of the difficulties which appeared in the particular research design used. These studies are not only of theoretical interest but it is essential to use the experience of such research if we are to understand the types of problem which lie in the way of any attempt to improve supervisory performance. The same difficulties that appear in the research design will undoubtedly appear in any practical exercise of this kind.

LIMITATIONS OF RESEARCH DESIGN OF PREVIOUS STUDIES

It will be seen that few of these studies show evidence of attempts to gather comprehensive and reliable data on the work behaviour of supervisors in the situation studied. Many of the studies rely exclusively on questionnaire evidence of work behaviour, reflecting either perceptions of workers or ratings of peers and superiors. The activity sampling used by Davis[5, 6] mentioned in Table 4.1 is also

TABLE 4.1

Some important studies of supervisor behaviour and performance

Main hypotheses tested	Sets of variables involved	Research methods used	Main results	Difficulties arising
(A) WESTERLUND, 1952[1] Production units under line supervisors show higher productivity and job satisfaction than those under functional supervisors.	*Individual characteristics* – *Supervisor work situation* Line v. functional organization *Supervisor work behaviour* Level 3. *Effects of supervisor work behaviour* Production records. Number of mistakes. Job satisfaction.	Self-observation of supervisors. Output data.	This was a field experiment in a telephone exchange handling long-distance calls. The units with line supervision showed fewer rest-breaks, higher output in most respects, and more contact with the supervisor. The work load was more evenly allocated within the group. These supervisors spent more time on training and supervision without workers perceiving that the supervision was more thorough.	1 Study is limited to a service situation with female labour. 2 Possible Hawthorne effect.

Main hypotheses tested	Sets of variables involved	Research methods used	Main results	Difficulties arising
(B) KAHN & KATZ, 1953[2]				
1 The supervisor with a more differentiated role has a higher productive unit.	*Individual characteristics* Attitudes of supervisors. Beliefs about supervisory role.	Estimates of foremen's behaviour of subordinates. Supervisors' interview data. Perceptions of foremen's behaviour and attitudes by subordinates.	This study attempted to find correlations between styles of leadership, behaviour among supervisors and production records. Job satisfaction	1 Study does not take technological or most situational variables into account.
2 The supervisor who practices 'open' supervision has a higher productive unit.	*Supervisor work situation* Degree of prescription of tasks. Norms and expectations of superior.	Subordinates' job satisfaction interview data. Records of productivity.	was seen as an intervening variable. In some situations productivity and job satisfaction were seen to have common determinants,	2 Reliance on perceptions and estimates of behaviour and no independent evidence of manifest behaviour given.
3 The supervisor who is oriented towards the needs of his subordinates rather than to production requirements has a higher productive unit.	*Supervisor work behaviour* Level 1. Level 2. *Effects of supervisor work behaviour* Cohesiveness in work group. High job satisfaction. High productivity.		but it was noted that high job satisfaction can co-exist with low productivity and vice versa.	3 Relevance and reliability of data on productivity records is doubtful.

Main hypotheses tested	Sets of variables involved	Research methods used	Main results	Difficulties arising
(C) FLEISHMAN, HARRIS & BURTT, 1955[3] (Effectiveness study) 1 There is a correlation between the degree of considerate behaviour shown by foremen and their effectiveness and that of their work groups. 2 There is a correlation between the degree of initiating structure shown by foremen and their effectiveness and that of their work groups.	*Individual characteristics* — *Supervisor work situation* Age, education, marital status, skill and seniority of subordinates. Method of pay. Hazards. Pleasantness of job (effect of above factors was estimated). Distinguished production and non-production sections. *Supervisor work behaviour* Subordinates' perception of behaviour. *Effects of supervisor work behaviour on local production system* Absenteeism (not permitted). Accidents. Grievances. Employee turnover. Appraisal of foreman and foreman's behaviour by workers. *Effects on total organization* Proficiency ratings of foremen by superiors	Development of questionnaires (Supervisory Behaviour Description) to measure perception of supervisor work behaviour (by subordinates). Decontamination of objective criteria by elimination of effects of other variables. Use of 'paired comparisons' for superiors' ratings. Use of scaling technique for describing how workers liked foremen.	Correlations existed between styles of foremen behaviour and effectiveness as hypothesized, but varied between production and non-production departments. 'Objective' criteria and workers' likings correlated positively with consideration and negatively with structure. Superiors' ratings correlated positively with structure and negatively with consideration. Departments with tight production schedules correlated positively with structure.	1 Study design correlates supervisor's scores (for consideration and initiating structure) with various criteria, *assumes* the validity and relevance of such scores. Little account is apparently taken of the subjective character of subordinate perceptions which may be based on stereotypes (contacts between foremen and workers may be extremely low). 2 Superiors' ratings may suffer from similar lack of knowledge. 3 Highest correlations are between workers' perceptions of the supervisory role, workers' appraisals of that role and workers' absenteeism. This could be quite independent from supervisor behaviour.

Main hypotheses tested	Sets of variables involved	Research methods used	Main results	Difficulties arising
(D) WESTERLUND & STRÖMBERG, 1965[4] The frequency of the contacts of foremen with their superiors and peers is related to the performance of employees in the foremen's production system.	*Individual characteristics* Age. Length of service, etc. *Supervisor work situation* Volume and quality of and variations in production. Company organization structure. Degree of mechanization. Personnel structure of each department. *Supervisor work behaviour* Recorded interactions between foremen and others. *Effects of supervisor work behaviour on local production system* Costs. Absence. Turnover. Quality and quantity produced. Number of suggestions.	Care was taken to compare departments within companies, where the foreman's work situation was roughly comparable. The frequency of inter-actions was then compared with a large list of criteria of performance and behaviour of the workers concerned.	No definite evidence of any correlations between the frequency of contacts and any criteria.	This study was part of a larger investigation (see text), which attempted to measure correlations between a large set of criteria of the performance of foremen. The data collected proved to be very unreliable (much of it came from company records) and in particular little data on supervisor work behaviour was collected. The hypothesis tested in this case has little plausibility.

a

Main hypotheses tested	Sets of variables involved	Research methods used	Main results	Difficulties arising
(E) DAVIS & VALFER, 1966[5] and DAVIS, 1966[6] An increase in the authority and responsibility of supervisors (by giving them direct control over all operational and inspection functions) will result in lower total cost and greater need satisfaction for all their subordinates.	*Individual characteristics* Not recorded. *Supervisor work situation* Organizational goals. Organizational changes (change from process to product organization and change to integrated production inspection responsibility). Type of production system. Type of supervisory system. Number and type of prescribed supervisor tasks. Norms and expectations of supervisor behaviour held by workers. Situation of local labour market. Level of demand for company's products and rate of growth. *Supervisor work behaviour* Activity sampling (level 2). *Effects of supervisor work behaviour* Attitudes and job satisfaction of workers. Costs (personnel and production). Quality.	In this study two organizational changes involving new responsibility for supervisors was followed through. Supervisor work behaviour was recorded by activity sampling and attitudes, costs, quality and output figures were also collected over 24 months. Control groups were used.	Lower total costs resulted in one change, not in the other. Quality improved in one change, not in the other. Personnel costs were not affected. Productivity did not change. Positive attitudes were expressed by workers and supervisors. Supervisors changed orientation from personnel to technical problems.	1 Organizational change presents severe problems for supervisors and some of the effects may be due to their success or failure in meeting the problems rather than due to the new authority or responsibility. 2 Data on supervisor work behaviour were too general and too difficult to interpret. 3 As the progress of the changes was being worked out over two years, it may have been too soon to jump to conclusions about the permanent effects, e.g. moves towards 'technical supervision'.

(F) FIEDLER, 1967[7]

The style of leadership which is the most effective depends on the situation.

The degree to which a leader has influence in his group depends on:

(a) task structure,

(b) leader-member relations, and

(c) relative leadership power.

Individual characteristics

Two crucial scales used are measures of least preferred co-worker (LPC) and assumed similarity between opposites (ASO). The scores on these scales were correlated with a large number of other individual variables, viz:

22 biographical variables, 13 response-set variables, 19 personality measures, 2 intelligence measures and 20 interpersonal perception measures.

Supervisor work situation

Task structure, relative power of leader in organization, group climate and group homogeneity were all used as variables.

Supervisor work behaviour

A behaviour-description questionnaire used in some studies, but not fundamental.

Effects of supervisor work behaviour

Work group and organizational performance measures.

Rating scales, questionnaires, personality measures and production data.

Correlations computed between leadership style attributes and work group performance data.

The demonstration of the critical nature of the organizational situation for leadership performance. This leads to an argument for changing organizations to fit the leadership styles for individuals (which is related to their need structure) rather than using training to modify leader style.

Such studies depend on utilizing production criteria and rating measures. The performance data are often of doubtful validity. The ratings of co-workers on scales of friendliness etc. are also of doubtful validity as they are based on a probable wide number of different criteria held by individual raters. Further weaknesses of the approved measures lie in the selectivity of the variables used to describe the work situation and the lack of information about work behaviour. There is little interest in such studies in distinguishing supervisory situations from other leadership situations.

Main hypotheses tested	Sets of variables involved	Research methods used	Main results	Difficulties arising
(G) LENNERLÖF, 1968[8] There exist associations between individual and behavioural variables for groups of supervisors within similar situations.	*Individual characteristics* 23 different variables (e.g. age, length of service, mechanical comprehension, capacity for study, need of achievement, need of affiliation, need of power, consideration, structuring, mutual attitudes towards striving for personal achievement, desired authority in production matters). *Supervisor work situation* 36 different variables (e.g. replacement value of equipment, number of subordinates, worker levels of skill, proportion of women, proportion of aliens, differences of workers' tasks, pressure on department to produce, barriers to verbal communication, mutual attitudes towards striving for personal achievement as per superior and as per subordinates, desirable consideration and structuring as per superior, and as per subordinates, authority delegated in matters of personnel administration as per superior).	Use of company records pertaining to the supervisors, their departments and their subordinates. Data from selection testing were available. A TAT-like projective instrument was developed and presented to the supervisors. A questionnaire on supervisory role expectations as perceived by superiors, subordinates and supervisors was used. A Swedish version of the Ohio questionnaire on the leadership dimensions of consideration and initiating structure was presented to supervisors, to superiors and to subordinates.	This was a field study of production and service supervisors in two manufacturing companies. The expectations held, the behaviour descriptions made and the reactions voiced by the role incumbents were found to be influenced to a high degree by role-centric and individual factors. Behaviour ratings based on a short observation and interview period and made by external industrial psychologists were much less sensitive to individual differences between the raters than descriptions from role incumbents.	In deciding to use a relatively large number of variables in each of the four sectors, the scope for working with larger samples of supervisors was limited. A large number of variables used were based entirely on questionnaire and rating scale data and were subject to the limitations of such methods.

Main hypotheses tested	Sets of variables involved	Research methods used	Main results	Difficulties arising
	Supervisor work behaviour 23 different variables (e.g. general [versus close] supervision, informal [versus formal] regulation of behaviour, pressure to produce, degree of activity, constructive [versus primitive] discipline, information to subordinates, consideration and structuring as described by external observer, by supervisor, by superior, and by subordinates. *Effects of supervisor work behaviour* 44 different variables (e.g. number of suggestion makers, unexplained absency and separations in relation to departmental size, relations to superiors, colleagues, staff and service personnel, and to subordinates as per superior, general fitness as supervisor as per superior, interest and involvement in work among subordinates, attitudes of subordinates supervisor's personnel treatment, and to opportunities for promotion and advancement, interest and involvement in work among supervisors, attitudes of supervisors to strenuous working conditions, to physical conditions, to physical conditions at the workplace, to immediate superior's personnel treatment, and to immediate superior's degree of general [versus close] supervision, psychosomatic symptoms among supervisors).	A questionnaire on present and desired authority was answered by supervisors and their superiors. A job satisfaction questionnaire for workers and one for supervisors was used. Ratings from superiors. Observations and interviews were used as a basis for situational and behavioural variables.		

at a very general level and information is given in terms of time spent in particular functions. Much of this information on work behaviour, therefore, attempts to describe the supervisory role or style with little evidence of any detailed approach to task performance.

One of the main reasons for this fact is the basic approach and interest of perhaps the majority of researchers in this field. The classic studies of Kahn & Katz and Fleishman and his colleagues are couched in terms of examinations of the relationship between (*a*) styles or dimensions of leadership and (*b*) the relative performance of work groups supervised by foremen who show varying degrees of such leadership styles. The interest in leadership has been one of the main approaches to the study of supervision itself, and it is, therefore, not surprising that studies of supervisory effectiveness should be designed in this way. Behind the concern with leadership lies an interest in worker motivation and the possibilities of supervisors stimulating and encouraging better economic performance. In the personnel field, the indices used, i.e. absence, grievances, labour turnover, accidents, etc., are a direct attempt to show the effect of considerate or employee-centred supervision on the attitudes and responses of workers or work-groups.

Davis's study, on the other hand, comes from an interest in job enlargement and job design, and attempts to show the effects of the enlargement of supervisory authority in terms of departmental performance. A third approach is represented by the Westerlund & Strömberg study, which is partly methodological and partly concerned with demonstrating correlations between aspects of supervisory work behaviour and objective and subjective criteria of performance. This approach, therefore, is more concerned with an objective scrutiny of the relationship which exists between particular aspects of supervisory work behaviour and performance rather than testing hypotheses about leadership styles or job enlargement.

Fiedler's book[7] summarizes his research of fifteen years into his definition of leadership style in terms of the measures LPC (least preferred co-worker) and ASO (assumed similarity between opposites). He investigated a large number of correlations with scores on these scales, and shows that both task-oriented leaders and relationship-oriented leaders are able to perform effectively, given appropriate conditions. This approach leads also to improving leadership performance through organizational engineering. His policy implications, therefore, approach those of Professor Davis.

Lennerlöf[8] is one of the few investigators who tried to take up variables in all the boxes listed in Figure 2.4. In particular, he introduced more sophisticated measures of satisfaction for supervisors' subordinates, i.e. effect variables. These included interest and involvement in work, attitudes to work strain and attitudes to a supervisor's personnel treatment. He also dealt with the question of the degree of job satisfaction and subjective personal adjustment on the part of the supervisors themselves. The variables used were similar to those used for subordinates. He tried to measure psychosomatic symptoms in supervisors. Another strong point of this study was the large number of variables used to measure aspects of the work situation. However, his attempt to use a 'clinical' or diagnostic 'slice' of selected observation and interview (averaging three hours per supervisor) can be criticized as the data may be untypical. A more fundamental criticism is that his study was mostly devoted to exploring relationships between variables in various areas without any prior hypothesis. Zero correlations in such a study mean much research without any theoretical advance. Lennerlöf's contribution is to have demonstrated some examples of possible correlations between variables in the areas discussed; and, although he produces rather few significant correlations, his approach does again lead to an emphasis on the importance of variations in the work situation and on differences in individual characteristics.

Most studies, as we have seen, are extremely selective in the type of variables chosen for measurement. This may be partly because the researchers considered that the only possibility of controlling the study was to centre on relatively few variables, but partly it appears to be from underestimation of the complexity of the problem. The Westerlund & Strömberg study does show considerable awareness, however, of the number and types of variables which might affect the performance of foremen and their workers. In particular, these two researchers examined in detail the difficulties of comparison between companies and between departments within companies. They reported that this problem could be overcome by very careful selection of the type of department, level of mechanization, etc., but it is a point which forms a serious objection to some of the earlier studies, such as that of Kahn & Katz. They also had an impressive list of individual characteristics which were taken into account, and they were very much aware of the fact that different criteria are likely to measure performance in different ways and in different directions. The whole study was largely an examination of this problem. Much of the negative evidence in the study is extremely salutary. Most of the hypotheses suggested were proved to have little supporting evidence. Most of the correlations supposed between types of criteria did not exist. It is clear from this that any future studies must reflect on the reasons why such correlations did not exist. This particular study challenges any research workers or consultants working in this field to think through the problem a little more thoroughly. This means that the distinction made by Fleishman between objective and subjective criteria, although useful in its time, is not sufficient to solve the problem. All these criteria attempt to measure performance at far too general a level.

Another deficiency of most of the studies quoted is that they were working with a concept of the individual supervisor rather than with any understanding of supervision as a type of social system. The idea of the supervisor in charge of his group of men, which was a very accurate picture at earlier stages of industrialization, has lingered on, and is highly misrepresentative of many situations in modern technology, where supervisors are extremely dependent on each other and working together with other supervisors and functional specialists. The studies, therefore, have tended to assume that one could draw a clear line around the supervisor and his department and measure the effects of the leadership behaviour of the supervisor on the performance of his subordinates. In reality, the supervisor may, as Westerlund & Strömberg point out, have little possibility of influencing the performance in many areas of his subordinates' work. Both workers and supervisors are engaged in collective tasks and open to the pressures of the total organization. If the work situation is studied as a series of socio-technical administrative systems, it becomes more possible to clarify the type of effects which supervisors can reasonably be expected to have on their environ-ment and on their subordinates. What seems clear is that the earlier models of the supervisory situation were oversimplified and that this has been a major problem for research into supervisory effectiveness.

Another way into the study of supervision has been that of concentration on descriptions of supervisory roles. The classical studies were those of Walker, Guest & Turner[9] and that of Ponder.[10] Ponder was also interested to show the relation-ship between foremen who practise certain tasks, e.g. planning, and the degree of their efficiency. O'Neill & Kubany in a useful critical study[11] showed that much of the observational information commonly gathered about supervisory work behaviour was of little value for understanding such behaviour or for studies of effectiveness. They argued that a breakdown by time spent shed little light on the supervisory role, and that it was necessary to understand in detail the degree to which certain tasks were performed well or poorly, as well as study-ing the significance of certain ways of attempting to solve problems displayed by the foreman on the job. Studies by the authors in Sweden[12] and in the United Kingdom,[13] however, confirmed the importance of attempting to collect detailed and comprehensive information of supervisory behaviour at level 3 (task level) by observation and interview methods.

Some of the studies aimed at evaluating the effect of the training of super-visors are also useful for our purpose here in that they underline some of the most important variables which appear to be critical. Fleishman and his asso-ciates, in the first phase of their study, placed a major emphasis on the leadership climate of the organization within which the supervisor had to work. Similar studies have been repeated throughout the world, e.g. in Japan,[14] Sweden,[15] Norway,[16] Netherlands,[17] United Kingdom,[18] and the U.S.A.[19]

Much of the American work on the effectiveness of supervision was discussed by Dubin.[20] This collection of essays is a highly significant one in that it marks the recognition of the limitations of the simple leadership/productivity equation. Dubin makes three statements:

'Supervisory behaviour affects the productivity of individuals by being appro-priate to the work setting' (p. 46).

'There is no "one best" method of supervision' (p. 47).

'As far as empirical data take us, it seems clear that the influence of supervisory behaviour on productivity is small' (p. 47).

The work of Hesseling[21] has also emphasized the importance of the organiza-tional climate for training. A study by Sykes confirmed that there could be considerable conflict[22] between the values and beliefs imported through training to supervisors and the senior management. Much of the evidence of the studies of evaluation of training[23] has been of this negative character, showing the importance of such organizational factors compared with the training effect. More recent research in the United Kingdom has, significantly, tried to concentrate on the behavioural effects of training programmes.[24]

It would appear to be very clear from this brief survey of research studies of supervisory performance and from that of other studies,[25] that most of them lack a comprehensive approach and tend to exaggerate the amount of measurement possible. In particular, the significance of the negative results in the Westerlund & Strömberg study has never been fully appreciated. There is grave doubt as to whether there is any real purpose in designing studies which purport to measure supervisory effectiveness as a single and discrete problem.

Notes and References

1 WESTERLUND, G. (1952). *Group leadership—a field experiment.* Nordisk Rotogravyr, Stockholm.

2 KAHN, R. L. & KATZ, D. (1953). Leadership practices in relation to productivity and morale. In D. Cartwright & A. Zander (eds.), *Group dynamics, research and theory.* 2nd ed. Row, Peterson & Co., Evanston, Ill., and Tavistock, London.

3 FLEISHMAN, E. A., HARRIS, E. F. & BURTT, H. E. (1955). *Leadership and supervision in industry.* The Ohio State University, Columbus, Ohio.

4 WESTERLUND, G. & STRÖMBERG, L. (1965). Measurement and appraisal of the performance of foremen. *British Journal of Industrial Relations,* Vol. 3, pp. 345–62.

5 DAVIS, L. E. & VALFER, E. S. (1966). Studies in supervisory job design. *Human Relations,* Vol. 19, pp. 339–52.

6 DAVIS, L. E. (1966). The design of jobs. *Industrial Relations,* Vol. 6, pp. 21–45.

7 FIEDLER, F. E. (1967). *A theory of leadership effectiveness.* McGraw-Hill, New York.

8 LENNERLÖF, L. (1968). *Supervision: Situation, individual, behavior, effect.* Report No. 57. Swedish Council for Personnel Administration, Stockholm.

9 WALKER, C. R., GUEST, R. H. & TURNER, A. N. (1956). *The foreman on the assembly line.* Harvard University Press, Cambridge, Mass.

10 PONDER, Q. (1958). *Supervisory practices of effective and ineffective foremen.* Ph.D. Dissertation, Columbia University, New York.

11 O'NEILL, H. E. & KUBANY, A. J. (1959). Observation methodology and supervisory behaviour. *Personnel Psychology,* Vol. 12, pp. 85–95.

12 WIRDENIUS, H. (1958). *Supervisors at work.* Swedish Council for Personnel Administration, Stockholm.

13 THURLEY, K. E. & HAMBLIN, A. C. (1963). *The supervisor and his job.* DSIR, London.

14 Misuni, J. & Shirakasi, S. (1966). An experimental study of the effects of supervisory behaviour on productivity and morale in a hierarchical organization. *Human Relations*, Vol. 19, No. 3 (August), pp. 297–308.

15 Gustavsson, B. (1963). In R. Meigniez (ed.), *Evaluation of supervisory and management training methods*, p. 110. OECD, Paris.

16 Kile, S. (1963). Some results from the evaluation project of the Institute of Industrial Psychology and Personnel Relations of the Norwegian School of Economics and Business Administration. In R. Meigniez, (ed.), *Evaluation of supervisory and management training methods*, p. 105. OECD, Paris.

17 De Sitter, L. U. (1970). *Leiderschapsvorming en leiderschapsgedrag in een organisatie*. N. Samson N.V., Alphen aan den Rijn.

18 Argyle, M. (1957 and 1958). The measurement of supervisory methods. *Human Relations*, Vol. 10, No. 4 (November 1957), pp. 295–314, and Vol. 11, No. 1 (February 1958), pp. 23–40.

19 Sales, S. M. (1966). Supervisory style and productivity, review and theory. *Personnel Psychology*, Vol. 19, pp. 275–86.

20 Dubin, R., Homans, G. C., Mann, F. C. & Miller, D. C. (1965). *Leadership and productivity, facts of industrial life*. Chandler Publ. Co., San Francisco, Calif.

21 Hesseling, P. (1966). *Strategy of evaluation research*. van Gorcum, Assen.

22 Sykes, A. J. M. (1962). The effect of a supervisory training course in changing supervisors' perceptions and expectations of the role of management. *Human Relations*, Vol. 15, No. 3, pp. 227–43.

23 Handyside, J. D. (1956). *An experiment in supervisory training*. NIIP, London.

24 Bird, M. (1969). Changes in work behaviour following supervisory training. *Journal of Management Studies* (February).

25 *Note.* There are, of course, a large number of other possible references on supervisory roles, leadership behaviour and performance, particularly from the United States. See in particular:

   a Kay, B. R. (1963). The foreman's role. Theme with variations. *Personnel*, Vol. 40, No. 6 (November/December), pp. 32–7.

   b Kay, B. R. (1963). Prescription and perception of the supervisory role. *Occupational Psychology*, Vol. 37, No. 3 (July), pp. 219–27.

   c Kay, B. R. (1959). Key factors in effective foremen behaviour. *Personnel*, Vol. 36, No. 1 (January/February), pp. 25–31.

   d Evans, C. E. (1957). *Supervisory responsibility and authority*. Research Report No. 30. A.M.A., New York.

   e Evans, C. E. (1957). Contrasting views of the foreman's responsibility. *Personnel* (July/August), pp. 32–3.

   f Wray, D. E. (1949). Marginal men of industry : The foremen. *American Journal of Sociology* (January), pp. 298–301.

   g Guest, R. H. (1956). Of time and the foreman. *Personnel*, Vol. 32, No. 6 (May), pp. 478–86.

h TURNER, A. N. (1957). Foreman, job and company. *Human Relations,* Vol. 10, No. 2, pp. 99–112.

i McGREGOR, D. (1946). The foreman's responsibilities in the industrial organisation. A case study. *Personnel* (March), pp. 3–11.

j PONDER, Q. E. (1957). *The effective manufacturing foreman.* Proceedings of 10th Annual Meeting of I.I.R.A., Madison, pp. 41–54.

k YANOUZAS, J. N. (1964). A comparative study of work organisation and supervisory behavior. *Human Organization,* Vol. 23, No. 3 (Fall), pp. 245–53.

l JASINSKI, F. J. (1956). Foreman relationships outside the work group. *Personnel,* Vol. 33, No. 2 (September), pp. 130–36.

m KUBLY, H. E. (1966). The inspectors and the foremen. *Wisconsin Commerce Report.* (June). Bureau of Business Research and Service, Graduate School of Business, University of Wisconsin, Madison, pp. 81–91.

n HUTCHINSON, J. H. (1963). *Managing a fair day's work.* Report No. 15. Bureau of Industrial Relations, University of Michigan, Ann Arbor.

o JOHNSON, A. (1967). The changing duties of today's foremen. *Management of Personnel Quarterly* (Winter), p. 44.

p FAMULARO, J. J. (1961). *Supervisors in action.* McGraw-Hill, New York.

q ROSEN, N. A. (1969). *Leadership change and work group dynamics.* Cornell University.

r KORMAN, A. K. (1966). Consideration, initiating structure and organisational criteria. A review. *Personnel Psychology,* Vol. 19, pp. 349–61.

s PELZ, D. C. (1952). Influence : a key to effective leadership in the first-line supervisor. *Personnel* (November), pp. 209–17.

t WIKSTROM, W. S. (1967). Can the foreman be a manager? *Conference Board Report* (July), p. 12.

u PATTEN, T. H., Jr. (1968). *The foreman: forgotten man of management.* AMA, New York.

5. Analysis III: Methods

DATA COLLECTION AND MEASUREMENT PROBLEMS

Analysis is a concept which implies concern for hard facts. This seems straightforward enough until one asks who is gathering the facts and for what purpose.

We can designate the objective of the social scientist in studying a supervisory system as one of understanding its structure and identifying the main variables. He will be concerned with the relationships between such variables inside the system and will use this understanding to construct a model to give him an adequate explanation of behaviour within the system. Finally, he will wish to be able to predict behaviour and the effects of postulated actions by actors within the system.

The main interest of managers, consultants or advisers to management will probably lie in utilizing models provided by social scientists. They will, of course, have to add to them their own insights and understanding of their own organizational system if they wish to use the model for prediction. Successful prediction for management means greater control.

Table 5.1 provides a classification of such objectives and underlines the way different studies may require differing types of analysis of data and differing types of explanation. There are differences in the purposes of managers, con-

TABLE 5.1
Objectives for study of supervisory systems

A	Social scientist	Pure research	Explanation at a general level by use of hypothesis and postulated models
B	Researcher or consultant	Diagnosis of nature of particular system	To provide a detailed historical explanation in one case or to isolate choices open or to make predictions
C	Change agent	Study of system to prepare for changes	To provide a model with emphasis on the dynamics of the system and areas ripe for change
D	Manager and supervisor	Modification of his existing 'working model' of system assumed in his actions	To allow his existing expectations over behaviour and results to be modified by more accurate data, greater allowance for certain factors, etc., i.e. to improve his possibilities of accurate control

sultants or change agents and these affect the 'facts' seen as significant. To be involved in the creation of a model, therefore, leads to the task of collecting the many types of data to be used for describing the relationships between variables or for testing those relationships. The problem of *validity* is a problem both for the scientist and for the manager. The social scientist is concerned with the degree to which the data he collects *measure* what he intended to measure. He is concerned with the problem of the *relevance* of the data collected to the theory which he hypothesizes will explain the phenomena he is investigating. The manager is concerned with validity in the sense that he hopes that the data which he has collected describe the situation accurately. The manager, in so far as he is relying on scientific theories for explanation, is, therefore, dependent on models and explanations provided by a social scientist. Parallel with and included in the validity question is the problem of *reliability*. The question of reliability arises when one is collecting data or making observations or tests under equivalent circumstances, i.e. where the conditions are as similar as one can get them, and the results are different. A third problem is the problem of *comprehensiveness*. The data collected must be representative in the sense that they must be collected from and descriptive of variables throughout the supervisory system and not restricted to variables in one sub-area of the system. The first three questions which must be asked about any scientific data are accordingly:

(*a*) Is the data likely to be reliable?
(*b*) Is it likely to provide a comprehensive picture of the variables we wish to cover?
(*c*) Is it likely to provide valid information?

These questions provide general criteria for judging the usefulness of data collection methods and particular researcher roles.[1, *]

In this chapter, descriptions will be given briefly of various measures and methods of collecting data for the areas in our model in Figure 2.4. There are five aspects of data collection which determine the answers to the questions listed above:

(*a*) Whether the collection of data is made by a person 'outside' or 'inside' the supervisory system. The terms 'outside' and 'inside' refer to the question of how far the role of the research worker (or consultant or investigator) is seen by those inside the supervisory system to be independent of it. If an investigator, as we shall see later, has a role which is partly contained within the social system he is observing, then the data collected by that person will be likely to be affected by his role position. Similarly, if a person is collecting information from a largely independent position, the type of information that he can obtain, his understanding of it, and his interpretation of the data will be affected by his independent position.[2]
(*b*) Whether the method is one that can be broadly described as *observational* or *perceptual*. Observation relies on picking up information directly

* *See* page 64 or references.

through the participation of the investigator in the situation under study. This data is selected or filtered according to the frame of reference of the observer. This frame of reference, interpreted in a systematic manner, is intended to ensure that the data collected are selected also in a precise and systematic way. In the case of a perceptual method, information (stimuli) is first received and perceived by persons in the situation. Afterwards, the persons concerned are asked, through a questionnaire or interview, to retail their understanding and their perceptions of what actually has occurred. This information will then be systematized by the research worker or investigator. The problem in the second case is that, through lapses of memory and because of the normal way in which the brain structures perceptions, the information given will be biased or 'twisted' before collection by the research worker. On the other hand, it is extremely valuable for the investigator to have some understanding of the process of bias and structuring which is going on inside the minds of the supervisors and others in the social system under study. The interpretations of actions by the actors and others is always of considerable importance. All actions are subject to interpretation, and this meaning is related to the structuring process. In this way, systematic observation and perceptual information are complementary.

(c) Methods of collection of data can be categorized by how far they are undertaken under conditions which are closely controlled by the person making the study. In the first stages of any investigation, the amount of control which the investigator has over the situation is very low indeed. He is concerned mainly with the collection of facts about the environment, with preliminary perceptions of the situation, and perhaps with the collection of some elementary observations. At a later stage in a study, he may structure the investigation so that his observations, for instance, are undertaken according to set codes. If the investigation goes so far to be designed as an experiment, with formal predictions and observations to test such predictions, then we can say that the type of data collected is in a relatively controlled situation. To that extent it has a different significance from data collected in the earlier stages of the study.

(d) Data collection can also be classified by the level at which the analysis is being undertaken. In large organizations there is some necessity to collect comparative statistical information. This could include data on individual characteristics, the work situation, and behavioural variables and effect variables (at a general level). Labour turnover and absence figures, for example, or age data could be collected for the whole organization. The need to provide explanations and predictions, however, means that it is also necessary to collect data about specific supervisory situations and systems. The methods outlined and variables named in this chapter are all at a specific level. This can be seen as a type of 'clinical' approach.

(e) The nature of the data itself must also, of course, be considered. There is firstly the question of the ease with which it can be broken into 'units' and measured. The variables already suggested as relevant are partly quantitative and partly qualitative in character. That is, some lie near the end of the continuum of measurability and can easily be dealt with statistically; others lie at the opposite extreme and can only be measured in terms of some type of systematic judgement, such as a rating scheme. It is important to emphasize the need to include such variables in a world in which the possibility of computer data analysis pushes the social scientist towards sole reliance on quantitative variables.

A further problem is the comparability question. The need for comparison leads to the use of standardized instruments which may or may not be acceptable or comprehensible to the actors themselves in the situation under study. In observational studies, the very detail of the observations makes it difficult to provide standardized categories except at a general level. The researcher always seems to be coming across new tasks or activities which he has never met before. We can only conclude here that there is a case for both comparative standardized data and for specific unique data (for longitudinal studies, for example). This point is linked with (c) above. It is clear that relatively unstructured data collection does have its place, particularly in the early stages of an investigation.

Lastly, there is the thorny question of the unidimensionality of variables chosen. The measurement-minded researcher will place great value on achieving measurements along so-called single dimensions and will be rightly critical of loose categories and general variables. On the other hand, those concerned with interpretations and change processes (as is the general orientation of the authors) must insist on the importance of retaining variables which have some meaning for the actors concerned and on the need to possess a model of a situation, which will almost certainly mean including 'common-sense' general variables.

If we return to the question of the contrast between observational and perceptual methods, we can express this simply as in Figure 5.1. Here the research worker is seen as making direct observations of behaviour within a supervisory system, and at the same time perceptions of behaviour and events inside this supervisory system are being collected by interview (or by paper and pencil methods) with the supervisors concerned. The point to notice is the screen of bias through which such perceptions are being given.

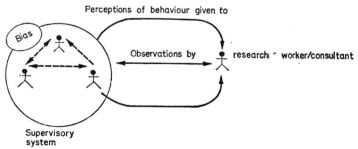

FIGURE 5.1   Simple model of observation and perception

This is, of course, a highly oversimplified picture. Figure 5.2 shows a more complex situation. Here the social system has been broken down into a number of different social groupings, work groups, functional management departments and line management departments. Each of these groups can be seen as perceiving certain aspects of supervisory behaviour. It may be that the work study officer only meets particular foremen once or twice a week and it may be that any such meeting deals with entirely trivial matters so that the perceptions made during that meeting leave no trace in his general stereotype of the supervisory situation. Given, however, a few disagreements, given the experience of being there just at 'the right time', it is easy to see how stereotypes can be amended and built up. If there is a power problem, or a clash between the supervisors and a functional staff department, it may be that the interpretation given to the events observed and the behaviour perceived by each party will tend to reinforce

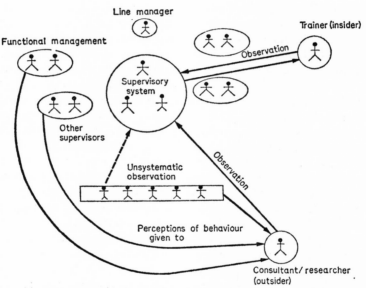

FIGURE 5.2 Complex model of observation and perception

attitudes held and protect defence mechanisms. In this way, conflict may lead each social group to consolidate stereotypes held by individuals within the group.[3, 4] In Figure 5.2 we show an outside consultant or research worker and a manager engaged in trying to understand the supervisory system. We should note that the outsider can have the advantage of receiving perceptions from the various groups in the situation which the insider may not be allowed to receive. It may be that the information given to the outsider is too dangerous to give to the person 'inside' the situation.

On the other hand, the 'inside' manager already has access to information and understanding of the situation from his own managerial position which may provide certain clues that are lacking to the outside research worker. Observations, if we turn to this problem, are also different considered from the point of view of the insider and the outsider. The outsider has a chance of using a clearer and a more formal frame of reference, but suffers severely from lack of understanding of the behaviour which he observes and which he may indeed misclassify and misinterpret. The insider has often the advantage of understanding more of the situation which he is observing, but he is likely to cause more observer effect. In this way, not only observation and perception can be seen as complementary, but also the role positions of the inside researcher and the outside researcher are also complementary.

We have assumed so far that the information collected in such investigations will be descriptions of supervisory behaviour or evidence concerning variables affecting such behaviour. In reality, however, there are a number of other questions which might be asked about supervisory behaviour. What, for example, is the person doing at this moment? This is the usual starting point. What should he be doing? What is he going to do in the future? What has he just done? These questions can be seen as covering differing aspects of work behaviour, dealing with the ideal and the actual and the difference in the time reference of the behaviour. The interpretation of behaviour and its effects clearly involves an understanding of the way the actors in a situation perceive it, the way they intend their actions to be carried out, and the results expected from such actions. Data have to be collected describing such perceptions before, for example, disturbance-handling can be adequately explained. As we shall see, it is necessary to explain actions in building up an understanding of the nature of supervisory systems.

In the following sections, we will discuss each of the areas described in Figure 2.4 and try to assess the techniques available for measuring variables included in them. In the case of individual characteristics and the supervisory work situation, our discussion will be restricted to listing typical variables and possible measures. We will merely indicate briefly some of the main methods available for measuring the most crucial variables. Bearing in mind the large range of such variables which may be important in any particular case, it is, unfortunately, not possible to give a comprehensive guide to all the measures that might be necessary. When dealing with supervisory work behaviour, however, we will attempt a more systematic coverage of methods available. The discussion of the *effects* of supervisory work behaviour will deal with the problem of selecting the most appropriate criteria and with finding practical methods of measurement. The measures of supervisory work behaviour will be summarized briefly, describing the aim, the preliminary work necessary, and the methods available for carrying out the data collection. The persons who seem most suitable for carrying out the method, their training, and the resources required will also be briefly discussed. Lastly, the limitations and merits of each method will be discussed, listing problems of reliability, validity and any practical difficulties. Examples will be given with each technique.

The reader should bear in mind that each technique will be discussed in terms of its importance in helping training officers, consultants or researchers to analyse the system of supervision. The methods discussed below vary in the degree of training required and in the degree of sophistication which has been achieved in the design of such instruments. Some, therefore, should not be used by training officers or personnel officers without fairly lengthy training, which would apply, for example, to projective methods such as the TAT test. Others require skilled advice, but can be used without too much difficulty and fear of misapplication by any manager or consultant. In each case it is important to distinguish the degree of training necessary and to consider this before use.

Notes and References

1 GALTUNG, J. (1967). *Theory and methods of social research.* George Allen & Unwin, London.
2 DENZIN, N. K. (1970). *The research act in sociology.* Butterworths, London. (There is a very useful discussion in this book of interactionist theory applied to the research process itself, i.e. showing the implications of the role of the researcher.)
3 KAHN, R. L. *et al.* (1964). *Organizational stress. Studies in role conflict and ambiguity.* John Wiley & Sons, New York.
4 SHERIF, M. (1967). *Group conflict and co-operation: their social psychology.* Routledge and Kegan Paul, London.

INDIVIDUAL CHARACTERISTICS

The problems of trying to measure individual characteristics of supervisors have been mainly explored by occupational psychologists in studies of selection or promotion methods. There have also been studies of attitudes, personality characteristics, and aptitudes in connection with the evaluation of supervisory training. Some of the measures developed by such studies have been used for actual selection or evaluation procedures but in many cases they have only been used for research purposes. Table 5.2 shows examples of some of the most commonly measured types of variables.

There are, of course, an infinite number of characteristics of any one unique human being. Any analysis of a large group of supervisors requires a study of a large number of variables, as is common in psychological research. Our task, however, is to give guide-lines for the analysis of the most relevant individual characteristics for specific supervisory systems.

In the research literature, there are a number of attemps to draw up basic lists of critical individual characteristics of supervisors, usually from the viewpoint of effective performance. It is not easy to get reliable performance criteria for foremen, as we noted in Chapter 4, and as indicated by the work of Rothe and Nye.[1], * Halsey, in his book on supervisory selection,[2] argues that it is best to take basic traits which are generally agreed to be relevant to supervisory performance

* *See* page 72 for references.

TABLE 5.2

Examples of individual characteristics measured

Variables	Measures used
Age	
Basic education	
Technical training	Documentary and written evidence
Industrial experience	Career inventories
Length of service as a supervisor	
Verbal fluency	
Verbal ability	
Logical-inductive ability	
Spatial ability	Mental performance tests
Numerical ability	
Mechanical comprehension	
Planning ability	

and which can be measured relatively easily by using well-known instruments with established high reliability scores or which can be observed in off-the-job or interview situations. He lists sixteen such basic traits. The problem is not, unfortunately, as simple as this assumes.[3] Two examples will make this clear.

The most carefully prepared approaches to selection of 'successful' supervisors in industrial psychology have tried to classify the basic factors relevant to performance by factor analysis of field ratings (either superiors, peers or subordinates) or actual success in their jobs over a long period. Roach[4] is an example of the first method. He isolates fourteen factors (Table 5.3):

TABLE 5.3

Example of basic supervisory individual factors seen as relevant to performance

Personal compliance (degree to which supervisor does what is expected of him and acts as example)
Job knowledge
Direction of group performance (ability to plan/organize/carry out procedures)
Rewarding performance and thoroughness of employee evaluation
Company loyalty
Acceptance of responsibility (and decision-making)
Group spirit
Personal drive
Impartiality
Poise and bearing
Consideration
Open-mindedness
Cheerfulness
Approachability

It can be seen from this list that some of these characteristics are attitudinal; some are questions of motivation; some indicate mental ability and some acquired knowledge and skills. Many are likely to be affected by the work situation (for example, organizational climate). Some might be detected by measures of individual characteristics and some are more related to work *behaviour* (for example, consideration).

A second example comes from the impressive study of Dicken and Black.[5] They develop seven 'global' personal supervisory traits from a number of commonly used aptitude tests[6] by the device of asking psychologists to make clinical interpretations of the individual data. These were then correlated with field ratings and measured against actual success over a number of years, Table 5.4.

TABLE 5.4

Example of basic personal traits for supervisors used in 'clinical' study

Personal traits	Reliabilities reported
Effective Intelligence	0·98
Personal Soundness	0·92
Drive and Ambition	0·94
Leadership and Dominance	0·90
Likeableness	0·86
Responsibility and Conscientiousness	0·85
Ability to co-operate	0·86

In this case, the factors are of a more homogeneous type and appear to have been useful in predicting success. The number of supervisors tested was extremely small, however (fifty-seven), and this is typical of most studies of this type. If we accept the basic argument above about the importance of viewing supervisory behaviour in terms of a supervisory system, then it follows that the interrelations between the parts of the system, the interrelations of the individual with the system and the interrelationships of the system and its environment[7] are all likely to be important in showing variations in significance of each individual factor.

The problem therefore lies in the fact that although for each system there may be rather few crucial variables, they will be likely to differ in significance, system by system. Our approach here can only be to offer the reader a loose operational classification of areas of variables, together with some selected examples of variables which have been important in recent studies. There is no generally accepted scheme for classifying such variables, although certain authors (Cattel,[8] Thurstone,[9] Eysenck[10]) do attempt a broad division of areas and levels distinguishing, for example, between the areas of personality, drives, and intellectual capacity and between the levels of personality traits, value systems, attitudes, and opinions. For practical purposes, it does not appear to be too useful to distinguish such levels. In Table 5.5 the fourteen areas already mentioned in Figure 3.2 are repeated and some examples of selected variables are given which may be useful.

TABLE 5.5

Broad classification of areas of importance for supervisors' individual characteristics

Areas	Selected variables	Suggested type of method
1. Age and sex	Degree of difference from workers	Documents
2. Type of family background	Extent of family commitment	Interview
	Degree of conflict within parental and own family	Career inventory[12]
3. Social background and occupational history	Degree of occupational mobility	Interview
	Knowledge of work-group culture	Documents
4. Education and general knowledge	Length and timing of education	Interviews
	Formal qualifications	Documents
	Travel and personal experience	
5. Technical knowledge	Extent of knowledge about current production methods	Achievement tests
		Interviews
		Ratings
6. Skills	Writing reports	Achievement tests
	Handling a meeting	Group tests
		Ratings
7. Opinions, attitudes, perceptions and expectations on work roles	Consideration	Questionnaire
	Initiating structure	(*see* Table 5.7)
	Least Preferred Co-worker	
8. Personal requirements for work satisfaction	Desired degree of task structure	Interviews
	Desired level of rewards	
	Type and level of ambition	
9. Ideology and values	Type of authority preferred	Interviews
	Work orientation	Questionnaires
10. Intellectual capacity	Verbal fluency	Aptitude tests
	Memory	Ratings
	Logical-inductive ability	(*see* Table 5.7)
	Spatial perception	
	Mechanical comprehension	
	Numerical ability	
	Mental alertness	
11. Personality traits	Flexibility	Personality tests
	Neuroticism	Performance tests
	Contact ability	Interviews
	Field independence	Ratings
	Dominance/Submission	
	Stress tolerance	
12. Interests	Social situations	Interviews
		Interest inventory
13. Drives and motivation	Need of achievement, affiliation and power	Interviews
		Ratings
	Ambition for training	Projective tests[13]
14. Physiological capacity and health	Activity level	Ratings
	Hearing and eyesight	Sickness record
	Ability to stand and walk	Performance tests
	Degree of tolerance of minor complaints	

Definitions

1. Age and sex	Differences arising from physical and mental factors connected with age and sex and social expectations
2. Family background	Differences of responsibilities and social pressures
3. Social background	Differences of occupational, ethnic and socio-economic group experience
4. Education	Differences of length and type of education
5. Technical knowledge	Differences of amount and type of technical knowledge
6. Skills	Differences of number and type of skills learnt – manual, social and conceptual
7. Opinions, attitudes, perceptions and expectations on work role	Differences of norms and actual expectations
8. Personal requirements for work satisfaction	Differences of level and type of pay-off from job wanted
9. Ideology and values	Differences of type of values, behaviour and intensity of belief
10. Intellectual capacity	Differences of types of mental ability
11. Personality traits	Differences of personality structure
12. Interests	Range of types of interest and intensity of attachment
13. Drives and motivation	Differences of types and intensity of drives present in individual
14. Physiological capacity and and health	Differences of physical abilities

This checklist of selected variables in Table 5.5 is, of course, an extremely arbitrary one. In any particular situation, some variables might be far more important than the others. Specific attitudes, for example, prejudice against foreign labour, might be a key to understanding a situation, but this is not included in the list as it is irrelevant to supervisory performance in many countries. The checklist is, therefore, only a list of variables which are possibly relevant arising out of previous studies. Clearly, it is open-ended and should be revised with experience.

We can classify methods also as in Table 5.6.

TABLE 5.6

Classification of types of methods of measurement

1. Documents and written evidence
2. Interview data (from structured, semi-structured or unstructured interviews)
3. Written questionnaires (with closed or open questions)
4. Ratings: various types of scales, including ranking[11]
5. Measurements of character, including: (a) expressions (handwriting, etc.), (b) projective techniques, (c) mock performance tests (group tests)
6. Performance tests

Some of these methods are complex, for example, the interview, which may combine observation, oral and written questioning, and ratings. Some methods are qualitative, and some are quantitative. Some measures require professional assistance, and some could be used by most people.

By a 'performance test' is meant any attempt to measure capacity by asking persons (in a situation where competition is perceived to be present) to perform certain tasks under specified conditions. Although such tests may be more or less sophisticated, and more or less standardized by being tested for reliability in large populations, it does not follow that they are necessarily relevant for supervisors or for the specific supervisors under study. A choice between these methods has to be made and usually this comes down to considering:

(*a*) the reliability of the method;
(*b*) the validity of the method; and
(*c*) the ease of access to the data.

In Table 5.5 there are some general recommendations as to the most suitable method. Sometimes there may be alternatives available. The only safe approach would seem to be to maintain scepticism with *all* methods and then to be extremely systematic in listing the advantages and disadvantages of each method in turn. We can, however, refer the reader to some relatively well-used instruments and these are shown in Table 5.7.

The references quoted are, of course, not comprehensive but generally illustrate the type of result found when the instrument in question was used for measuring some trait of supervisors. Two points deserve some further elaboration.

First, there is a lot of evidence of the importance of measures of mental alertness and mental capacity in supervisory work. Tiffin and McCormick[23] place great emphasis on it. Stockford, in a classical study also emphasizes intelligence.[34] We can quote from the conclusion of the Neel and Dunn report,[18] which was a comparison of the Wonderlic, How Supervise, and 'F' Scale instruments in supervisory training programmes.

'In generalizing about the predictive value of the three tests, it appears that without specialized supervisory training, intelligence seems to be the primary factor in application of knowledge to supervisory problems. The "How Supervise" Scale appears not to be an achievement test as it was originally conceived, but is to a large extent an attitude or aptitude test. It predicts how much one can learn about supervision rather than what one already knows, whereas the F Scale is a more basic aptitude test which predicts better, after completion of training, how well one can apply knowledge to a supervisory problem.'

Secondly, there is growing interest in the importance of the field dependence/independence variable as an indicator of supervisory and managerial capacity. The Witkin and other tests purport to measure the degree to which individuals are affected by the environment in their tasks. Bearing in mind the constant interruptions in the typical supervisory job, this has at least some face validity. The Weissenberg and Gruenfeld article[15] is an extremely interesting attempt to try to correlate the Fleishman and Fiedler measures with the Embedded Figures Test. They found that there was no linear correlation between the measures, but

TABLE 5.7

**Examples of possible instruments for measuring individual
characteristics of supervisors**

Area	Variable	Instrument	Reference	Ref. No.
7.	Consideration	Leadership Opinion	Fleishman & Harris	14
	Initiating structure	Questionnaire	Weissenberg &	
			Gruenfeld	15
	Least Preferred	LPC Questionnaire	Fiedler	16
	Co-worker		Weissenberg &	
			Gruenfeld	15
	Learning capacity for	How Supervise	File & Remmers	17
	employee centred		Neel & Dunn	18
	supervision		Rosen	19
9.	Authoritarianism	Californian 'F'	Adorno	20
		Scale	Neel & Dunn	18
			Kile	21
10.	Mental alertness	Adaptability test	Tiffin & Lawshe	22
			Tiffin & McCormick	23
			Lawshe	24
	Logical inductive ability	Wonderlic Personnel	Wonderlic	25
		Test	Holmes	26
			Neel & Dunn	18
	Logical inductive ability	Otis Self Administering	Harrell	27
		Test	Dicken & Black	5
	Logical inductive ability	Ravens Matrices	Raven	28
11.	Field Dependence	Embedded Figures	Witkin	29
		Test	Weissenberg &	
			Gruenfeld	15
	Dominance/Submission	Bernreuter Personality	Richardson &	
	Self confidence	Inventory	Hanawalt	30
	Neuroticism			
12.	Interest in dealing with	Strong Vocational	Shartle	31
	others	Interest Blank		
13.	Need for achievement	TAT	Cummin	32
	Need for achievement	Industrial TAT	Lennerlöf	33

The reader is advised to consult the references and tests of the instruments quoted before
using them in any investigation.

a curvilinear relationship. In particular, field independent supervisors scored
low on consideration, but those intermediate on Field Dependence discriminated
most between their preferred and least preferred workers (the Fiedler measure).
We can conclude from this that the degree of dependence or independence from
environmental stress may be related to the capacity to adopt certain styles of
supervision, but not others. Once again, any one- or two-dimensional measure is
clearly a great oversimplification.

There has been no comprehensive classification of physiological factors created
which is relevant to supervisors, but a number of measures are being developed.
Examples include: vision, hearing and touch tests; balance tests; general health
tests.

This field is developing fast and falls generally into the subject of Ergonomics. Most of the work here has been concerned with measurement of fatigue and heavy work, labouring, lifting etc. Attention is now being focused on these factors in relation to supervisors. A typical instrument being developed by the researchers in this field would be the 'Bicycle Ergo-meter' which measures respiration, circulation and pulse rates of subjects undergoing a work test.[35]

More controversy exists about 'personality theory' than about any other aspect of psychological theory. However, many of the personality instruments, whatever their theoretical foundations, have been of some value in the prediction of behaviour. Two types of instrument will be described here. First, there are instruments to be applied and marked under strictly standardized conditions, such as paper-and-pencil tests. Secondly, there are semi-standardized instruments, where subjects are put in miniature or real-life situations and their behaviour is rated by observers. The latter type of instrument can be useful where group reactions are needed, though they are highly dependent on the skill and insight of observers. The reliability of these instruments can therefore be questioned, but would seem probably higher than that of measures (discussed below) which are dependent on the judgement of participants in a situation. Measures of personality, however, are often inaccurate and unreliable when compared with the performance tests described above.[36]

Certain types of performance tests are of use indirectly in this area. For instance, emotional stability and fluctuations in performance could be measured by a long series of reaction-time tests. It has been found, for example, that unstable people cannot concentrate for a long time. Eysenck has also developed body-sway tests to measure neuroticism.[37]

Quite promising results, however, have been achieved from constructing or simulating real-life situations and measuring some of the ways in which people undertake their various tasks. Again the purpose of the measure is not so much the actual results or performance in the situation as the technique and style used in achieving the result.

A useful development of this technique was used by the British War Office Selection Board during the Second World War.[38] A number of officer candidates were put into a rigged situation and given a task to perform with certain rules attached. Observers rated the performance of these individuals on a number of given characteristics. Thus in 'a leaderless group' problem, with the assignment of the task of moving a heavy object over a set of obstacles, individuals can be rated for the degree to which they dominate over others in the group. This is argued to be of value in industrial situations for isolating such qualities as leadership, initiative and co-operation. It is also seen as a way of measuring the social reactions of candidates to their fellows (rather than to the tester). It is nevertheless completely dependent on the skill, experience and impartiality of observers. Another example is described by Hesseling.[39] Various groups of departmental managers were asked to solve a communication problem where the rules restrict the communication to written notes. The style of the group and the part played by individuals in the group can be rated by observers. Simulated stress situations can also be of some value in assessing reactions and styles of behaviour, as well as the degree and the amount of emotional stability.

Projective techniques, on the other hand, are mainly paper-and-pencil exercises designed on psycho-analytical principles and intended to provide a means through which a subject expresses or projects his personality structure. They reveal personality by the effects of some stimuli on the subject's perception. Thus, the Thematic Apperception Test (TAT) has been tried in industrial situations by Lennerlöf.[33] Here supervisors are asked to interpret industrial pictures and invent stories to explain them. Some psychologists have thought it possible to measure, by these means, the subjects' interests as well as the level of organization of their thinking and their maturity. The main pitfall of such measures lies in the marking and interpretation, and much depends on the perspectives of the person doing the task. TAT tests, however, are more difficult to fake than other paper-and-pencil tests.

The interview is still the most common method used in industry for appraising individual characteristics, but it should be treated with some caution. Typically, interviews can be used to get basic background information about individuals and are of course used in this way in personnel departments. There is a much greater problem in using interviews as a measure of assessing personality. Many psychologists have been critical and have stressed the unreliability of interviews; others have emphasized the importance of training and how the skilled interviewer can succeed in reaching much more accurate conclusions than those without any standard training.[40]

In the light of the evidence of many supervisory studies, both in Sweden and in the United Kingdom,[41] it seems clear that there is a considerable variety of supervisory situations and supervisory work behaviour, and this would seem to imply that it is unlikely that *one* type of personality or individual characteristics will be critical in every industrial situation. It seems more reasonable to assume, therefore, that each industrial situation may put at a premium different types of supervisory qualities. In particular, in the process industry, where considerable routine exists, and where it is extremely important that supervisors are highly motivated to make consistent inspection rounds and checking of instruments, the qualities of supervisors needed are probably completely different from those demanded by small-batch production. In the construction industry, for example, where there may be an exceptional number of contingencies and interruptions to programme (and the distribution of blame for these failures among supervisors), it is essential for supervisors to be able to cope with such a varying situation and with a great deal of role stress.

Notes and References

1 ROTHE, H. F. & NYE, C. T. (1958). Output ratios among coil winders. *Journal of Applied Psychology*, Vol. 42, pp. 182–6.

2 HALSEY, G. D. (1955). *Selecting and developing first line supervisors*. Harper & Bros., New York.

3 *Note:* Even apart from the interrelation of the work situation and individual

variables there is the question of the variation of personality traits by culture and, of course, variation of expected and desired behaviour.

4 ROACH, D. E. (1956). Factor analysis of rated supervisory behaviour. *Personnel Psychology*, Vol. 9, pp. 487–98.

5 DICKEN, C. F. & BLACK, J. D. (1965). Predictive validity of psychometric evaluations of supervisors. *Journal of Applied Psychology*, Vol. 49, pp. 34–47.

6 *Note:* The tests included : Strong Vocational Interest Blank, M.M.P.I., Otis Quick Scoring Mental Ability (Gamma) Test, General Clerical, Bennett Mechanical Comprehension Test, Minnesota Paper Form Board, Test of Practical Judgement, How Supervise.

7 LAWRENCE, P. R. & LORSCH, J. W. (1969). *Development of organisation, diagnosis and action*. Addison-Wesley Series on Organisation Development. Addison-Wesley, Reading, Mass.

8 CATTEL, R. B. (1966). *The scientific analysis of personality*. Aldine Publ. Co., Chicago.

9 THURSTONE, L. L. (1924). *The nature of intelligence*. Harcourt, Brace & World, New York.
Also: *Measurement of values* (1959). University of Chicago, Chicago. (Collected papers.)

10 EYSENCK, H. J. & EYSENCK, S. B. C. (1969) (with help of A. Hendrickson *et al.*). *Personality structure and measurement*. Routledge & Kegan Paul, London.

11 WHISLER, T. L. & HARPER, S. F. (1962). *Personnel appraisal, research and practice*. Holt, Rinehart & Winston, New York.

12 Nihon Sangyo Kunren Kyokai (Japan Industrial and Vocational Training Organisation) have developed a Career Inventory, based on a number of questionnaires, which gives profiles, scoring seven main factors; viz.: Health, Family life, School life, Social life, Economic consciousness, Interests and Values. Preliminary results show marked differences for managers and supervisors, compared with other grades of staff.

13 McCLELLAND, D. C., ATKINSON, J. W., CLARK, R. A. & LOWELL, E. L. (1953). *The achievement motive*. Appleton-Century-Crofts, Inc., New York.

14 FLEISHMAN, E. A. & HARRIS, E. F. (1962). Patterns of leader behaviour related to employee grievances and turnover. *Personnel Psychology*, Vol. 15, pp. 43–56.

15 WEISSENBERG, P. & GRUENFELD, L. W. (1966). Relationships among leadership dimensions and cognitive style. *Journal of Applied Psychology*, Vol. 50, pp. 392–5.

16 FIEDLER, F. E. (1964). A contingency model of leadership effectiveness. In L. Berkowitz (ed.) *Advances in experimental social psychology*. Vol. 1. Academic Press, New York, pp. 149–90.

17 FILE, Q. W. & REMMERS, H. H. (1948). *How supervise*. Psychological Corporation, New York.

18 NEEL, R. G. & DUNN, R. E. (1969). Predicting success in supervisory training

programmes by the use of psychological tests. *Journal of Applied Psychology*, Vol. 44, pp. 358–60.

19 ROSEN, N. A. (1961). How supervise. 1943–1960. *Personnel Psychology*, Vol. 14, pp. 87–99.

20 ADORNO, T. W. *et al.* (1950). *The authoritarian personality.* Harper, New York.

21 KILE, S. (1963). In MEIGNIEZ, R. *Evaluation of supervisory and management training methods.* OECD. op. cit., pp. 105–9.

22 TIFFIN, J. & LAWSHE, C. H. (1943). *The adaptability test.* A 15 minutes Mental Alertness Test for use in personnel allocation. Science Research Associates, Chicago.

23 TIFFIN, J. & McCORMICK, E. J. (1958). *Industrial psychology.* 4th ed., pp. 118–19. Prentice-Hall, Englewood Cliffs.

24 LAWSHE, C. H. Jr. (1949). How can we pick better supervisors? *Personnel Psychology*, Vol. 2, pp. 69–73.

25 WONDERLIC, E. F. (1945). *The Wonderlic Personnel Test.* Psychological Corporation, New York.

26 HOLMES, F. J. (1950). Validity of tests for insurance office personnel. *Personnel Psychology*, Vol. 13, pp. 57–69.

27 HARRELL, T. W. (1940). Testing cotton mill supervisors. *Journal of Applied Psychology*, Vol. 24, pp. 31–5.

28 RAVEN, J. C. (1938). *Progressive matrices.* H. K. Lewis, London.

29 WITKIN, H. A. (1950). Individual differences in ease of perception of embedded figures. *Journal of Personnel*, Vol. 19, pp. 1–15.

30 RICHARDSON, H. & HANAWALT, N. G. (1944). Leadership as related to the Bernreuter Personality Measures: III. Leadership among adult men in vocational and social activities. *Journal of Applied Psychology*, Vol. 28, pp. 308–17.

31 SHARTLE, C. L. (1943). A personnel approach to foremanship. *Personnel Journal*, Vol. 13, pp. 135–9.

32 CUMMIN, P. C. (1967). TAT correlates of executive performance. *Journal of Applied Psychology*, Vol. 51, No. 1, pp. 78–81.

33 LENNERLÖF, L. (1966).*Dimensions of supervision.* Swedish Council for Personnel Administration, Stockholm.

34 STOCKFORD, L. (1947). Selection of supervisory personnel. *Personnel*, Vol. 24, pp. 186–99.

35 EDLUND, E. & LUNDGREN, N.)1957). *Hälsotillstånd och fysisk arbetsförmåga.* Swedish Council for Personnel Administration, Stockholm. (Summary in English.)

36 CATTEL, R. B. & WARBURTON, F. W. (1967). *Objective personality and motivation tests. A theoretical introduction and practical compendium.* University of Illinois Press, Urbana.

37 EYSENCK, H. J. (1966). Body sway suggestibility as a function of drive and personality. *Bulletin of British Psychological Society*, Vol. 19, pp. 1–28.

38 Morris, B. S. (1949). Officer selection in the British army. *Occupational Psychology, N.I.I.P.*, Vol. 23, pp. 219–34.
39 Hesseling, P. & Können, E. (1969). Culture and subculture in a decision-making exercise. *Human Relations*, Vol. 22, No. 1, pp. 31–51.
40 Glazer, R., Schwarz, P. A. & Flanagan, J. C. (1958). The contribution of interview and situational performance procedures to the selection of supervisory personnel. *Journal of Applied Psychology*, Vol. 42, pp. 69–73.
41 Thurley, K. E. & Hamblin, A. C. (1963) and Wirdenius, H. (1961). op. cit.

THE WORK SITUATION

The phrase 'supervisory work situation' stands for a highly complex network of interrelated factors and any discussion of these needs to start with a clarification of the terms used. The supervisory situation can be interpreted to signify the factors in the supervisor's immediate environment which impinge on his behaviour, but it can also be widened to include more general variables in the organization where he is working which have an overall and long-term effect on his work and problems. It is necessary, therefore, to make some general division according to the *level* at which these factors are operating. The fifteen examples of areas of variables shown in Figure 3.3 are classified in Table 5.8 into three levels:

(a) Supervisory system variables.
(b) General internal organizational variables.
(c) Extra-organizational variables.

This classification should not be seen as anything other than a convenient way of conceptualizing the 'environment', as in any real situation factors at one level very much influence factors at others and overlap with them, and the distinction is not always easy to make. Nevertheless, there is some logic about this division: it is necessary to classify before analysis.

It is, however, clearly important for those seeking to understand the supervisory situation to make a model to structure hypothetical interrelations *for the particular system under investigation.*

Many of the pressures on supervisors come from middle management downwards, indicating that certain methods and certain tasks may be prescribed by such managers. An example of this is a possible demand for reports on a weekly basis or a demand that supervisors make inspection tours of their departments every few hours. Some demands may be extremely subtle and are very definitely *not* confined to formalized minutes, job descriptions or circular letters. Similarly, certain supervisors may be highly successful in manipulating or changing the direction of these demands in a way not immediately apparent to the outsider. Many of the job demands from the work situation (from the plant, material and operative behaviour) are also difficult to quantify and, again, they may not be apparent to anybody other than the supervisors concerned.

This reminds us that it may be more important to understand the way supervisors perceive situational variables than to measure the variables themselves.

TABLE 5.8

Examples of important situational variables

Supervisory system variables	Selected variables		
1 Number and type of subordinates	Level of skill of workers. Proportion of skilled workers. Type of ethnic group.	Occupational background of workers. Dispersion of workers and work area. Local culture of works.	Range of worker's task. Age of subordinates.
2 Behaviour of workers	Extent and type of work group organization. Type of leadership style expected. Type of incentive payment scheme.	Degree of group cohesiveness. Existence and power of informal leaders.	
3 Rewards and sanctions for workers			
4 Type of production system	Process continuity. Level of mechanization. Degree of predictability of production system. Work flow rigidity.	Type of occupational culture. Economic consequences of mistakes in handling disturbances. Inter-dependence of operations.	Physical barriers to verbal communication. Degree of risks at work. Production maintenance and inspection functions.
5 Rate of technical change	Frequency of introduction of new machines, new materials, new layouts, new products, manning scales.		
6 Type of supervisory system	Number of levels of supervision. Amount of specialization within system. Degree of inter-changeability.	Number and type and quality of staff assistants. Degree of role overload.	Complexity of supervisory system
7 Number and type of supervisory tasks prescribed	Degree of ambiguity in prescribed tasks. Proportion of problem solving tasks.	Difficulty of problems. Type of search procedures required (logical – intuitive).	
8 Rewards and sanctions for supervisors	Extent of relationship between rewards and performance criteria. Relative differentials of pay between workers and supervisors. Fringe benefits. Management control over career prospects.	Frequency of use of sanctions. Specificity of evaluation of operations.	

General internal organizational variables	Selected variables	
9 Type of management administrative system	Number, range and type of staff, departments, relationships and communications. Type and number of administrative procedures and reports required of supervisors. Degree of organizational role conflict.	Contextual variables (1): Origin and history. Ownership and control. Size. Charter. Location. Resources. Criteria for supervisory performance.
10 Behaviour of superiors	Degree of pressure from superior. Style of leadership. Degree to which superior can be influenced. Area of pressure for results.	
11 Values of other supervisors (peer group pressures)	Degree of professionalization of supervisors. Leadership norms (consideration, initiating structure). Range and intensity of demands on supervisors.	

Extra-organizational variables	Selected variables	
12 Trade union organization	Degree of effective demand for work regulation.	
13 Situation of labour market	Degree and type of labour shortage and surplus.	
14 Level of demand	Degree of unpredictability of changes of demand.	Degree of dependence for business strategic decisions on external organizations.
15 Community constraints	Health and welfare regulations Safety regulations.	

The focus of our attention is on the explanation and prediction of supervisory behaviour and this distinguishes it from the various attempts by organizational behaviour theorists to draw up conceptual schemes for classifying organizational structure *per se*.[1, 2, *] Many of these studies produce schemes which are difficult to operationalize,[3] but some previous work is relevant here. Pugh and his colleagues, over the past ten years, have been exploring the possibility of comparing organizations along scales of dimensions of structure and bureaucracy[4] and some of his measures and variables appear in Table 5.8. He divides his variables into organization processes, aspects of structure, contextual variables and performance variables.[5] His empirical work leads him to isolate seven types of organization structure[6] according to the location and degree of structure. His methods of measuring operations technology are particularly relevant.[7]

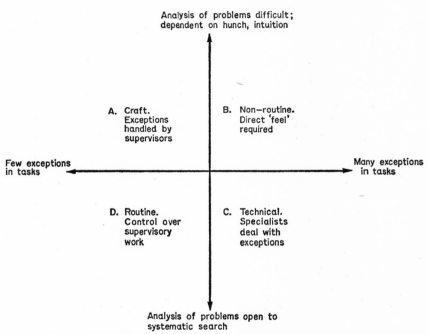

FIGURE 5.3   Types of task structure (adapted from Perrow[10])

The previous emphasis of Woodward[8] and Burns and Stalker[9] on the importance of technology and environmental demands on organizational behaviour is a starting point for many writers. Of particular use is the scheme produced by Perrow.[11] He suggests some highly significant dimensions of task structure for supervisory behaviour and these are reproduced below (Figure 5.3 and Table 5.9).

Perrow's two main dimensions are:

* *See* page 81 for references.

1. The number of exceptional cases encountered at work, or the degree of familiarity with problems met.
2. The nature of the search procedures used when exceptions to routine occur.

He distinguishes situations where problems can be analysed systematically from those where the only course is to use hunch, intuition or experience, i.e. non-logical methods.

This allows us to distinguish four types of situation for supervisors. The nature of task structure can be said to be likely to correspond to four types of organizational situation, as measured by:

(a) The degree of discretion (or choice of means and judgement for critical individual tasks) for supervisors, compared with technical specialist staff.
(b) The degree of power, for example, to mobilize resources, for supervisors and technical staff.
(c) The type of co-ordination practised (by planning first or by feed-back after action).
(d) The degree of inter-dependence of groups.

Table 5.9 illustrates these distinctions.

TABLE 5.9

Types of organizational situation, corresponding to task structure

		Situations		
Technical control	A	B	C	D
Discretion	Low	High	High	Low
Power	Low	High	High	High
Co-ordination	Planning	Feedback	Feedback	Planning
Interdependence of groups	Low	High	Low	Low
Supervision				
Discretion	High	High	Low	Low
Power	High	High	Low	Low
Co-ordination	Feedback	Feedback	Planning	Planning
Interdependence of groups	Low	High	Low	Low
Examples				
	Shoe industry	Research and development (e.g. electronics)	Engineering industry	Steel industry

Source: Perrow[12]

The situations in the Table are only types, of course, and are therefore only intended to provide some type of 'map' to allow the work situation to be diagnosed. The task structure is only one aspect of the work situation, however, and Perrow also attempts a classification of the types of goals and orientations of those within the organization (organizational climate). He distinguishes four types:

1. Social identity (community-based).
2. Organization goal identification.
3. Work or task identification.
4. Instrumental identification (rewards or pay-off).

Again, these types are a useful classification of the types of pressures within which the supervisors have to work. The problem here, however, is the difficulty of measurement.

Table 5.10 summarizes the methods which seem to be most suitable for assessing the variables mentioned above.

TABLE 5.10

Examples of methods available for assessment of the work situation

Supervisory system variables	*Type of method best suited*	*Example/Reference*
1. Number and type of workers	Documents. Interview Work study data. Observation	Turner & Lawrence[13]
2. Workers behaviour	Questionnaire. Interview Observation	Lupton[14] Trist *et al.*[15]
3. Rewards and sanctions for workers	Documents. Questionnaire Interview	NPIB Report[16] Baldamus[17]
4. Production system	Documents. Ratings. Interview	Hickson,[18] Crossman[19] Bright,[20] Woodward[21]
5. Technical change	Documents. Interview	Touraine[22]
6. Supervisory system	Interview. Observation	Thurley & Hamblin[23] Kahn *et al.*[24]
7. Number and type of tasks	Interview. Observation Documents	Deeks *et al.*[25] Wirdenius[26]
8. Rewards and sanctions for supervisors	Documents. Interviews Questionnaires	Chester,[27] Herzberg[28] Gruenfeld[29]
General internal organizational variables		
9. Management system	Documents. Interviews Ratings	Pugh,[30] Burns[31]
10. Behaviour of superiors	Interview. Observation Questionnaire	Pelz,[32] Coates[33] Fleishman[34]
11. Supervisory value system	Ratings. Questionnaire Interview	Stogdill & Coons[35] Jasinsky,[36] Kipnis[37]
Extra-organizational variables		
12. Trade unions organization	Interview. Observation	Kuhn,[38] Dalton[39]
13. Labour market	Documents. Statistics	Labour Market Board Reports[40]
14. Demand	Documents	Turner *et al.*[41] Lawrence & Lorsch[42]
15. Community constraints	Documents	Dunlop[43]

For many of these variables, there are no precise measures. However, the literature referred to will show various contemporary attempts to make assessments (for different purposes) on a comparative basis. Some types of norms are clearly necessary, in order to make such data meaningful. Survey information is therefore of considerable importance here.

Notes and References

1 PUGH, D. S. *et al.* (1963). A conceptual scheme for organisational analysis. *Administrative Science Quarterly*, Vol. 8 (December), pp. 289–315.
2 BLAU, P. M. & SCOTT, W. R. (1964). *Formal organisations: A comparative approach*. Routledge & Kegan Paul, London.
3 ETZIONI, A. (1961). *A comparative analysis of complex organisations*. Free Press of Glencoe, New York.
4 PUGH, D. S. *et al.* (1969ᵃ). An empirical taxonomy of structures of work organisations. *Administrative Science Quarterly*, Vol. 14, No. 1, pp. 115–26.
5 PUGH, D. S. *et al.* (1969ᵇ). The context of organisation structures. *Administrative Science Quarterly*, Vol. 14, No. 1 (March), pp. 91–114 esp. p. 92.
6 PUGH, D. S. *et al.* (1969ᵃ). op. cit., Table 2.
7 HICKSON, D. J. *et al.* (1969). Operations technology and structure. *Administrative Science Quarterly*, Vol. 14, No. 3, pp. 378–97.
8 WOODWARD, J. (1965). *Industrial organization*. Oxford University Press, Oxford.
9 BURNS, T. & STALKER, G. M. (1961). *The management of innovation*. Tavistock, London.
10 PERROW, C. (1967). A framework for the comparative analysis of organisations. *American Sociological Review*, Vol. 32, pp. 194–208.
11 PERROW, C. (1967). ibid., p. 196 (See also PERROW, C. (1970). *Organizational analysis: A sociological view*, pp. 80–5. Tavistock, London.)
12 PERROW, C. (1967). ibid., p. 199.
13 TURNER, A. N. & LAWRENCE, P. R. (1965). *Industrial jobs and the worker*. Graduate School of Business Administration, Harvard University Press, Boston, Mass.
14 LUPTON, T. (1963). *On the shop floor*. Pergamon Press, Oxford.
15 TRIST, E. L. *et al.* (1963). *Organisational choice*. Tavistock, London.
16 National Prices and Incomes Board (1968). *Payment by results*. Report No. 65. HMSO, London.
17 BALDAMUS, W. (1951). Type of work and motivation. *British Journal of Sociology*, Vol. 2 (March), pp. 44–58.
18 HICKSON, D. J. *et al.* (1969). op. cit.
19 CROSSMAN, E. R. F. W. (1966). *Taxonomy of automation*: State of the art and prospects. Manpower aspects of automation and technical change. *European Conference Supplement to final report*, p. 75. OECD, Paris.
20 BRIGHT, J. A. (1958). Does automation raise skill requirements? *Harvard Business Review*, Vol. 36, No. 4 (July/August), pp. 85–98.
21 WOODWARD, J. (1965). op. cit.
22 TOURAINE, A. (1965). *Workers' attitudes to technical change*. OECD, Paris.
23 THURLEY, K. E. & HAMBLIN, A. C. (1963). *The supervisor and his job*. HMSO, London.

24 KAHN, R. *et al.* (1964). *Organisational stress.* op. cit.

25 DEEKS, J. *et al.* (1967). *Problem solving behaviour in construction management.* Anglo–Swedish Conference on 'Human factors in the construction process' (September) (mimeographed).

26 WIRDENIUS, H. (1961). *Förmän i arbete.* Swedish Council for Personnel Administration, Stockholm.

27 CHESTER, C. M. (1952). Supervisory compensation – direct and indirect. Practical approaches to supervisory and executive development. *Personnel Series,* No. 145. A.M.A., pp. 27–37. (See also : ROSENSTEEL, D. H. (1957). Supervisory compensation – an interim report. *Personnel* (January), p. 357.)

28 HERZBERG, F. (1965). The motivation to work among Finnish supervisors. *Personnel Psychology,* Vol. 18, No. 4 (Winter), pp. 393–402.

29 GRUENFIELD, L. W. (1962). A study of the motivation of industrial supervisors. *Personnel Psychology,* Vol. 15, No. 3 (Autumn), pp. 303–14.

30 PUGH, D. S. *et al.* (1969[a]). op. cit.

31 BURNS, T. (1967). The comparative study of organisations. In VROOM, V. (ed.) *Methods of organisational research.* University of Pittsburg Press, Pittsburg, pp. 118–70.

32 PELZ, D. C. (1952). Influence : a key to effective leadership in the first-line supervisor. *Personnel* (November), pp. 209–17.

33 COATES, C. H. & PELLEGRIN, R. J. (1957). Executives and supervisors. Self views and views of each other. *American Sociological Review,* Vol. 22 (April), pp. 217–20.

34 FLEISHMAN, E. A. *et al.* (1955). *Leadership and supervision in industry.* Bureau of Educational Research, Ohio State University, Columbus.

35 STOGDILL, R. M. & COONS, A. E. (eds.) (1957). *Leader behaviour: Its description and measurement.* Bureau of Business Research, Ohio State University, Columbus.

36 JASINSKY, F. J. (1956). Foreman relationships outside the work group. *Personnel,* Vol. 33, No. 2 (September), pp. 130–36.

37 KIPNIS, D. (1960). Some determinants of supervisory esteem. *Personnel Psychology,* Vol. 13, No. 4 (Winter), pp. 377–91.

38 KUHN, J. W. (1961). *Bargaining in grievance settlement.* Colombia University Press, New York.

39 DALTON, M. (1954). The role of supervision. In KORNHAUSER, A., DUBIN, R. & ROSS, A. (eds.), *Industrial conflict.* McGraw-Hill Book Co., New York.

40 Swedish Labour Market Board Reports, published monthly.

41 TURNER, H. A., CLACK, G. & ROBERTS, G. (1967). *Labour relations in the motor industry.* Allen & Unwin, London.

42 LAWRENCE, P. R. & LORSCH, J. W. (1967). *Organisation and environment.* Managing differentiation and integration. Harvard University Press, Cambridge, Mass.

43 DUNLOP, J. T. (1959). *Industrial relations systems.* H. Holt, New York.

WORK ACTIONS

What should be measured?

We have already discussed two main concepts in the area of supervisory work actions: the idea of *levels* of behaviour (Table 3.1) and the concept of the role as a 'portfolio of problems'. It is now important to introduce a third concept, that of *types of perceptions* of work behaviour.

If the record of Foreman Pat in Table 3.4 is re-examined, we are looking at the work behaviour of this supervisor as perceived and described by an observer. In this case, the observer was trained to observe certain aspects of behaviour according to some simple criteria. In the Walker study[1, *] the dimensions given in its appendix show such items as the topic of work, type of activity and so forth. We can say, therefore, that such an attempt to observe work behaviour systematically and to record aspects of it without bias is an attempt to measure *actual behaviour*. This is still subject to selective perceptions, but if care is taken to control bias, it is reasonable to suppose that this concept of actual behaviour will produce descriptions of a relatively objective type.

If we now go further in our investigation and ask *why* the behaviour is taking place, we will be forced to consider many of the variables already discussed. Among those variables are two which also relate directly to behaviour: the prescriptions of managers or of those in authority, *prescribed behaviour*; and the expectations of workers, managers, peers, staff employees, etc., about the behaviour of the supervisors in question in a particular period of time, *expected behaviour*. These are both situational variables in the main model. Prescriptions could include oral or written instructions and rules concerning desired supervisory behaviour. Expectations include all types of anticipated behaviour for a future period of time and they range from formal conscious expectations to the semi-conscious. They might be extremely detailed or vague, and they could refer to different levels and aspects of behaviour. It is very common to find conflicts between expectations held by different parties in the situation, for example, workers and management.[2]

The supervisor, himself, of course, also has his own intentions about his behaviour or actions over the next period of time. This we call *intended behaviour*. In the analysis of strategy or tactics, it is necessary to try to get 'inside' the supervisor and find out what he thinks he is doing. This type of data, therefore, belongs to the central box of supervisory work actions along with actual work actions. They are only the same if the supervisor acts exactly according to his intentions or plans. In fact, this is rarely so, as the supervisory action is taking place in a field where disturbances are common. Such disturbances, being by definition unexpected at the moment when they appear, are among the main reasons for a gap between *intended* and *actual* behaviour.

The supervisor, managers and other parties also have certain beliefs about

* *See* page 99 for references.

possible behaviour in the future, although this may be vague. In Chapter 1, the criticisms of supervisory performance imply the existence of beliefs about ideal or possible behaviour. The processes of bringing about change, already discussed in Chapter 2, showed the emergence of a gap between the variables describing the current situation, individual characteristics, behaviour and effects, and those in a possible new hypothetical system. We refer to *potential work behaviour*, therefore, when such a change is discussed and the implications are perceived in terms of behaviour. The process of determining potential behaviour is discussed in Chapter 6.

This classification of types of perceptions of supervisory work behaviour is brought together in Table 5.11.

TABLE 5.11

Types of perceptions of work behaviour and possible methods for data collection

	Area of variables in model	Persons perceiving	Methods used
Actual behaviour	Supervisor work actions	Anybody who can observe	Direct observation Ratings Questionnaires Interviews Combined methods
Prescribed behaviour	Supervisor work situation	Management Society	Documents Questionnaires Interviews
Expected behaviour	Supervisor work situation	Anybody who has contact with supervisor	Interviews Questionnaires Ratings
Intended behaviour	Supervisor work actions	Supervisor himself	Interviews Questionnaires Ratings Direct observation
Potential behaviour	Potential system	Anybody	Interviews Questionnaires

If we take an example to illustrate these differences of meaning for types of behaviour, the case of a drama or play is convenient. The *actual behaviour* is the performance of the actor as seen by the audience. The *prescribed behaviour* is the script and stage directions. The *expected behaviour* is the way the part is expected to be played by the director and the other players. The *intended behaviour* is the way that the actor sees himself playing the role. The *potential behaviour* could be seen as the type of performance desired by a drama critic, who could like to see a better actor in the part.

TABLE 5.12

Methods and instruments for appraising work behaviour

Level of behaviour		Selected variables	Type of unit of data	Type of method	Specific instrument
Actual	*Intended*				
	Strategy in role	Leadership style Participation in external work flows Monitoring role	Frequency Importance	Questionnaire Interview Direct observation Rating Combination	Ohio State Questionnaire[3] Likert scales[4] Long term self recording[5]
Function	Tactical	Functions performed Sequences of action in problem solution Time reference of function Cause of function	Time spent Frequency Importance Sequence	Interview Questionnaire Direct observation Rating Combination	SISCO[6] (*See* Appendix) Continuous observation[7]
Task	Disturbance handling	Tasks performed (e.g., social, manual, administrative, technical) Source of information Content of communication Meetings	Time spent Frequency Importance Sequence Incident Disturbance handling behaviour	Direct observation Rating Interview Combination	SISCO Sampling or continuous observation Critical incident method[8] Card sorting[9] Paired comparison[10]
Activity		Physical activity Contact activity Initiator of contact Communication channel	Time spent Frequency	Direct observation Rating	Sampling or continuous observation[11] Card sorting Paired comparisons Simple estimates[12]

Table 5.12 shows a classification of levels of work behaviour, some crucial variables and the types and range of methods available. It can be noted that *intended behaviour* is more important at the general level than it is at the specific. *Actual behaviour* is important at the specific level and follows a reverse pattern. It is clear that the analysis of supervisory style at the general level may produce stereotyped expectations which conflict with actual behaviour as perceived by onlookers. If the role of the perceiver allows such direct observation, then this conflict will be unlikely to persist. It may persist, however, when the perceiver has little contact with the supervisors in question.

TABLE 5.13

Summary of methods for assessing work behaviour

Method of data collection	Agent	Type of unit of data	Examples of dimensions of behaviour[13]
Direct observation	Researcher	Time spent	Place
Continuous	Consultant	Frequency	Activity
Sampling	Supervisor (self)	Importance	Contact status
Rating	Staff specialist	Sequence	Contact department
Questionnaire	Superior	Incident	Communication type
Interview	Subordinate	Disturbance	Subject of function
Unstructured	Peer	handling behaviour	Time reference of
Semi-structured			function
Structured			Cause of function
Combined method			Search for information
			Initiator of contact
			Consideration
			Initiating structure
			Authoritarian
			Democratic
			Laisser faire
			Bureaucratic
			Manipulative

Table 5.13 shows the range of types of method available for assessing work behaviour. We can discuss this best by concentrating on a number of possible techniques. There are twelve main methods which will be reviewed in detail. They are:

1. Observer continuous diary
2. Self-completed continuous diary
3. Distant work sampling
4. 'Following-after' work sampling
5. Work sampling with interview
6. Self work sampling
7. Superiors' distant work sampling
8. Superiors' ratings
9. Self-ratings

10. Semi-structured interview after continuous observation
11. Semi-structured interview after self-observation of critical incidents, disturbances or problems
12. Combination of group discussions and questionnaires, after self-observation of critical incidents, disturbances or problems

Method 1: Observer continuous diary

1 *Examples*

The most notable example is that of Guest.[7] Other examples include Wallace & Gallagher,[14] Westerlund [15, 16] and Thurley & Hamblin.[17]

2 *Purpose*

The aim of this method is to make a continuous record of the sequence of events in one or more days of a supervisor so that both the time spent, frequency and the sequence can be recorded accurately.

3 *Description*

Preliminary work. The method may be used as an exploratory one at the beginning of a study, and therefore the only preliminary work necessary is to familiarize the observer with the equipment and personnel in a department.

Carrying out the method. The observer can use two different approaches. The most common one is to follow after the foreman as a 'shadow'. An alternative method is to observe inside the department or unit from one position, which could be used, for instance, in cases where the supervisor does not leave the department very often.

Analysis. The observations are classified on several dimensions by taking incidents as 'units'. The definition of the incident varies between authors but it can, for instance, be defined by a change of location or contact or function. After the diary has been made, it can be either reported as a sequence of events or classified and quantified so that the frequency of incidents and time spent in them may be calculated.

4 *Reliability*

The first problem of reliability lies in the question of defining the term 'incident'. Very often in these studies the observer himself decides what is an incident, frequently without a clear frame of reference, and it is therefore probable that two or more observers will come to different definitions of the term 'incident'. It can be defined by the use of the criteria of contacts, location or function, but there are cases where one changes and the others do not. This makes it very difficult to be precise and clear as to when one incident ends and another one begins. The second problem is that a supervisor's work behaviour has significance on a large number of dimensions. Because the numbers of problems dealt with by supervisors are often very large and do not necessarily occur very frequently, an observer cannot normally hope to make a comprehensive account of what is going on. Selection of information is involved and selection can mean that the personal interest of the observer introduces a bias.

As this is a time-consuming method, it is usually not possible to be able to study supervisors for more than one day each. With the fluctuations in work cycles according to seasonal variations and from week to week, which exist in many supervisory jobs it becomes plain that a sample of one day, or even one week, may give an unreliable picture of the supervisor's job over the long term.

5 *Validity*

A main problem in validity here is the question of observer influence. The observer can influence the data in three ways. First, by unconsciously persuading the foreman to change his behaviour, because of his presence, in a direction intended to impress the observer. Secondly, because the foreman changes in order to be friendly towards the observer, he might spend much time talking to the observer. Thirdly, other managers or staff in the department may change their behaviour because the observer is with the foreman for that day.

If the period of observation is short, for example, two hours per day, it is likely that the supervisor will concentrate on certain jobs when he is under observation. In such a case data may be extremely unrepresentative and mirror mainly the 'interesting' sides of supervisory behaviour.

6 *Practical value*

The greatest advantage of this method is that it is simple and straightforward and can provide the observer with considerable insight into the sequence of events and of the type of critical problems with which supervisors have to deal. The great defect is that any statistical data worked out from even the most carefully classified observer diary information is liable to gross error for the reasons stated above. The problem of coding the material has also practical difficulties. It can be a very laborious process, particularly if, as in the Guest example, there is an undertaking to show the account of the day to the supervisor concerned shortly after the observation period. One good reason for using this method is that it can give insight into training needs and this has been demonstrated by Nightingale.[18]

Method 2: Self-completed continuous diary

1 *Examples*

Westerlund;[16] Jacobson;[19] Westerlund & Strömberg;[20] Lehesmaa;[21] Stewart;[22] Hesseling;[23] Weinhall;[24] Burns.[25]

2 *Purpose*

There are two types of studies, one dealing with all aspects of behaviour recorded by the supervisors themselves, and one dealing with contacts or communication only.

3 *Description*

Preliminary work. Here supervisors need basic instructions and training in filling in diaries. Considerable efforts may be needed to secure co-operation in getting supervisors to add to their normal duties.

Carrying out the method. The usual method is to issue each supervisor with a book, in which he writes down all the events which occur to him. Sometimes the book is pre-coded so that only ticking is necessary, sometimes it is left blank. A third variety is to have the subjects put down anything unusual or special occurring in a day (critical incidents, difficult situations).

Analysis. The books are recovered from supervisors and coded by the researcher. The researcher may interview each supervisor and check observations made. After this the diary is processed as in Method 1.

4 *Reliability*

The reliability of this method is usually very low, because supervisors vary in their willingness and capabilities in completing such a return. Moreover, as in Method 1, problems of definition, comprehensiveness, and representativity are difficult to escape.

5 *Validity*

The validity of this method is consequently bound to be low. The same problems exist, which have been discussed in Method 1, e.g. the tendency of supervisors to select incidents according to their interest and perception. A practical problem is to get the necessary time to keep these records. Sometimes they are completed at night, when some of the events have been forgotten.[26] The ticking method may induce a supervisor to tick certain things just to make sure that he has a good coverage of activities.

6 *Practical value*

The value of this method for obtaining a valid picture of the supervisor's work day is extremely limited, as indicated. It is, however, useful as a method of high-lighting critical problems, as seen by supervisors, particularly if combined with a series of interviews by skilled interviewers based on the records kept by the supervisors. In one instance in the early LSE research, a supervisor diary provided considerable insight into supervisor/manager relationships. The method has the same practical difficulties as Method 1.

Method 3: Distant work sampling

There are five main types of sampling observation methods, which should be discussed here (Methods 3–7 in this text). For all of them it is necessary to use the statistical theory of sampling as described in the text-books available.[27, 28] The basic points can be summarized as:

(*a*) The use of normal randomization methods, e.g. random tables, for pre-determining the times or order of the observations.

(*b*) Making sure that every instance which is observed has the same chance of being selected as any other instance.

(*c*) Making sure that the supervisor does not know at which instance the observation will take place.

(*d*) The possession of a coherent system of dimensions and categories for classifying the observations.

1 *Examples*

Thurley & Hamblin;[17] Kelly;[29] Wirdenius;[11] Hesseling.[30]

2 *Purpose*

The intention of the distant work sampling method is to sample the supervisor's day by using an observer walking at random times round predetermined routes in a factory or department.

3 *Description*

Preliminary work. Preliminary work is necessary (besides the four points mentioned above) to determine the classification and train the observers in the interpretation of the classification. Secondly, it is necessary to decide on routes for the tour in such a way that certain types of observation will not be more likely than others. For example, the tour should not include too much corridor (non-working area).[31] Thirdly, several choices of tours should be arranged and tours should be undertaken in different directions. Fourthly, observations are made by adopting the rule that the first time the observer sees the supervisor, at that 'snap point', the observation is made.

Carrying out the method. The observer carries out a large number of tours at randomly determined times, taking observations of supervisors at any point of time, when he first sees these supervisors on his list. If not seen, supervisors are not pursued or followed into other parts of the factory away from the route.

Analysis. The analysis is done by coding observations and calculating percentages according to the various categories of the classification.

4 *Reliability*

Reliability is high in the 'objective' dimensions, i.e. those which require little inference on behalf of the observer, and low in those that do require inference. The experience of both authors indicates this.

5 *Validity*

The validity question depends entirely on what dimensions are being observed. For certain dimensions, like location, activity, and contacts, this method seems to produce a more accurate picture of supervisors' time and work than any other. Observer influence is low, and it is possible to make observations without supervisors really being aware of when they are being carried out. All supervisors should, of course, be warned and their co-operation should be secured for undertaking such a study. Even so, it is probably advisable to instruct observers to notify supervisors that they have been observed in the preceding minute.

6 *Practical value*

This method is valuable for obtaining rather precise measures of particular activities, for example inspection, and could be used, for instance, for determining the effects of a training course for these particular categories. The data, however, do not help with the isolation of training needs and do not generally highlight critical aspects of the supervisor's work. It is, therefore, most useful in conjunction with other methods which investigate more fundamental aspects of behaviour.[32]

Method 4: 'Following-after' work sampling

1 *Examples*

Wirdenius & Lönnsjö;[33] also standard interval sampling, with continuous observation (SISCO method) used by Thurley, Hamblin & Pinschof.[6]

2 *Purpose*

The aim of these methods is the same as the other sampling methods; to give a valid picture of the supervisor's work activities.

3 *Description*

Preliminary work. As in Method 3, although there is much greater need for 'rapport' from the supervisors concerned.

Carrying out the method. One procedure is the 'following-after method' used in the Wirdenius studies. This involves an observer shadowing a supervisor and sampling his day at random intervals. Another method, the SISCO technique, involves a non-random sampling by an observer every two minutes. The argument for this is that the repetitive routine part of a supervisor's job is small and that there is little risk, therefore, of biasing the results by choosing observations for fixed work cycles. Both methods use snap reading as described above for their observation.

Analysis. Similar to methods described above.

4 *Reliability*

Reliability is rather high at least in the first type of study (see Table 5.14). In SISCO, some evidence emerged of discrepancies between observers. This would seem to be due to lack of training and the difficulty of making inferences with the classification used (see standard classification in Appendix to this book).

TABLE 5.14

Agreement of independent codifications made by paired observers in house-building

Behaviour dimension	Percentage average agreements (over and above that determined by chance)
Place	92
Physical activity	84
Mental activity	79
Contact object	78
Number of contact persons	89
Method of communication	80
Contact person	88
Initiator of personal contact	78
Function	88
Time aspect of function being carried out	75
Method of carrying out function	71

Source: Wirdenius and Lönnsjö[33]

5 *Validity*

The problem here is observer influence as discussed for the observer diary method. Otherwise, validity can be seen to be quite high in the sense that the interpretation of an inference made by the observer can be more accurate, as he is on the spot and has followed the history of problems and sequence of events all day and is less likely to misunderstand the situation.

6 *Practical value*

These methods are of considerable value in the measurement of supervisory functions and the reasons for his behaviour. They enable the observer to penetrate beyond the rather superficial level of information obtained from the distant sampling, without some of the problems of the diary method. On the other hand, observer influence cannot easily be minimized. There is also the basic resource problem, as with the diary method, of studying enough of the whole range of behaviour.

Method 5: Work sampling with interview

1 *Examples*

Wirdenius;[11] several Swedish company studies have been made with this method, for example by Sack;[34] Thurley.[35]

2 *Purpose*

The intention here is to penetrate beyond the observational information and try to get the supervisors' perceptions in order to understand and interpret the events and activities seen, and to check the accuracy of the observations.

3 *Description*

Preliminary work. As above.

Carrying out the method. The interview is carried out immediately after the observation, although sometimes the observer may have to wait a minute or so until he finds a convenient moment.

Analysis. As above.

4 *Reliability*

Reliability is rather high (Table 5.15).

TABLE 5.15

Agreement of independent codifications made by paired observers in three textile companies

Behaviour dimension	Percentage average agreements (over and above that determined by chance)
Place	97
Physical activity	88
Mental activity	65
Contact object	71
Number of contact persons	89
Method of communication	60
Contact person	83
Initiator of personal contact	78
Function	75
Time aspect of function being carried out	60
Method of carrying out function	59

Source: Wirdenius[36]

5 *Validity*

Validity is also rather high, apart from possible observer influence due to the fact of continual interview on the job.

6 *Practical value*

The practical value of this method seems considerable, if enough support from the company can be assured and if the supervisors concerned are prepared to collaborate with the study.

Method 6: Self work sampling

1 *Examples*

Wirdenius & Lönnsjö;[33] Stewart.[37]

2 *Purpose*

The aim of this approach is to find a cheap method enabling one to gain information about a very large number of supervisors over a long period.

3 *Description*

Preliminary work. A great deal of importance should be laid on the training of supervisors in classifying their observations correctly.

Carrying out the method. A type of self-timing device is used, either a clock or a wrist watch or a signal, so that the supervisors know precisely when to make their observations.

Analysis. As for normal work sampling, apart from the necessity for a checking device by the person conducting the investigation, i.e. by interview every shift or day.

4 *Reliability*

There is no complete evidence on this, but one study[38] showed agreement between parallel supervisor and specialist observer of almost the same level as that between two specialist observers. The same study indicates that self-observation data may be biased in comparison with specialist observer data, giving an idealized picture of supervisor work behaviour.

5 *Validity*

Some doubt exists on the validity of these observations, but no comprehensive examination has yet been made.

6 *Practical value*

The obvious difficulty here is that supervisors may postpone the time of writing down their observations, because the timing device may go off at an inconvenient moment. The observation then may be the wrong one or the one that the supervisor wishes to record. It is difficult to see how this can be avoided.

Method 7: Superiors' distant work sampling

1 *Example*

Wirdenius.[11]

2 *Purpose*

The intention here was to use a method of gaining information to compare with observer methods, which would cause as little observer influence as possible.

3 *Description*

Preliminary work. Superiors have to be trained in the use of the work sampling method and in classifying their observations.

Carrying out the method. As above.

Analysis. As above.

4 *Reliability*

Reliability depends upon the accuracy of the coding made by the superior, and upon the opportunities he has to make observations strictly according to the random time schedule. Selective perception may also operate and give rise to biased information.

5 *Validity*

Here observer influence, i.e. due to the effect of the presence of the superior, may be considerable, because the manager has a role which itself influences supervisory behaviour.

6 *Practical value*

This approach may be resisted by supervisors who may well see it as an underhand method. Excessive superior work load or absence may create practical difficulties.

Method 8: Superiors' ratings

Estimates or ratings of supervisor behaviour could be made by an observer, by peers, by the superior, by subordinates, or by the supervisor himself. An example of the first type is when an observer is asked to estimate behaviour after doing an observation study of the type above. This is sometimes very valuable, in that it draws on the practical experiences of the observer on the job, especially in the 'follow-after' method. Peer ratings have not been tried for supervisors in the sense of estimating time spent on work. One experiment was carried out for middle management in a study at Churchill College, Cambridge,[39] where the managers in an organization were asked to estimate the time spent in various activities by a trainee manager. Estimates of subordinates have been tried,[11] but this was not successful due to the lack of knowledge of the operatives of what the supervisor was doing.

Two types of methods can be discussed here in detail, namely superiors' ratings and self-ratings; and we start with the first one.

1 *Examples*

Wirdenius;[11, 31] Westerlund;[16] Hamblin, Thurley & Pinschof, unpublished;[40] Argyle.[41]

2 *Purpose*

The purpose of this method may be to merely confirm the inaccuracies of the perceptions of senior management about the role of their supervisors, but it can, of course, be used as a way of stimulating organizational change.

3 *Description*

Preliminary work. The classification of behaviour and the definition of terms have to be worked out in detail and adapted to raters.

Carrying out the method. Several procedures can be followed, but a useful technique is to have a rather tight standard classification, and to train the managers in estimating according to the terms and definitions laid down by investigators. Any open-ending questions are much less reliable.

Analysis. All types of rating techniques could be used, paired comparison, card sorting, etc. Also training could be used to eliminate or minimize the biases to be expected in this sort of estimating.

4 *Reliability*

Reliability will depend on the type of technique used. Generally paired comparisons have high reliability.

5 *Validity*

Here the important question to ask is the type of work norms accepted by the managers. For instance in certain companies, personnel functions may be exaggerated by the superiors' rating.[42] Sometimes the opposite may be true depending on the type of situation.

6 *Practical value*

It would seem to be of considerable advantage to develop these methods of estimating, because in certain types of situation, and with certain allowances, the degree of accuracy obtained may approach that of the observation study, if the biases are known and can be allowed for.

Method 9: Self-ratings

1 *Examples*

Westerlund;[16] Wirdenius;[31] Stogdill & Coons;[43] Thurley & Tawara;[44] Hatchett.[45]

2 *Purpose*

The intention here is again to develop a rather cheap method of estimating own behaviour but also combining this with an 'inside' knowledge of intended behaviour.

3 *Description*

As above.

4 *Reliability*

The matter of reliability is of crucial importance. The training problem is a very difficult one. It is possible that with adequate training supervisors could be developed to the point at which they could make reliable estimates of their own time, but it would be difficult to know that this performance was being kept. The possibility of cheating is extremely large.

5 *Validity*

For the reasons stated above, there is still considerable doubt as to the validity of this sort of method.

6 *Practical value*

At the moment, this method is not really of much practical value, although it has some potentialities for the future with training.

Method 10: Semi-structured interview after continuous observation

1 *Examples*

Herbert, Martvall & Wirdenius;[46] Hamblin;[47] Lennerlöf;[48] Sayles.[49]

2 *Purpose*

The intention of this method is to analyse behaviour at a more general level than for previous techniques, i.e. where the behaviour is structured in a more complex pattern around functions or tactics.

3 *Description*

The supervisor is observed for one day or so and this prepares for a lengthy interview around a number of key topics (functions, disturbances, etc.).

4 *Reliability*

No data are available, but reliability may be low owing to the importance of the skills of the interviewer and the willingness of the supervisor to talk.

5 *Validity*

This may be low, if the observation period is short, and not representative of the role (Lennerlöf's clinical method).[48] It may be high, if a number of periods of observation are carried out over time, to build up the observer/interviewer's understanding of the situation.

6 *Practical value*

This is of some practical value, as it is one of the main methods for analysis of organizational relationships and problems.

Method 11: Semi-structured interview after self-observation of critical incidents, disturbances or problems

1 *Examples*

Herbert, Martvall & Wirdenius;[46] Marples;[50] Docherty;[51] Jackson.[52]

2 *Purpose*

To clarify and examine special aspects of behaviour which appear to the supervisors to be important and crucial.

3 *Description*

Supervisors are requested to carry out self-observations of a selective type and are trained in the method. These self-recordings can be general and free descriptions and form the basis of an interview at regular intervals (or at one time).

4 *Reliability*

Reliability is likely to be low, as method is dependent on the supervisor's perceptions and bias in relation to own behaviour.

5 *Validity*

Validity can hardly be checked, but over time and with growth of confidence, this method may give a good indication of problems perceived to be critical by the supervisor.

6 *Practical value*

This procedure has considerable practical value in gathering information about intended behaviour and possibly potential behaviour. It could be a useful starting point for analysis.

Method 12: Combination of group discussions and question-naires, after self-observation of critical incidents, disturbances or problems

1 *Examples*

Thurley & Tawara;[44] Wessex Hospital Board study.[53]

2 *Purpose*

To discover a range of perceived incidents and problems as a preliminary to change.

3 *Description*

Supervisors are asked to attend in groups for completing questionnaires and discussing aspects of their role. This is preceded by the collection of incidents, by self-observation for a short period.

4 *Reliability*

Reliability cannot be high, but superior to Method 9.

5 *Validity*

No data available as yet, but methodological tests could be carried out in the future.

Practical value

This method promises to be a useful and quick way into discovering the type of critical incidents likely to be found in a group of supervisors. It may be more valuable for studying the work situation than work behaviour.

Summary

It should be clear from the above descriptions of methods that there is no one perfect method of measuring supervisory work behaviour by observers or by anybody else. Each method has its own limitations and its own virtues, depending on the situation at hand.

Clearly, the *purpose* of the study is the first thing to consider. For some purposes it is not necessary to have the same degree of accuracy in measurement as is needed for others. In general, however, one can conclude that the more reliable methods of 'heavy' observation, i.e. 'following-after' work sampling with interviews and distant work sampling, should not be used as main methods of approach but more for *checking* information secured through quicker procedures.

Many of the references in this field are from current research, and some are only published at the moment in the form of restricted reports. The selection here is therefore biased towards those studies of which the authors have direct knowledge. There are clearly many experiments going on in measuring work behaviour, particularly by those influenced by an 'engineering' approach, for example, Sayles & Chapple,[54] Marples[55] or Mintzberg.[56] This chapter, therefore, should be seen as merely a current report on the state of the art.

Notes and References

1 WALKER, C. R. *et al.* (1956). *The foreman on the assembly line*, pp. 151–9.

2 WARR, P., BIRD, M. & RACKHAM, N. (1970). *Evaluation of Management Training*, p. 34. Gower Press, London.

3 FLEISHMAN, E. A. (1957). A leader behavior description for industry. In R. M. STOGDILL & A. E. COONS (eds.), *Leader behaviour: Its description and measurement*. Ohio State University, Columbus.

4 LIKERT, R. (1967). *The human organisation*. McGraw-Hill Book Company, New York.

5 There are few, if any, examples of supervisors who have observed themselves systematically and then written down their own perceptions of their role. There are, of course, articles by supervisors who are writing from their experience. See, for example :
BENNETT, W. E. (1961). Why don't they give us more authority? *Supervisory Management* (January), pp. 2–8.
LYTTON, A. H. (1964). Supervisors have feelings too! *Training Directors Journal* (March), pp. 21–4.
One of the most famous self-observation studies of supervisors concentrated at the level of recording interactions, rather than role behaviour, is :
ATTESLANDER, P. M. (1954). The interactio gram : A method for measuring interaction and activities of supervisory personnel. *Human Organisation*, Vol. 13, pp. 28–33.

6 Standard Interval Sampling with Continuous Observation was used by K. E.

Thurley, A. C. Hamblin, M. Pinschof and J. Tawara in various studies, e.g. PINSCHOF, M. (1964), A note on the role of production foremen in one case study. *International Journal of Production Engineering*, Vol. 3, No. 4, pp. 333–9.
Also, PINSCHOF, M. (1962). *Systems of supervision. Report on a methodological experiment*. London School of Economics (mimeographed).

7 GUEST, R. H. (1956). Of time and the foreman. *Personnel*, Vol. 32, pp. 478–86.

8 FLANAGAN, J. C. (1954). The critical incident technique. *Psychological Bulletin*, Vol. 51, pp. 327–58.

9 Used by M. Pinschof in the study quoted above and other studies to obtain estimates of time spent and importance of tasks carried out. Also used by Wirdenius (see 11) and by Argyle (see 41).

10 See WHISLER, T. L. & HARPER, S. F. (1962), op. cit., for a general discussion.

11 WIRDENIUS, H. (1958). *Supervisors at work*. Swedish Council for Personnel Administration, Stockholm.

12 Many studies have used managerial estimates of supervisory time for comparison with observed data. In many cases, they are probably very inaccurate.

13 Examples of dimensions are given in the Appendix, and in the appendix to Wirdenius. The term 'style' is often used in the same meaning as dimension. See discussion in PATTEN, T. H., Jr. (1968), *The foreman: forgotten man of management*. A.M.A., New York.

14 WALLACE, W. L. & GALLAGHER, J. V. (1952). *Activities and behaviours of production supervisors*. Washington, D.C.: Personnel Research Section, AGO, Department of the Army (PRS Report No. 946).

15 WESTERLUND, G. (1952). *Behaviour in a work situation with functional supervision and with group leaders*. Nordisk Rotogravyr, Stockholm.

16 WESTERLUND, G. (1953). Analys och klassifikation av arbetsledares arbetsuppgifter. In ELMGREN, J. (ed.), *Förhandlingar. Andra Nordiska Psykologmötet i Göteborg*. Borås.

17 THURLEY, K. E. & HAMBLIN, A. C. (1963). *The supervisor and his job*. DSIR, London.

18 NIGHTINGALE, M. B. L. (1963). Unpublished report from Clarks Ltd., Street, Somerset, U.K.

19 JACOBSSON, M. (1955). *Trestadshusen. Byggkostnader och arbetsorganisation i Stockholm, Göteborg och Malmö*, pp. 195–200.

20 WESTERLUND, G. & STROMBERG, L. (1965). Measurement and appraisal of the performance of foremen. *British Journal of Industrial Relations*, Vol. 3, pp. 345–62.

21 LEHESMAA, M. (1956). Arbetsledarens dag. Preliminära resultat av en undersökning. *Industritidningen* (Finland), Vol. 37, pp. 28–9.

22 STEWART, R. G. (1967). *Managers and their jobs*. Macmillan, London.

23 HESSELING, P. Since the publication of his *Strategy of evaluation research* in 1966 (van Gorcum, Assen), the research group at Philips, Eindhoven, has

concentrated on the use of interviews, gaming and self-recorded contact information. The latter has usually been on middle management level, but some data on supervisors have been included. (*See* thesis by Graves comparing communications patterns in a French and English factory : GRAVES, D. (1970). 'The comparison of management role behaviour in three factories of an international electronics company.' M.Phil, thesis, University of London.)

24 WEINSHALL, T. D. (1966). The communicogram. In J. R. Lawrence (ed.) *Operational research and the social sciences*, pp. 619–33. Tavistock, London.

25 BURNS, T. (1954). The direction of activity and communication in a departmental executive group. *Human Relations*, Vol. VII, No. 1, pp. 73–97.

26 WEINSHALL, T. D. (1960). *Effects of management changes on organization relationships and attitudes.* Cambridge, Mass. : Graduate School of Business Administration, Harvard University MBA Thesis. (Weinshall argues that *remembered* incidents are also important incidents and that completing a diary after the events have taken place is a satisfactory way of recording important perceived incidents.)

27 BARNES, R. M. (1957). *Work sampling.* (2nd ed.). John Wiley & Sons, New York.

28 HEILAND, R. E. & RICHARDSON, W. J. (1957). *Work sampling.* McGraw-Hill Book Company, New York.

29 KELLY, J. (1964). The study of executive behaviour by activity sampling. *Human Relations*, Vol. 17, No. 3, pp. 277–87.

30 HESSELING, P. (1961). Multimomentopnamen een vergeten waarnemingstechnick. (Time sampling as an observational technique.) *Sociologische Gids*, Vol. 8, pp. 157–70.

31 A banal point, but the very fact that the observer has to use certain paths in approaching his observees means a certain bias in the location of the observations and the activities observed. See WIRDENIUS, H. (1961). *Förmän i arbete*, pp. 23–4.Swedish Council for Personnel Administration, Stockholm.

32 O'NEILL, H. E. & KUBANY, A. J. (1959). Observation methodology and supervisory behaviour. *Personnel Psychology*, Vol. 12, pp. 85–95. The criticism here of observational methods is not a fundamental one, but does make some useful points.

33 WIRDENIUS, H. & LÖNNSJÖ, S. (1964). *Functions of supervisors in the building industry.* The National Swedish Council for Building Research (Foreign Language Series, No. 2), Stockholm.

34 SACK, J. G. (1961). *Arbetsledarnas ställning i organisationen, arbetsuppgifter, befogenheter, utbildningsbehov.* Hofors : SKF, Hofors Bruk (unpublished report).

35 THURLEY, K. E. & TAWARA, J. (1967). Industrial supervision in Japan and Europe. A research report. I–IV. *Nihon Sangyo Kunren Kyokai* (Japan Industrial and Vocational Training Association), Vol. 13, No. 5 & 6. This study, in one Japanese steel mill, used the Wirdenius method of interview after observation as well as a SISCO method. (In Japanese.)

36 WIRDENIUS, H. (1958). op. cit., pp. 202–5.

37 STEWART. (1962). Unpublished internal report of study of chargehands in one process plant. Self-recording was found to be a useful technique, if combined with a continual checking of codings used.

38 WIRDENIUS, H. & LÖNNSJÖ, S. (1964). op. cit., pp. 16–17.

39 GILCHRIST, P. J. & MARPLES, D. L. (1966). *The Churchill College Management Course 1961–64*. ATM Occasional Paper No. 7. Churchill College, Cambridge.

40 THURLEY, K. E., HAMBLIN, A. C. & PINSCHOF, M. Study of XY Company (unpublished report). Managers and supervisors were asked to estimate frequency and importance for a list of defined task areas, using a card-sorting method.

41 ARGYLE, M. (1957). The measurement of supervisory methods. *Human Relations*, Vol. 10, No. 4 (November 1957), pp. 295–314.

42 PINSCHOF, M. (1964). op. cit. This was found to be the case in one large company where there was a well developed personnel department with an impressive supervisory training programme (LSE research).

43 STOGDILL, R. M. & COONS, A. E. (1957). op. cit.

44 THURLEY, K. E. & TAWARA, J. (See 35 above.) The method used was to ask supervisors in a gang interview situation to fill in a questionnaire, estimating the tasks which they carried out and rating them for importance. This was also done with contingencies.

45 HATCHETT, M. (1967). Unpublished study of the Construction Industry Training Board in the U.K. where supervisors were asked to complete questionnaires on their estimates of tasks and the importance of those tasks. The list of tasks numbered 214.

46 HERBERT, A., MARTVALL, K. & WIRDENIUS, H. (1969). *Byggarbetsledning och produktionsstörningar (Site management and production disturbances)*. Summary in English. Statens institut för byggnadsforskning, Stockholm.

47 HAMBLIN, A. C., has developed a new method of analysis of roles and functions after observation based on the SISCO classification. He argues that the observation can provide the starting point for a detailed investigation. The method is said to be a potent one for analysis of interrelated behaviour.

48 LENNERLÖF, L. (1968). op. cit. (Supervision.)

49 SAYLES, L. R. (1964). *Managerial behaviour. Administration in complex organisations*. McGraw-Hill Book Company, New York.

50 MARPLES, D. L. (1968). Roles in a manufacturing organisation. *Journal of Management Studies*, Vol. 11, No. 2 (May), pp. 183–204.

51 DOCHERTY, P. (1970). *A study of perceived contingencies in a Swedish building company*. (Ph.D. thesis). University of London.

52 JACKSON, P. (1970). *Organisational change and supervisory effectiveness*. (Ph.D. thesis). University of London.

53 Wessex Hospital Board (U.K.) (1968). Unpublished study of training needs of nurses, in which one of the authors took part. The group questionnaire was followed by discussions triggered off by the questionnaire. The project is discussed in A. Gould & P. Thornley, Partners in management training.

Industrial Training International, Vol. 5, No. 12 (December 1970), pp. 504–10.

54 SAYLES, L. R. & CHAPPLE, E. D. (1961). *The measure of management*. Macmillan, New York.
55 MARPLES, D. L. (1967). op. cit.
56 MINTZBERG, H. (1972). *The nature of managerial work*. Harper & Row, New York.

EFFECTS

Types of criteria

In Chapter 3, we gave examples of possible measures of the effects of supervisory work behaviour in terms of the *direct* relationship of actions to the performance of subordinates or their relative satisfaction. These measures were mostly familiar indices of the *output* of a logical production system, i.e. the degree to which managerial standards of physical output, quality, cost, waste, machine component, and personal utilization were being achieved (Figure 3.4). They also included the conventional indices of worker satisfaction, namely absenteeism, sickness, and turnover figures. Measures of the *indirect* effects on organizational performance were also suggested. These ranged from meeting customer requirements to measures of organizational effectiveness in terms of standards of profit per unit of output, per unit of capital employed or per employee. The degree to which organizations successfully adapted to new environments and maintained satisfactory working relationships were also mentioned (Figure 3.5). Besides these types of criteria, one could also mention the effects of particular supervisory actions on the supervisors themselves (Figure 3.7) and the possible effects on parties in other organizations, such as subcontractors or trade unions (Figure 3.6).

Most of these measures of supervisory performance can be found in the literature on supervisory effectiveness, for example in Westerlund & Strömberg[1] and in Lennerlöf.[2] We have commented already on the almost universal failure, in any rigorous study of supervisory effectiveness, to obtain significant correlations between styles or patterns of supervisory behaviour and such criteria.

There are two basic reasons for this failure. Firstly, writers have attempted correlation analysis without using any conceptual model of supervisory behaviour, and consequently related variables which belong at different levels of analysis. Even the extensive and systematic study of Lennerlöf reviewed in Chapter 4, which tried to find correlations between individual, behaviour and effect variables within different situation groups, was largely ineffectual.[3] There is little attempt here, for example, to separate effect variables by their relative closeness to the field of supervisory action.

The second and most fundamental error, however, in the literature on effectiveness is the search for *general* measures which can be applied to *all* supervisory situations. As argued in Chapter 3, supervisory behaviour can be conceived, at different levels of particularity, to be composed of activities, tasks, tactics, strategies, and roles. A certain type of tactical behaviour in one situation may be profoundly significant and yet be totally irrelevant in another. In the first situation, one can trace a set of events arising from the supervisory action, which may multiply its effects as time goes by. In the second situation, the supervisory action can be compared to a stone which falls into a pond and hardly causes a ripple; in popular language, it does not 'connect' with reality as defined by other parties in the situation and is, therefore, perhaps simply ignored or not noticed.

An example which demonstrates this vividly was observed by one of the authors in a plant in Japan. Following a mistake with the handling of a hot tube in a steel mill, the supervisor ran up and attempted to take command, giving many instructions. He ignored the fact that the situation was already being dealt with by the gang boss and the work group in question, who quietly ignored the supervisor in turn and themselves proceeded to arrange for the travelling crane to lift the tube. The supervisory action appeared to be of no consequence.

It can be seen, therefore, that *general* measures or *basic* criteria of effectiveness are unlikely to be available as the actual effects of supervisory action are dependent on the particular way in which variables in all the boxes of our conceptual model mesh together, *at a particular point in time*, in that production system. If it were possible, for example, to use absenteeism figures or scores on a worker job-satisfaction scale as a general measure of supervisory effectiveness across all supervisory situations, then this would imply that one could hypothesize the set of relations between crucial variables in all supervisory systems and treat these as constants. If, again, one found that an increase in 'initiating structure' elements in a supervisor's job behaviour was always accompanied by some increase in absenteeism figures and in a decline in worker job-satisfaction scores, then it would be clear that the other and intervening variables which might affect such scores *must* be constants in all supervisory systems. This, of course, is not so, and it follows that the quest for such general criteria and measures which have been the objective of so much painstaking research is indeed a will-o'-the-wisp.

Relationships of cause and effect

Should we then abandon any attempt to measure effects of supervisory action? Surely not. Common sense and experience tell us that there *are* situations in which decisions and actions taken by supervisors have had and will have profound effects on events. There is still meaning in referring to 'supervisory performance', good, bad and indifferent. The failures of research have been in the way that the problem has been conceived.

The first clue lies with the concept of supervisory actions as being bound up with problems, difficulties or contingencies. In Table 3.1 we emphasized that behaviour could be conceptualized on a number of levels and that the higher the level, the more far-reaching or the more long-term was the purpose of the action. Criteria, therefore, differ by level. For each level, we can distinguish both the nature of discretionary behaviour (or the reality of the choice situation for the

supervisor) and the type of effects of that choice. At level 4, for example, in thinking of *activities*, choice has little meaning beyond the possibilities of changing
habitual responses to given stimuli. At level 3, we can discuss task performance
and *disturbance handling* in terms of the patterns and sequences of actions
accepted as appropriate responses. At level 2, *tactical* behaviour in meeting perceived problems clearly involves a great number of choices, influenced by both
values held and facts perceived. In any discussion on level 1, we are in the realm
of *'style'* or *'strategy'*, in which values and beliefs are most important and social
choice is most significant. This is why most studies have tried to find correlations
between perceived 'style' (such as the leadership style, or 'consideration') and
generalized data on the measures of output from a section supervised by a foreman. The difficulty is not only that other factors are important as intervening
variables. It lies with two facts: firstly that there is little evidence that supervisors
themselves or their role set partners actually conceptualize their behaviour at
this level. The perceived meaning and explanation of their actions and its effect
could be highly misleading if the analysis is 'above' the actual level of interpretation. Secondly, at the level of strategy or style, there is much more difficulty in
demonstrating effects in terms of causal links of various events. It seems as
though we are faced with a problem in that the greater the significance of the
type of choice of behaviour, the more general the criteria and the greater the
difficulty of measurement.

Table 5.16 shows some examples of supervisory actions seen on levels 1, 2 and
3. The type of effects likely and possible measures of these effects are shown. In
these examples, it is clear that there are considerable difficulties in finding precise
statistical measures which would establish the degree to which certain effects
actually took place or not.

There would seem to be two ways in which the effects of supervisory actions
could be monitored. In the first case, a system of recording of disturbances or of
difficult problems made by supervisors in different departments might pick up
the repercussions of action by one foreman in a particular case and show the
extent and the area over which the repercussions of this action have actually
spread. Secondly, any investigation by supervisors themselves or by organization
and method teams or by a researcher into the case would be able to judge, in as
systematic a way as possible, the extent to which effects had taken place and the
possible further effects which might be expected to follow.

The implication is, therefore, that such crucial pieces of supervisory behaviour
could be followed up on a case-by-case basis if it is thought that the time and
energy and resources necessary to establish the effects in that situation are really
worth while. This means that any effective system of monitoring the effects of
supervisory action would be selective and restricted to problems where supervisors themselves and management felt that a minimum payoff could come from
an investigation.

The failure of the attempts at demonstrating general cause-and-effect relationships therefore turns us towards the possibility of a *selective* approach in which
only a sample of actions (chosen as likely to be critical) are taken for analysis. It

TABLE 5.16

Examples of critical supervisory work actions and their effects

Level of work behaviour	Examples of critical work behaviour	Local effects	Organizational effects	Possible measures
STRATEGY (Level 1)	Consistently tries to deal with all problems on a construction site himself and seldom refers issues to the contracts manager.	Quick solutions. Arbitrary and biased judgements.	Contracts manager is left free to deal with commercial problems but knows little about site problems.	Observation of contracts manager job behaviour and number of grievances reported above site level.
TACTICAL BEHAVIOUR (Level 2)	A certain line of products give a high reject rate from the inspection department. The supervisor feels this which is partly due to the methods of his workers and partly due to the tight standards of the inspectors. The production department workers resent criticism and the supervisor takes up the matter with his boss, blaming the inspectors.	Trust of workers in foreman is reinforced.	Argument and dispute develops between inspection and production.	Judgement of supervisor himself only possible guide to measuring dissatisfaction of workers *against* possible harm of dispute with inspection.
DISTURBANCE HANDLING (Level 3)	Machine in section starts to produce faulty work. Foreman calls maintenance department foreman who promises to send man. Nobody comes for 30 minutes and foreman starts to repair machine himself.	Maintenance man arrives after 45 minutes and complains that foreman is repairing wrongly. Foreman gets angry	Exasperate relations between maintenance and production departments. Possible industrial dispute (UK example, not Sweden!)	If no formal grievance is recorded, difficult to get a direct measure of the effect. Possibility that case could be reported by foreman to supervisory council.

also suggests strongly, that analysis should be concentrated at levels 2 or 3 in terms of supervisor tactics or disturbance-handling behaviour.

Types of effect situation

At this point in the argument, however, the critic might reply somewhat justly that practising managers have known this or intuitively understood it for a long time. The practical solution, he might say, to the problem of supervisory effectiveness will never be a general solution, it must be tailor-made for a *type* of supervisory system or, if even this is impossible, for a particular supervisory system over time. These two approaches are attractive possibilities and deserve some attention.

In the first case, the use of the term 'type' assumes that it is possible to classify supervisory systems and that within such a classification, hypotheses could be made about the interrelationships between variables, both background and intervening. In this view, we would be able, in certain sets of circumstances, to predict the possible effects of shifts of supervisory behaviour on production and personnel indices. In theory, this seems quite possible, providing one could identify the main 'structural' variables which would determine the other variables and, therefore, make up the main criteria forming the classification.

What type of variables would these be? The most obvious example would seem to lie with the technological factors, as in the classification of Miss Woodward.[4] This division of production systems into 'unit', 'small batch', 'mass production', 'process', etc., depends on their general position on a continuum of 'technical complexity' defined as 'the extent to which the production process is controllable and its results predictable'.[5] On examination, this continuum breaks down into a number of subsidiary factors, measuring the type of production and assembly arrangements, the cycle time of production, the type and complexity of the product, the size of the batch produced, etc.[6] More seriously, there seems ample evidence that the production systems concept, which has had such useful repercussions in the last fifteen years in directing research and argument to a more particular level, has itself been greatly overrated by the followers of the Woodward school.

To begin with, economic and market factors are clearly bound up with the purely technological in that mass production arrangements are only developed in a certain market context. (This was clearly recognized in the Tavistock model of a 'socio-technical system'.[7]) The snag here is that such market factors are volatile in the extreme, and this means that one has to use the concept of a production system, not as a simple production engineering system, but in terms of this system in the context of varying levels of demand. Mass production systems, therefore, are rarely at peak output and exhibit differing constraints on behaviour according to output levels.

A second limitation on the usefulness of the 'production system' concept is that the way production arrangements are related to the behaviour of workers, managers and supervisors is, like all situational variables, partly explained by the perceptions and beliefs about the production system which are held by the 'actors' inside and around the system.[8] The growing weight of international comparison of production systems demonstrates the variance in human behaviour possible within similar technologies, but under different cultural and social conditions. An example would be a recent comparison of supervisory behaviour in Japan and the United Kingdom.[9] If such differences are possible, this casts much doubt on the validity of using production systems as units for classifying situations. If we try to do this, it follows that we also have to assume a great deal about the 'support' of each type of system in terms of economic, social and cultural factors. Although it is conceivable that particular 'clusters' of such variables do exist in a persisting form, which would enable such prediction to take place successfully (this is argued by Professor Lupton of the Manchester Business School),[10] as yet there are no concrete examples which could be quoted. It would also seem to be likely that, even if such clusters exist, they may be islands of structure in a sea of uncertainty and, therefore, that there is little hope of a general solution to our problem from this approach.

The second suggestion offered above was that of tailor-making a set of criteria and measures for each supervisory system by itself. There is clearly much sense in this approach, bearing in mind our discussion up to this point. If we mean by this, however, that it is possible to design measures that are particularly appropriate for a given situation and then leave them as a form of managerial control, we should still be cautious in accepting it.

There are limitations here which depend on the degree of permanence of the structural elements in the supervisory system under appraisal. In cases where products, markets, production methods and labour force are relatively permanent and stable, there might be every possibility of working out specific criteria of effectiveness and of using these to monitor supervisory performance. (A margarine or tobacco factory would be a good example, as Crozier[11] shows.) The construction industry gives us the opposite situation, where in a 'new works' contract, the environmental situation changes daily, even hourly. A rise in labour turnover could be very significant for supervisory behaviour at one point in the contract and irrelevant at another. Specific measures can hardly be developed here; there is only the possibility of sampling the individual disturbances handled by supervisors and attempting to evaluate the relative success of such actions, case by case.

A further complicating factor lies not with the environment but with the narrow situation, the degree of individual autonomy. At one extreme, there are the situations where individual supervisors possess real freedom of action, in that they are in a position to decide what to do and how to do it. The results of individual actions could then be traced back to the original action without much confusion. At the other extreme, supervisors could be perceived to exist continually dependent on the actions of others, either managers, workers or other supervisors or ancillary workers. Any evaluation of the effects of individual supervisory action is here impossible. There is only the possibility of tracing col-

lective goals or collective problems and of trying to ascertain the relative degree
of success in achieving such goals or solving such problems.

Four differing approaches

Figure 5.4 summarizes the differences between these situations which relate to
the problem of evaluating the effects of supervisory actions.

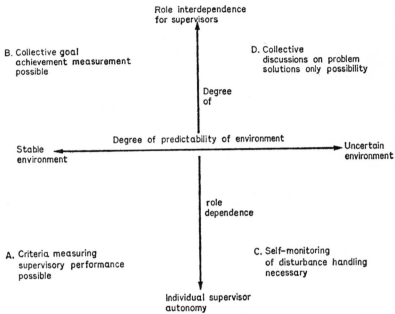

FIGURE 5.4   The problem of evaluating supervisory effects: various situations

It shows four typical situations which would all require a different approach
for measuring the effects from supervisory behaviour.

In situation A, the stability of the structural factors in the supervisory system
is such that it is possible and desirable to build up a determinate model of the
main variables in the system. This would, of course, require considerable analysis
of a large number of the variables mentioned already in the various boxes of the
model in Chapter 2. If this was carried out, it would then be necessary to observe
and test possible relationships between supervisory actions and a range of particular criteria: production achieved, wastage figure, labour turnover and
absenteeism, cost figures, etc. From this analysis it would be possible to select
those indices which showed high correlations and to use these over a long period
to indicate trends.

In situation B, it is not possible to isolate the effects of individual behaviour in
any meaningful way. Here one would follow the same procedure as with A, with
the exception that the analysis of actions would concentrate on classification and

TABLE 5.17

Examples of important effect variables

Areas of effects	Examples of selected variables	Types of measures that are appropriate
I *Extra-organizational* (goals)		
The customer	1 Response of customers after quality defects	1 Monitoring of a sample of disturbances tracing their effects and analysing supervisory actions in detail, e.g. accident report procedure
The supplier	2 Response of customers after broken delivery dates	
Trade unions	3 Response of trade union committee after dispute	
State agencies	4 Response of factory inspectorate after accident	2 Use of consumer survey techniques (questionnaires, interviews, discussions)
Family system	5 Response of Race Relations Board after a dismissal	
II *Organizational* (goals)		
Productivity	6 Effect on programming of subsequent processes of delays in delivery	1 Monitoring of sample of disturbances
Morale		2 Consultation and managerial group appraisal sessions
Conformity	7 Necessity for quality control departments to use resources for renovation of final products following manufacturing defects	
Adaptiveness		3 Examination of production and personnel indices comparing departments
Institutionalization	8 Idle time created by industrial relations stoppage	
Goal achievement	9 Bottle-necks in production caused by unwillingness to change procedures or methods	
	10 Managerial time required following rise in costs	
III *Supervisory system* (objectives)		
Control system performance	11 Relative success in meeting organizational targets, following disturbances (output, quality, cost, machine component, and labour utilization measures)	1 Examination of production and personnel indices over time
Autonomy		2 Monitoring of sample of disturbances
Survival		3 Use of rating scales
Job satisfaction	12 Difference between *potential* consequences of disturbances and *final* effects	4 Use of non-directive interviews
Power structure		5 Use of supervisory group discussions

Areas of effects	*Examples of selected variables*	*Types of measures that are appropriate*
Problem solution	13 Level of worker job satisfaction following supervisory action	1 Medical examinations
	14 Relative power of work group leaders/supervisors/managers	2 Counselling interviews
	15 Rate of introduction of innovations and relative success	3 Self-appraisal of success with new task
IV *Personal* (needs and objectives)		4 Supervisory club discussions (outside working hours)
Needs fulfilment	16 State of physical health related to work load	
Learning	17 State of mental health related to work load	
Individual objectives	18 Effect on family obligations of work role obligations	
	19 Increase in value of personal knowledge and skills from work experience	
	20 Extent of frustration/satisfaction from daily work experience	

E

measurement of supervisory behaviour taken as a whole, i.e. for *all* supervisors within that discrete production system. Clearly, it is more difficult to measure accurately the interrelated role behaviour of six or a dozen supervisors than it is for one supervisor. It would be necessary to rely more on ratings and estimates than on detailed observation. The objective, however, would be to isolate certain characteristics of the styles and strategies used by the group of supervisors as a whole and *then* to test out the relationship with a number of particular criteria of organizational effectiveness: costs, output, performance, quality achieved, etc. It should be possible here to show some general relationships between the styles of behaviour and such criteria. If this was achieved, then these too could be used over time to show improvements.

In situation C, we are dealing with an autonomous supervisory role which is mainly made up of disturbance or contingency handling. In this case, there is no hope for using any standardized measures and the only approach would be to develop a systematic method of sampling cases of disturbance handling. In each of these sampled cases, there would be some attempt to trace the story of the disturbance: the actions taken, the intended consequences, the actual results, both intended and unintended, and the repercussions of these events outside the supervisory system, within the larger organization and beyond this. Some of this could be found by a self-monitoring process; greater validity would be achieved if the investigations were partly carried out by external parties with no interests at stake.

In situation D, we have the greatest problem for tracing effects of actions. The same technique for monitoring disturbances could be used, but in this case much more emphasis on the use of collective appraisal sessions would be necessary. The case studies are more complex and the task of unravelling the part played by supervisors would be similarly more complicated. External observers could be asked to help with the collection of data by interview sessions and by recording the process of group discussions.

There is no means of knowing the relative proportion of actual supervisory situations which fit into each of these ideal-type situations. From the studies carried out by both authors in the last fifteen years, however, it would appear that a large proportion of supervisory situations would fall into categories C and D, particularly the latter. Those in the relatively straightforward category A were not so common, although there were perhaps a few more in category B.

Types of effects and appropriate measures

We turn now to the range of types of effects which might be met with in any of the investigations suggested above. There are several possible ways of classifying effects, but it seems convenient here to distinguish (*a*) the area of the effect and (*b*) some possible types of objective within each area.

Table 5.17 summarizes such areas of effects. It suggests possible objectives which might be effected by supervisory action. It gives some concrete examples and shows the broad range of measures which would appear to be most appropriate for each area.

It is immediately apparent that the frame of reference for measuring effects is much wider here than in the classical studies reported in Chapter 4. Effects on the supervisor himself, on his family and trade union, and on customers, suppliers and other organizations are all included, besides the conventional subjects of organizational goals.[12]

The justification for broadening the frame of reference in this way rests with the fact that, in so many supervisory situations, the goals of the organization are relatively distant from the personal objectives of the various actors in the situation. Any evaluation of supervisory behaviour, therefore, which takes place purely in terms of such managerial criteria may be very limited and possibly in conflict with the ways that different parties in the situation tend themselves to evaluate the behaviour. If we wish to understand the dynamics of any supervisory system, therefore, it is necessary to be prepared to consider a wide range of possible effects of behaviour and to use a number of differing criteria, according to the area and objective of the analysis.

It will be noted from the list of twenty variables suggested for criteria that the majority are fairly specific. They would mostly seem to be useful when used in evaluating a particular case of disturbance handling. Some, however, are more general items, from which one could design standardized instruments, for use in A and B type situations. In all situations, it seems necessary to design a particular approach for evaluation which is most appropriate for the variables in that single supervisory system. The list of measures, therefore, offers suggestions which all need further designing to take account of crucial local details. A standard methodology cannot be offered to the reader.

Notes and References

1 WESTERLUND, G. & STROMBERG, L. (1965). Measurement and appraisal of the performance of foremen. *British Journal of Industrial Relations*, Vol. 3, pp. 345–62.

2 LENNERLÖF, L. (1968). *Supervision: situation, individual, behaviour, effect.* op. cit.

3 LENNERLÖF, L. (1968). ibid., pp. 317 and 319.

4 WOODWARD, J. (1965). *Industrial organization.* Oxford University Press, London.

5 WOODWARD, J. (1958). *Management and technology*, p. 12. HMSO, London.

6 THURLEY, K. E. (1966). *Changing technology and the supervisor. Employment problems of automation and advanced technology. An international perspective.* (ed. J. STIEBER.) Employment problems of automation and advanced technology. Macmillan, London and New York.

7 EMERY, F. E. & TRIST, E. L. (1960). Socio-technical systems. In *Management Sciences: Models and Techniques*, Vol. 2. Pergamon, London.

8 GOLDTHORPE, J. H., LOCKWOOD, D., BECHHOFER, F. & PLATT, J. (1968). *The*

affluent worker: industrial attitudes and behaviour, p. 181. Cambridge University Press.

9 THURLEY, K. E. (1970). *Implications of the use of electronic computers for the future roles and behaviour of industrial and construction supervisors.* op. cit.

10 LUPTON, T. (1968). 'Operation research and the behavioural sciences'. Paper delivered to the Joint Operational Research Society Conference (December). London. Unpublished.

See also: BOWEY, A. M. & LUPTON, T. (1970). Productivity drift and the structure of the pay packet. *Journal of Management Studies*, Vol. 7, pp. 156–71.

11 CROZIER, M. (1964). *The bureaucratic phenomenon*, pp. 61–142. University of Chicago Press, Chicago and London.

12 PRICE, J. L. (1968). *Organizational effectiveness. An inventory of propositions.* Richard D. Irwin, Inc., Homewood, Illinois.

6. *Objective Setting I: Theory*

DEFINING POTENTIAL SUPERVISORY PERFORMANCE

In describing our main conceptual model in Chapter 2, the device was used of depicting perceptions of possible changes in a supervisory system by imagining a type of mirror image of the existing system at a certain distance from it. This mirror image shows possibilities for change – in behaviour, in the situation, in the individual characteristics or in the effects of behaviour – that are actually perceived by the actors within the supervisory system.

If such perceptions are seen clearly and strongly, it will throw up the contrast between the ideal and the actual. We argued that the crucial element in any change strategy rested in the perception of a 'gap' between the actual supervisory system and potential supervisory systems. To complete the motivation for change, there would also have to be a belief that the supposed 'gap' could be bridged. The persons concerned with the change would thus have to have some concept of what they were trying to change, what they wanted to change it to, and, practically, how they were going to do it successfully. The definition of potential behaviour and performance, in reality, involves all these *three* problems. It requires an understanding of the failures and shortfalls of the existing situation, which can come from a study of the effectiveness of supervisory behaviour as discussed in the last chapter. It requires some vision of what *could* be done, what *could* be achieved, if only . . . It also needs a developed plan or strategy which, it is hoped, will meet the situation and enable past failures to be avoided and potential objectives to be grasped and achieved.

THE MBO SOLUTION

The currently popular idea of 'management by objectives' (MBO) is an approach which can be described as trying to stimulate improvements by forcing the definition of potential performance levels and using the managerial authority system to apply pressure to achieve such results.[1] MBO has many interpreters, notably John Humble[2] in the United Kingdom. Approaches vary, especially in so far as they lay emphasis on (*a*) individual motivation or (*b*) the achievement of collective goals.

In the former case, the MBO programme seems to be mainly concerned with defining individual targets, so that each manager knows what he should be trying to achieve in a certain period. This is intended to provide a direct stimulus for individual motivation; ambiguity is seen as the refuge of the lazy or the over-cautious. Of course, the use of such mutually agreed targets in appraisal sessions between a manager and his subordinates also allows the manager to strengthen his control over his subordinates' activities. It reinforces the authority of the line.

In the latter case, the MBO programme is a way of breaking down collective goals, reached in long-term planning exercises, so that each level knows what is expected of them and how they can contribute to the overall goals. In this method, the MBO process will be started with top management and will work down the organization, level by level. It is intended to strengthen, not only line authority, but the commitment of each level to organizational goals. It is also possible in this approach to prescribe new patterns of roles and organizations in the process of determining individual objectives.

Another contrast within the MBO approach which has been rarely explicitly admitted is that between the programme which emphasizes the importance of a formalized strategy of goal setting and performance appraisal, and the alternative programme of allowing the definition of potential behaviour and performance levels to arise from a relatively unstructured process of discussion and 'brain-storming'.

The first approach has been largely favoured in the literature, so far. A good example is shown in a well-known paper by Marcus Knight.[3] We can also quote the definitions used by John Humble; viz.:

Performance Standard
By performance standard we mean 'a statement of the conditions which exist when the result is being satisfactorily achieved'. It is not a statement of the ideal results in ideal circumstances nor the minimum acceptable standard.[4]
Performance Review
The manager's superior analyses how far the Key Results and Improvement Plan have been met and seeks explanations for success and failure. He will, of course, have been doing this in detail as an integral part of his daily management job. *A formal review is, however, an essential discipline for creating a sense of accountability in both manager and superior* in a broader sense than is possible in day-by-day management.[5] (Our italics.)

These definitions lay bare some of the critical assumptions of the Humble approach. It is assumed (*a*) that it is possible to define the work of managers in such a way that satisfactory achievement of the results can be known in concrete terms. It is also assumed (*b*) that, although managers normally are engaged in chasing failures, they need a formal procedure to do it in a systematic and *accountable* way. The manager being appraised, like his boss, is assumed (*c*) to need the discipline of being formally accountable for his actions and achievements. Otherwise, what will be the result? It seems to be implied that managers without such external aids to accountability will be mainly concerned with their own personal objectives. This is all very much in the tradition of scientific management and classical management theory with its emphasis on the importance of structure and definition.[6]

The second alternative approach to MBO may be seen as one which starts with some scepticism as to whether potential managerial behaviour and performance could be defined precisely, in the way, for example, that a programmed learning specialist defines the 'terminal behaviour' he desires to achieve. There would be two reasons for this scepticism.

The first would lie with the recognitions of the pluralistic power structure within management[7] and the understanding that group and role conflict are endemic in organizational life. The facts of the 'power game' and its importance encourage different groups within management to perceive different objectives and underline the problem of reaching a consensual view on the nature of 'satisfactory results'.

The second reason lies simply with the fact of change, economic, social and technological. It is clearly more difficult to achieve a certain definition of potential performance levels under conditions of fast change and unpredictable change. The *need* to define potential performance, however, is just as great under conditions of uncertainty as it is in a predictable environment. It may, indeed, be greater as it is necessary to motivate individuals to cope with threatening prospects of change. A set of clear criteria of performance will protect and stimulate many individuals under such conditions. It is, of course, also probable that the perception of the possibility of improved performance levels will stimulate the process of adaptation to changed organizational demands. In a complex, indeterminate, and changing organizational situation, therefore, the MBO approach could be described as likely to be more pragmatic and short-term, building on a set of temporary agreements on targets which are continuously revised. Such agreements are more likely to be between colleagues and collaborating departments than between boss and subordinate, which is the crux of the first approach.

The setting of objectives, therefore, is a task that varies according to the type of organization situation. We can 'map' some of these differences by classifying them on a familiar two-dimensional diagram (Figure 6.1). The two dimensions which have been mentioned above are:

(a) The degree of uncertainty in predicted behaviour and effects (WX) (structure).
(b) The area of emphasis for improvement (YZ) – ranging from the individual job to formal organization performance (corporate goals).

Most of the literature on MBO undoubtedly follows a Type A–C approach (at least as published in the United Kingdom). A typical example was the short case-study on the Heath Street Division of G. K. N. Screw and Fasteners reported in *The Times*.[8] Here it is stated that 'the advantages of MBO [lie] in helping the company know itself, in making targets and objectives part of everyone's language, and in inducing a greater awareness of profitability . . . Looked at from the outside, the great advantages of MBO at GKN seem to be the improvement of communications, the sharpening of financial disciplines, and the involvement in profit making down to the foreman level . . . Bert Walters, the President of the Screw Nut Bolt and Rivet Trades Society, the main trade union, said: "It has made the foremen cost-conscious." ' One could paraphrase this by saying that it appears to be a strategy for convincing foremen of their involvement in top management objectives. In this sense, MBO is, or can be, a general strategy for 'raising the sights' of foremen, so that they realize more what they could do and how significant this could be to the business in which they work.

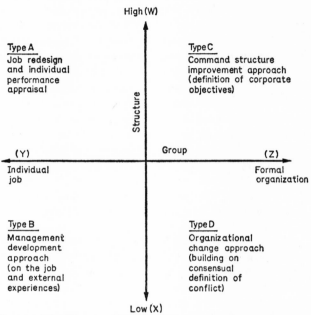

FIGURE 6.1   Types of Management by Objectives strategies

Developments which could be classified around the line B–D in Figure 6.1 are more difficult to describe as general strategies, as they are more likely to be indeterminate and particular to the actual situation to which they are applied. The philosophy behind Type B, for example, would emphasize the importance of developing the capacity of individual foremen for dealing with a wide range of possible problems. We will consider in the next chapter how this might be done, but it can be seen already that this could heighten conflict by sharpening the difference among foremen as to the priorities for the future and the relative importance of various ways of meeting problems. The thinking behind a Type D approach would *start* with this problem of individual and group conflict and would attempt to bring about understanding on joint action in areas where the perceived conflict was not inevitable or a matter of 'interest'. An example will demonstrate the concept here, and will also show some of the inherent problems of this approach.

Let us assume that the supervisors in question are dealing every day with strong pressure by work groups and shop stewards to 'control' bonus earnings under a financial incentive scheme. The situation in Jays Ltd. described by Tom Lupton in his book *On the shop floor* would be a typical case in point.[9] Workers perceive their interest to lie in 'systematic soldiering' or in arranging their performance under work study so that there is plenty of 'slack' to enable them to earn high bonus when the opportunity presents itself. Stewards may be judged, in such a situation, by their capacity to exploit the rules of the scheme, by claiming allowances for delays, and arguing for 'retimes' as and when there is an advantage in doing so. Work study officers may be quite aware of this process and are, of course, stimulated to put an end to it. As frequently happens, the work study department decides that management control has to be re-established: times have to be tightened up under a general restudy of the jobs and tasks in question. Supervisors are asked either to enforce existing times and rates more strictly or to support such a general restudy programme.

What can supervisors do in this case situation? It is not an easy problem to decide as there is a clash between different objectives and as supervisors are under pressure from a number of sources and groups, all of whom perceive the facts of the situation rather differently and who value the possible results differently, since they are using contrasting criteria. Table 6.1 gives a simplified decision matrix for this case.

TABLE 6.1

A simple decision matrix for supervisory action

	Criteria of various parties (and possible effects)				
Alternative actions	WORK GROUP More pay	WORK STUDY DEPT. Tighter rates	PERSONNEL DEPT. Industrial peace	SHOP STEWARDS Union strength	TOP MANAGEMENT Composite
Supervisors try to impose work standards by threat or persuasion	Go slow/ higher absenteeism	Support	Advise supervisors to 'go easy'	Organize worker resistance	Praise if successful
Supervisors accept the *status quo*	Dissatisfied but keep working	Criticise ineffective supervision	Support	Neutral	Try to instruct supervisors to act
Supervisors tacitly support work groups for dilution of rates	Improve personal relations with workers	Criticise supervision to top management	Neutral	Increased power and contact with management	Bargain with stewards directly
Supervisors support work study demands for tightening of rates	Probable stoppage	Support	Attempt to delay revision	Organize stoppage or non-co-operation	Blame supervisors for bad industrial relations

If supervisors try to enforce any measures making for a reduction in relative labour costs, they run the risk of alienating the work force and increasing industrial conflict. If they run with the men and tolerate the pressures for higher earnings, they may earn better relations but forfeit their authority. Any particular approach may gain support from one functional department, but antagonize another. If the supervisors look for a reduction in the amount of personal criticism which they have to face, it may be that the *status quo* is the best position to defend. Certainly, many supervisors act under this belief, leaving all innovation for others to carry.

An approach to improving the situation of Type D (Figure 6.1) would presumably attempt to study the facts of the case and would try to explore how far the dilemmas perceived in Table 6.1 were real. Was it true that work groups would react so strongly in defence of their interests? What were the vital interests of supervisors themselves? Production targets? Costs? Human relations? Methods? Were their objectives discrete ones? Was there any possibility of an overall deal which would safeguard their interests and those of the other parties? If the system of payment was changed, what differences would this make? Could a new set of joint objectives be agreed?

There are evident problems here in deciding whether perceived interests are necessary interests. A change in the institutions might alter roles and functions and interests. Nobody can know, however, with any certainty, how far such conflicts could be eased by changes in role and by discussions, consultation and bargaining.

The definition of potential behaviour and performance is therefore not likely to be a cut-and-dried affair whenever (as is likely) there are conflicts, submerged and visible, about objectives and methods. It remains an essential element in any improvement strategy. We have shown that there is a wide range of possible ways of trying to define potential performance and trying to achieve it. In particular, management may try to convince and coerce supervision into widening its perspective and beliefs about its objectives. An opposite approach lays emphasis on the existing conflicts and tries to negotiate beyond them. The selection of an appropriate way into such a definition of potential clearly depends on the organizational situation and on the nature of the supervisors and other parties concerned. A knowledge of the local environment and people is the first prerequisite for designing a successful strategy of change.

Most of the approaches in the literature to the definition of 'ideal' supervisory behaviour have used questionnaire methods. A typical example would be that of Michael Argyle,[10] who designed a number of statements of supervisory behaviour (Foreman Description Preference Test) and asked supervisors to say which one represented the ideal type for his situation. There is some possibility of developing a useful diagnostic tool on these lines, but it is fair to add that it could easily be a fatal short cut. The statements could be too general to be exactly applied to a particular situation, but the questionnaires would be filled in to satisfy the research worker. The result would hardly be an accurate measurement of norms or patterns of ideal behaviour.

Notes and References

1 DRUCKER, P. F. (1964). *Managing for results.* Heinemann, London.
2 HUMBLE, J. W. (1967). *Management by objectives.* Industrial Educational and Research Foundation. Occasional Paper, No. 2. London.
3 KNIGHT, M. W. B. (1966). *Management by objectives.* Smith Industries Ltd (mimeograph).
4 HUMBLE, J. W. (1967). op. cit., p. 10.
5 HUMBLE, J. W. (1969). *Improving management performance.* British Institute of Management, p. 34.
6 BRECH, E. F. L. (1965). *Organisation: the framework of management.* 2nd ed. Longmans, London.
7 DALTON, M. (1959). *Men who manage.* John Wiley & Sons, New York.
8 *The Times* (1969). Business Section. Management News. Monday, 21 July. London.
9 LUPTON, T. (1963). *On the shop floor.* Pergamon Press, Oxford.
10 ARGYLE, M. (1957). op. cit.

7. *Objective Setting II: Practice*

THREE CASES FOR DISCUSSION

We turn now to the use and application of the approach which has been developed in the preceding pages. The problem of objective setting is the problem of diagnosing from the data available, the nature of the main 'gaps' which exist between the potential and the actual situations. This diagnosis will inevitably take place with inadequate data and is not likely to be a once-for-all process. Bearing this in mind, therefore, it may be useful for the reader to study the cases given below, using the suggested model and classifications for summarizing the facts given and listing the 'gaps' which appear to exist from the clues present in the data and comment. In order to make for some reality, the cases are extracts from actual research studies. There has been no attempt to 'plant' clues in the text; rather the data are given as reported, with all the irrelevancies and waste data still present. There are no right answers to these exercises; they are given simply to allow for some practice in using the conceptual model described. Readers interested only in the theoretical argument, therefore, can afford to skip this chapter.

The situation in each case can be assumed to be that of a factory situation in which a preliminary report has been made by consultants on the nature of supervisory problems and behaviour. You can assume the role of a member of the steering committee of the project which has now to decide on the type of position which has been revealed by the analysis and the major objectives for any change programme which might be suggested.

The questions (for each case) are:

1. Can you classify the data given according to the model?
2. Can you identify likely crucial variables?
3. Do you need additional data? If so, what? How would you get it?
4. What 'gaps' appear most significant?
5. What objectives of change may be most realistic?

CASE A: A SMALL FIRM[1]

The Company (Johnsons Ltd.)

This report deals with the foreman and chargehand roles in a small shoe factory manufacturing ladies' fashion shoes and a variety of boots and sports shoes. At the time of the study, it employed about 150, of whom two-thirds were women. The firm had previously reached twice the number of employees, but had been forced to contract due to a decline in orders. One of the main outlets for the firm's products was through a mail order company, but there were also direct links with shoe retail shop chains. The size of batches of shoes ordered tended to vary considerably and this, combined with constant fashion changes in the lasts demanded and styles required, led to many production change-overs and problems of programming.

Johnsons was a private company, controlled by a family. The Managing Director and the Sales Director were brothers and took a strong personal interest in the running of the firm. Production was the responsibility of the Works Manager (Mr Brown) and under him was a simple line structure based on traditional divisions of labour in the shoe trade, with one or two specialist managers attached to it (Figure 7.1).

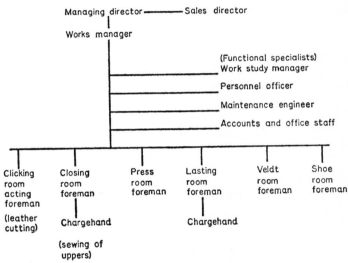

FIGURE 7.1   Organization of Johnsons Ltd.

The production process utilized at Johnsons was a simple one, based on the flow of work through the various stages as indicated in the organization chart. That is, the leather had to be cut from skins by hand and then the various parts of the shoe (uppers, heels, sole) were shaped, cut and machined, to be assembled around a last. Finally, there had to be a visual inspection and packing and despatch. The technology used consisted of machines for particular operations, for example, sewing; tools for hand tasks and trolleys for moving batches around the factory. Traditionally, certain tasks were performed by men, for example, pattern cutting; and some by women, for example, sewing and despatch. Supervision came from the department labour force and reflected the differences in sex and age and experience of those operatives.

The Investigation

A study was made of the job behaviour of the various members of the supervisory team in the factory. The purpose of this was twofold:

(*a*) to discover, by observational methods, the nature of the daily problems with which the supervisors have to contend, and the way in which they spend their time;

(*b*) to compare the observational data with their perceptions of their own jobs.

There were three stages to the study. In the first, Mr Brown and five foremen (all except the Shoe Room Foreman) and the two chargehands were accompanied on the job over two to three days by an observer. During this time, the observer made observations on the supervisors' behaviour at regular two-minute intervals and recorded it on eight dimensions (SISCO method, see Appendix). The second stage was an attempt to check the validity of the data obtained by the previous method. Two hundred and fifty tours were made by observers around the factory at random times, with 'spot' observations taken of supervisors when they were first seen. This conventional activity sampling information was then checked against the SISCO data on three dimensions (activities, location and contacts) using a Chi Square statistical test. (The results here showed a considerable fit between the two sets of data with the exception of those for the Works Manager.) The report concluded that the number of days taken for the data collection appeared to be a critical factor determining the degree of agreement between the figures. The third stage saw the use of questionnaires for foremen from four departments, to enable them to estimate the time spent on thirty-three key activities. These were then compared with the observational data. Finally, the researchers compared the observed data on certain main dimensions with those of a similar investigation in another shoe firm, whose effectiveness was rated very highly by managers and customers in the shoe trade.

The Results

For ease of presentation, a selection of tables (7.1 to 7.7) are given showing some of the main results. The categories have been simplified and the full definitions of each category are not given, although these are essential to any detailed diagnosis of supervisory behaviour and any valid comparison of data with other firms.

Table 7.1 shows the location of supervisory activities according to the SISCO data. The percentages of time at work exclude lunch or tea breaks.

The term 'office' or 'desk' refers to the desk in the production department used by production foremen. 'Work area' refers to production areas under control by the supervisor concerned. The Veldt Foreman has not been included, as he spent 89 per cent of his time in his own department, 84 per cent without contact with

TABLE 7.1

Location of supervisory work role

AREA	Works Manager	Clicking Foreman	Closing Foreman	Closing Ch/hand	Press Foreman	Lasting Foreman	Lasting Ch/hand
	Percentages of time at work						
Own work area	37	82	50	92	53	74	76
Own office or desk	41	—	19	—	25	1	9
Other depts. or offices	5	4	18	—	7	12	2
Other	17	14	13	8	15	13	13

anybody, and 76 per cent in manual work, i.e. working as a normal operative, during the period of the study.

Table 7.2 shows the time spent in various main activities by the supervisors in question (SISCO data).

TABLE 7.2

Activities of supervisors

ACTIVITIES	Works Manager	Clicking Foreman	Closing Foreman	Closing Ch/hand	Press Foreman	Lasting Foreman	Lasting Ch/hand
	Percentages of time at work						
Direct communication	63	21	45	37	11	26	21
Paper work	7	11	9	2	19	3	11
Inspection and direct supervision	10	4	13	8	16	29	5
Manual work	1	44	15	25	28	16	33
Other	19	20	18	28	26	26	30

Communication included telephone conversations. Paper work included all types of clerical work. Manual work included some operative tasks but also 'responsible' physical tasks.

Table 7.3 shows the time spent by the supervisors in various functions. Tasks were classified by whether they were *routine* (normal, repetitive tasks) or *contingencies* (abnormal, unexpected difficulties which required action).

The term 'production' functions includes dealing with the process, the production programme, the behaviour of the raw material, tools, plant, etc., and any routine production matter. The substantial figures for 'other' in these tables cover the use of time for walking around the factory, personal time and any time which could not be classified because the immediate purpose was unclear.

Table 7.4 shows the tasks carried out by supervisors classified by their 'time reference', i.e. whether it was concerned with the past, present or the future. This is useful in showing how far supervisors have resources and motivation to try to avoid future problems.

TABLE 7.3

Functions carried out by supervisors

FUNCTIONS	Percentages of time at work						
Routine	Works Manager	Clicking Foreman	Closing Foreman	Closing Ch/hand	Press Foreman	Lasting Foreman	Lasting Ch/hand
Production	49	57	27	40	69	41	56
Distribution of work	—	3	4	8	—	2	4
Personnel	4	—	14	1	—	2	—
Clerical	3	5	5	1	6	1	1
Total	56	65	50	50	75	46	62
Contingencies							
Technical	13	19	33	7	12	31	3
Human/ administrative	7	10	13	10	1	10	6
Total	20	29	46	17	13	41	9
Other	24	6	4	33	12	13	29

TABLE 7.4

Time reference of supervisory tasks

TIME REF.	Percentage of time at work						
	Works Manager	Clicking Foreman	Closing Foreman	Closing Ch/hand	Press Foreman	Lasting Foreman	Lasting Ch/hand
Investigations into past	9	21	24	19	19	29	7
Present activities	40	74	49	48	58	56	62
Planning future	26	—	19	2	9	3	7
Other (no function, etc.)	25	5	8	31	14	12	24

We can compare Table 7.3 with Table 7.5, which shows the data collected from the questionnaire. Foremen estimated time spent on thirty-three key jobs. As the supervisors did not allow for time spent in 'no function', the observed data is shown as recalculated as *percentages of time observed in some function*. This means that exact comparisons between Tables 7.3 and 7.5 are misleading. Instead, the observed data is shown in brackets after the estimated data.

Table 7.6 deals with the communications between the supervisors and the other members of the staff of Johnsons. One figure of interest is the percentage of time without contacts of any sort. The other point of interest is the time spent with various directions of communication, i.e. upwards or downwards, etc.

TABLE 7.5
Estimated time spent in various functions compared with observed times

	Works	Clicking	Closing	Press	Lasting
Routine	Manager	Foreman	Foreman	Foreman	Foreman
Planning and reports	22(18)	12(3)	10(4)	40(15)	3(2)
Production	22(30)	78(56)	27(18)	34(58)	67(37)
Personnel	18(8)	—(—)	16(18)	2(—)	4(3)
Contingencies					
Technical	21(30)	7(29)	35(46)	9(25)	6(44)
Human/Admn.	17(14)	3(12)	12(14)	15(2)	20(14)

Percentages of time observed in some function

TABLE 7.6
Persons contacted during work role

Percentages of time at work spent with various types of contact

CONTACTS	Works Mgr	Clicking Foreman	Closing Foreman	Closing Ch/hand	Press Foreman	Lasting Foreman	Lasting Ch/hand
No contact	22	64	31	40	72	46	55
Own operatives	13	14	28	39	14	26	12
Subordinate supervisor	21	—	7	—	—	5	—
Immediate boss	13	5	10	7	—	3	5
Other superiors management	17	9	20	1	4	10	14
Other dept. operatives	—	5	1	1	—	1	2

TABLE 7.7.
Comparison of activity sampling data from Johnsons and Evans

	Clicking		Closing		Lasting	
	Johnsons	Evans	Johnsons	Evans	Johnsons	Evans
ACTIVITIES	Foreman	Foreman	Foreman	Foreman	Ch/hand	Asst. Fm
Direct communication	21	30	35	34	46	46
Paper work	8	16	7	9	3	—
Inspection and supervision	4	12	11	11	10	8
Manual	36	14	10	16	13	18
COMMUNICATIONS						
Operatives	18	39	34	41	48	61
Other supervisors	7	8	4	19	9	23
Other staff	11	13	15	35	3	21

Percentages of time at work

This data is best studied together with the organization chart in Figure 7.1.

Finally, the researchers compared some of the data from the distant activity sampling exercise with that from a comparable firm (Evans). This is shown in Table 7.7.

Conclusions

It seems from the data presented that in some departments the foreman is little more than an operative with occasional supervisory duties; whereas in others, notably in the closing room, his functions consist of dealing with a tremendously wide range of unforeseen contingencies, leaving him only a limited amount of time for routine duties such as inspection. Chargehands rarely stood in for their foremen on such occasions. They tended to be concerned solely with the sorting and distribution of raw material to workers or, in the case of the lasting room, the keeping of records. It was clear that the two chargehands had the largest proportion of ineffective time. There seems to be a case for changing the responsibilities of supervisors in the closing and lasting rooms.

CASE B: A STEEL MILL[2]

The project was carried out at the Zion Tube Works. By steel industry standards it was fairly small, employing about 950 people. We were concerned with the two Production Departments, B and C, which rolled hot finished seamless tubes by the Rotary Forge Process from plain carbon and alloy steels. The tubes were produced in batches, ranging from small numbers to many hundreds of given specifications, being used for such things as oil-well casing, boiler tubes, and general engineering purposes.

The departments were adjacent to each other, though quite distinct, with C Department being very much larger than B Department. Each was divided into a mill and a finishing section, working a three-shift twenty-four-hour day for five days a week, plus normal overtime for the morning shift on Saturdays and some Sunday night overtime.

Despite the difference in size, B Mill had a larger establishment figure (48 men) than did C Mill with 42 men, whilst C Finishing had a labour force of 73 men, compared with 39 in B Finishing. The Mill difference was mainly due to the greater number of men required for the B Mill furnace, which was considerably older than that of C Mill; C Finishing was far larger than B Finishing because it had to deal with far greater variations and sizes of tubes. To the C Finishing labour force must also be added the 23 men employed in the relatively new C Alloy section. The two Mills were serviced by a Steel Stock section which had a work-gang of 13 men.

Sixteen foremen in all took part in the project. In the Mill and Finishing sections of both departments, three shift foremen were employed, making a total of twelve. At the time of the study, two of the usual foremen were ill, and their place was taken by their chargehands. The Finishing sections were both under the control of a day foreman. The other two people taking part were the foreman of the Steel Stock section and the C Alloy shift controller who came under the C Finishing day foreman. The day foremen and the last two mentioned all worked a day shift. Being the larger department, C Department was controlled by a superintendent, with a deputy holding the position of supervisor; B Department had a superintendent only. Both superintendents were responsible to the Assistant Works Manager.

Method of Production

In B Department tubes from 4in. to 6⅝in. o.d. were made to a maximum length of 50 feet from carbon and alloy steel rolled bars. The raw material in the form of bars was broken into the required lengths by a hydraulic press before being charged into the furnace. These billets were rolled manually in an old rolldown type furnace by means of long pokers. Heating was to 1250/1300°C, and took about four to five hours. On discharge they were centre-punched at one end, and then transferred to the piercer where the billets were rolled into hollow blooms over a plug. A mandrel bar which determines the final internal dimensions of the tube was then pushed through the bore of the bloom before conveying it to the Rotary Forge. Here, the tube was forged between rotating rolls, the red-hot bloom being converted into a long tube sliding forward off the mandrel as it was squeezed out by the rolls. When it had emerged from the mill, the bell-end containing impurities was sawn off and the tube checked for length. It was then sized in a single-stand mill, weighed, and passed on to the cooling racks.

In the Finishing section, the tube was straightened in a hydraulic press, given a first examination, and marked for cutting to lengths. After the ends were finished, it was further inspected for dimensional accuracy, and any minor defects removed. It could then be hydraulically tested before final inspection and despatch. Movement of tubes within the Finishing section was carried out by conveyors between different racks, otherwise they were rolled by hand along the racks.

In C Department, tubes of carbon and alloy steels from 6⅝in. to 16in. o.d. in lengths up to 80 feet and sometimes over, were rolled from cast or machined ingots. The furnace was automatic, the ingots being charged on to bogies which took up to eight hours to pass through, with heats of about 1250/1300°C. The red hot ingot was then taken to the pre-piercer where it was shaped into a 'bottle'. After this, the process was the same as in B Department, though on a much larger scale.

In the C Alloy section, special alloy tubes, usually in small batches of less than ten pieces, were finished and given preliminary inspections. Since each piece of tube is expensive, a lot of care had to be taken in removing minor faults, and in surface preparation. A recent addition was a shot-blasting machine to improve the work and inspection. Some tubes were also sent to this section after heat treatment for a further examination.

Background of foremen

A total of sixteen foremen took part in the study, two of whom were acting foremen at the time. All had started at Zion in jobs on the shop floor and had worked their way up through the section until they were appointed chargehand, and then foreman. Most had spent some time working in more than one section, though only two had been in both B and C Departments. In the Finishing sections, two of the foremen had worked for a time in the Inspection Department, and two others had worked as section clerks for a short time. All those who had worked in sections other than the one which they now controlled felt that the experience had been useful, and all felt that the best form of preparation for the foreman's job was to have worked one's way up from the shop floor.

Only one of the shift foremen had held his post for longer than five years, and, in fact, in both Finishing sections the position of foreman had only been created about two years previously; until then, the work-gangs had been controlled by chargehands under the overall control of the section day-foreman; all the shift foremen had been chargehands, though only one had had charge of a gang before the change. Again, the position of C Alloy shift controller was a recent creation though its holder had been leading hand in the section for some time. The Steel Stock foreman had held his job for a considerable time; both day foremen had risen from being shift foremen, though there had been no special preparation for their new appointment.

On actual appointment, it had been assumed that the foremen had picked up sufficient knowledge of the duties when they had been chargehands; in B Department, the superintendent was prepared to give informal help, whilst this was done by the supervisor of C Department; two of the Mill shift foremen had been appointed from other sections, and therefore needed some help. Several foremen felt that they could have had some induction into the paper work needed; this did not apply so much in the Finishing section, yet it was here that two of the shift foremen had spent a short time in the office after appointment.

All the foremen had attended various courses, both inside and outside Zion, yet only four of the shift foremen (all in C Department) and the day foremen had been on courses since their appointment. They had attended general supervision courses organized for the combine at Boxford, which had dealt generally with the history and development of the company, industrial relations and trade unions, the function of other departments in the company, and general ideas on supervision. The other foremen, including the two acting foremen, had attended various courses as chargehands; several had attended part or all of the Ministry of Labour TWI courses. Other courses attended had been smaller but still general ones at either Zion or Youe, which were the two most closely linked tube works. One shift foreman had attended a course organized by the Institute of Industrial Supervisors; only one man had been on a safety course which had lasted for two days. The courses annually organized at Zion were follow-ups, relating the other more general courses to the needs at Zion; these had usually taken the form of discussions rather than lectures and had been well received by the foremen, who all preferred this form of course.

The main criticism levelled by the foremen at these courses was that though they had given much background information, much of the work had been irrelevant to the needs at Zion. All felt that the most useful part of these general courses was the opportunity which it gave the foremen of having informal discussions with foremen from other works, with the exchange of information and discussion of mutual problems.

Overall, Zion was not very highly unionized, and none of the Finishing section gangs contained many union members; however, the union, in this case the Transport and General Workers Union, was quite well represented in both Mills. All the foremen in both departments and in all the sections had been or were

TABLE 7.8

Age of foremen studied

	Under 40	*41–50*	*50–66*	*Total*
Shift foreman	4	2	4	10
Acting foremen	1	1		2
Day foremen		1	1	2
Steel stock foremen			1	1
Alloy shift controller			1	1

TABLE 7.9

Length of service of foremen

	Less than 15 yrs	*16–30*	*30+*	*Total*
Shift foremen	4	5	1	10
Acting foremen	1	1		2
Day foremen		1	1	2
Steel stock foremen			1	1
Alloy shift controller			1	1

TABLE 7.10

Service as foreman

	Less than 2 yrs	*2–5 yrs*	*5 yrs +*	*Total*
Shift foremen	6	3	1	10
Day foremen		1	1	2
Steel stock foremen			1	1

still union members, either of the TGWU, or its clerical branch – the Clerical Workers Union. In B Department, all but the acting foremen in the mill had given up their membership on appointment as foremen. Three foremen, two from C Department and one from B Finishing, had been shop stewards, one in the Amalgamated Engineering Union; both acting foremen were members of the works branch committee of the TGWU.

Those who had taken such an active part in the union felt that this experience had been useful to them because it enabled them to have two views of problems on the shop floor. None of the foremen now took any active part in the unions, however.

Environment and general activities

The method of production at Zion has already been explained; this section will relate the main activities of the foreman to his place of work without going into detailed explanation of his activities, which will be described later in the report. It is based on the findings of the observations which are elaborated on later, bringing in the interviews and questionnaires to add further information. It does, however, give an overall picture of what the foreman was doing and where he was doing it.

In both departments the foreman spent at least 70 per cent of his time on the floor of his section, dealing with problems which arose there, and associating with the work of his gang. In C Department and B Finishing most of the rest of the time was spent in each section's office dealing with necessary paper work, and it was also here that the foreman spent his break-periods. In these sections, the offices were immediately adjacent to the sections; in B Mill, however, the office was some distance away and the foremen spent far less of their time in their offices than did the other foremen. Further explanation can be seen in the large number of breakdowns in B Mill which will be described later.

Both day foremen spent almost all their time in their section's office, which they shared with the shift foremen. In C Finishing the day foreman spent some of his time also in the C Alloy section, which came under his control. The Steel Stock foreman spent nearly all his time in his office during the period of observation, while the C Alloy shift controller was seen almost always on his shop floor.

All the foremen were only observed for one shift each, and it is possible that there would have been some distortion of where they usually spent their time; however, the tour observation, which saw all the foremen on nearly all the sixteen shifts, did substantiate the findings.

By far the most frequent activity of all the foremen was direct verbal communication in the form of giving and receiving information and instructions; this was above all a case of giving instructions to members of their own work-gangs.

This was linked to the next most important category of activity, that of direct supervision, which also covered the wide field of inspection of products and machinery, which was seen especially in the Mills. There was a lot of overlap in this category because of the problems of quality control and breakdowns, which varied in intensity between sections. In the Finishing sections on the other hand, there was considerable fluctuation in the amount of time spent on direct supervision and inspection.

Most of the foremen also did a fairly substantial amount of physical work, with variations between sections again depending on the size, the labour situation, and other needs of the shift.

In the Mills, most of the activity of the shift foremen was centred around problems of quality and quantity of products, machinery and labour, whilst the first noticeable characteristic of the Finishing sections was the variation in time spent on the various activities in different shifts. In each shift the activities in finishing were governed very much by what was going on in the Mill.

There was considerable communication between the foremen and their subordinates, especially, of course, on the night shift, in all the activities in which

TABLE 7.11

Summary of observations of shift foremen

Percentages of time at work (after 'following-after' SISCO observations)		
	MILL FOREMEN	FINISHING FOREMEN
Place	*Range*	*Range*
Own work area	65–89%	60–90%
Own office	8–25	9–23
Elsewhere	6–24	5–18
Main activity		
Talks	19–38%	28–52%
Clerical work	4–10	3–13
Supervision and inspection	23–36	6–32
Physical work	9–21	0–18
Not work related	8–32	9–32
Status of contact		
Operatives	25–83%	42–83%
Chargehand	12–38	0–42
Shift foreman	2–23	3–17
Day foreman	—	3–16
Supervisor ('C' Dept. only)	12–15	3–5
Superintendent (C/B)	3–8/23–27	0–4
Department of contact		
Own line	58–80%	61–77%
Other production sections	8–34	5–18
Maintenance	5–17	3–22
Inspection	—	5–9
Other functions	Less than 5	Less than 5
Type of communication		
Instructs that	16–35%	10–48%
Informs that	15–38	8–40
Is informed	11–32	14–40
Other forms	10–20	10–15
Function of activity		
Programming	0–1%	0–9%
Transfer of materials	3–14	4–33
Raw materials	5–11	2–4
Product	16–38	19–43
Tools and machines	16–38	6–37
Labour	0–8	0–10
Method of operation	2–33	4–23
Working himself	0–12	0–9
Non-work function	18–37	19–40

TABLE 7.12

Supervisors' estimates of contacts*

Name of contact	'B' DEPT. Mill		Finishing		'C' DEPT. Mill		Finishing		BOTH 'B' & 'C' Mill	Finishing
	Freqy	*Impce*	*Freqy*	*Impce*	*Freqy*	*Impce*	*Freqy*	*Impce*	*Freqy*	*Freqy*
General manager	0	1	0	2	0	0	0	0	0	0
Works manager	1	2	0	2	0	1	0	0	1	0
Dept. superintendent	10	6	11	6	8	4	5	3	18	16
Dept. supervisor	—	—	—	—	11	4	7	3	—	—
Other prodn. foremen in dept.	11	5	10	5	11	4	11	6	22	21
Steel stock foremen	8	1	1	1	4	3	0	0	12	1
Foremen in *other* prodn. dept.	5	0	6	4	4	0	6	3	9	12
Operatives of *other* prodn. foremen	0	0	4	0	10	3	6	2	10	1
Maintenance dept. superintentents	1	1	0	1	1	1	0	2	2	0
Foremen or workers of maintenance	11	4	11	6	11	4	11	6	22	22
Staff inspectors	5	3	12	6	4	0	9	4	9	21
Planning staff in dept.	8	3	10	4	7	2	8	5	15	18
Progress outside dept.	0	0	1	4	0	0	0	0	0	1
Drawing office, R & D.	0	0	0	1	0	0	0	2	0	0
Work study	1	1	0	3	0	1	1	3	1	1
Personnel & training	3	1	0	3	0	0	0	2	3	2
Wages & time office	2	1	2	4	3	3	3	3	5	5
Cost dept.	0	0	0	1	0	1	0	1	0	0
Safety & security	1	2	0	5	4	0	1	2	5	1
Stores	3	0	2	4	1	1	3	4	4	5
Clerical in own dept.	7	6	12	6	1	0	11	5	8	23
Other clerical	0	0	2	1	0	0	0	0	0	2
Union officials	1	3	4	2	6	1	2	1	7	6
Visitors	0	3	0	0	0	0	0	1	0	0

*Key to score   (i) *Frequency of contact*

Never or rarely	About once a week	About once a shift	2 or 3 times a shift	Very often a shift
0	1	2	3	4

(ii) *Importance of contact*

Very important	Important	Not so important
2	1	0

Questionnaires were given to the 3 shift foremen of each Mill and Finishing section in B and C Departments. Maximum score for 'Frequency of contact' is $3 \times 4 = 12$ and for 'Importance of contact' $3 \times 2 = 6$.

they engaged; due to the special problems of machinery, which were more apparent in some sections than in others, contact with maintenance workers was also fairly substantial. Within departments, the foremen of the two sections were fairly closely in touch. The Finishing day foreman naturally had a fair amount of contact with inspection and despatch.

TABLE 7.13

Supervisors' estimates of own functions carried out*

Duty	'B' DEPT. Mill		Finishing		'C' DEPT. Mill		Finishing		'B' & 'C' Mill	Finishing
	Freqy	Impce	Freqy	Impce	Freqy	Impce	Freqy	Impce	Freqy	Freqy
Personnel admin. & *labour control*										
1. Personal problems & complaints	3	2	9	5	7	5	9	5	10	18
2. Arranging training	3	5	2	6	4	2	7	5	7	9
3. Pay questions	0	3	6	6	6	4	3	3	6	9
4. Discipline	0	3	2	5	2	3	2	3	2	4
5. Selection & Transfer	0	4	1	4	0	1	2	4	0	3
6. Joint consultation	0	3	0	3	0	2	0	4	0	0
7. Reporting J.C. to workers	0	2	0	2	0	3	0	2	0	0
8. Allocation of work	3	1	2	6	7	4	10	6	10	12
9. Arranging supply of workers for overtime	1	1	4	4	7	3	5	4	8	9
Production control										
1. Planning work	1	4	12	6	0	1	3	0	1	15
2. Checking supply of raw materials, tools, etc.	7	2	9	6	4	2	4	2	11	13
3. Checking output figures	8	5	10	6	4	2	2	1	12	12
Quality control of:										
1. Raw materials	6	4	0	0	3	1	0	0	9	0
2. Intermediate product	12	6	12	6	12	6	9	6	24	21
3. Inspecting finished product	9	5	12	6	12	6	12	6	21	24
Technical control of:										
1. Performance of machinery & tools	10	6	12	6	12	6	12	6	22	24
2. Maintenance of machinery	11	6	8	5	4	2	12	6	15	20
3. Improving layout	1	2	0	0	0	0	0	0	1	0

TABLE 7.13 *continued*

Duty	'B' DEPT				'C' DEPT				'B' & 'C'	
	Mill		Finishiug		Mill		Finishing		Mill Finishin,	
	Freq y	Impce	Freq y	Impce	Freq y	Impce	Freq y	Impce	Freq y	Impce
Operations control of:										
1. Checking work methods	10	3	10	5	0	0	7	3	10	17
2. Accident prevention	9	5	12	6	8	6	12	6	17	24
3. Transfer of work	0	0	12	6	0	0	8	4	0	20
Cost control Calculating or using cost figures	0	0	0	0	0	0	0	0	0	0
Physical work	6	1	10	5	8	5	3	1	14	13
Writing reports	7	5	8	6	8	5	6	5	15	14

* Estimates as Table 7.12.

TABLE 7.14

**Rank ordering* of type of problem dealt with by foremen
(Supervisors' estimates)**

| Cause of problems | B | | C | | B & C |
	Mill	Fin'g	Mill	Fin'g	Together
Major faults in machines or equipment leading to work stoppages	1	3	4	1	1
Minor faults in machines or equipment	2	5	2	2	=2
Quality of labour available	3	2	3	3	=2
Minor faults or variations in product or materials	4	4	1	6	=4
Shortage of labour	5	1	5	4	=4

     * To find an average rank order of problems for each section of B and C Departments, and a overall ranking, each questionnaire reply was assigned the score of its respective ranking. Thes were added up by section to find the average rank-ordering. The figures in the table represe» this average ordering of work problem causes.

     Problems ranked in the bottom categories 9th–12th by each section: problems caused by (a) mi understanding with other departments, (b) misunderstandings within own section, (c) disput« with unions or with individuals, (d) problems given to the foreman by his superior or a sta« department, were all ranked low by the foremen.

Summary of findings

The work of the foremen in all sections was very closely concerned with the nee« to solve a number of problems which emerged along the production process, an« in the subsections which served the process; as a result, the methods of supervisio» used and the attitudes of the foremen were geared to these problems. In this sens« the role of the foreman at Zion was very much that of a problem-solver; the con cept of solving was, however, a short-term one since the problems of the sections were of the kind that had to be met perhaps several times a shift, and fairly frequently in a foreman's working week. This section is concerned mainly with the problems encountered by the foremen, and will act as a summary of the rest of the report, which describes the problems and how they were settled in detail, and also brings in that part of the foreman's work which was not directly linked with problem-solving, but was fairly continuous. As the descriptive report is examined, it will be seen that the problems were closely linked so that each tended to lead into or from another.

The main problem was that of quality – both of product and of machines. All foremen had to ensure that the production specifications were met, that the finished product was acceptable to the Inspection Department, and that tools and machinery were kept up to standard. In this, there had to be considerable liaison between the Mill and the Finishing section foremen, though there was some difference in their conceptions of quality control; it was rather difficult for the Mill foremen to alter the process from furnace to rolls once it had begun, whilst the Finishing foremen could be far more flexible.

All the foremen experienced considerable difficulties with the machinery and tools in their sections, and this was especially true of B Mill, which had a large number of stoppages during the period of the study. Although they all recognized that a lot of the trouble was caused by the age of the machinery, there was also considerable criticism of the maintenance department and its workers. There seemed to be little formal communication between production and maintenance departments, with complaints of delays in repairs and repairs proving only short-lived. The major complaint was that maintenance workers tended to be unfamiliar with machines because they did not specialize in a particular section. Both Mills had a definite advantage over the Finishing sections in this sphere, since they had priority when repairs needed to be made.

Linked with the problem of quality was that of production control. In formal terms, the foreman had nothing to do with planning production programmes. In the Mills, however, the foremen could alter programmes if certain sizes of ingots were in short supply or to maintain continuity of certain specifications; again, the Finishing foremen could be more flexible, though geared to mill production, provided that completion dates were met.

Labour was a considerable problem, both in quantity and in quality. Almost every section was undermanned by one or two workers, which could lead to a lot of additional work for the foreman; even those sections which met their establishment requirements had only been fully manned for a short time. The Mill foremen were again fortunate in having men in their work-gangs who had been at Zion for a fairly long time, and were perhaps capable of doing more than one job. The foremen had the final say in the selection of new labour, but the great shortage meant that nearly anybody would be taken on regardless of quality.

Lack of both quantity and quality meant a need for a lot of physical work by the foreman, and a need for close supervision of many workers who could not be left alone for too long. Problems of the training of workers were acute because the bad quality made it difficult for most workers to be trained for more than one job, and the training of any worker took a substantial amount of time; training usually had to be done by the foreman himself, or entrusted to one experienced operator. Bad quality of labour also led to some problems of safety, which was increased by the number of hazards apparent on the work-floor. The foremen were probably themselves most accident-prone since they were constantly on the move.

The labour shortage meant some limits on the disciplinary powers of the foremen; yet although bad timekeeping was a problem on the morning shifts in all sections, the foremen considered that by and large their men were dependable, and they did not need to be too strict most of the time.

From this, looking at human relations, it was apparent that whilst the foremen were critical of many aspects of their labour force, there was also a considerable amount of sympathy felt for the members of their work-gangs. Since the foremen had all risen from the shop floor, they recognized and made allowances for individual problems which could affect work-behaviour; all seemed to be on friendly terms with their gangs, and the attitude of the Mill foremen appeared to be 'the happier the gangs the better the work'. In all sections, the foremen thought it important to explain as much as possible of what was going on to their work-gang. In B Department, the foremen also attached importance to the building up of good relations with the outside departments, maintenance, inspection and despatch.

The Mill foreman's most constant link was with his 'chargehand'. In formal terms this part had been abolished a short time before the study took place; in fact, the Mill foremen all considered that one of their two rollermen was a *de facto* chargehand, on whom the foremen placed some responsibility, and work which would otherwise have added to their own duties. None of the shift foremen in the Finishing sections had a formal deputy, though, if necessary, one of their senior men could take over for a short time. The usual relief in C Department when a Finishing foreman was away was the C Alloy shift controller. At the time of the study two of the *de facto* chargehands in the Mill were acting foremen.

Of necessity, there was considerable contact between Mill and Finishing shift foremen, usually over quality control, or the Mills' need to borrow labour.

Apart from contact with the head of their own departments, there was surprisingly little contact between shift foremen and any other members of management, apart from the visit of the maintance head if a breakdown was important. In the Finishing sections most of the liaison with outside departments and superiors, apart from maintenance, was carried out by the two day foremen. In B Department, the superintendent, and in C Department the supervisor, who was second-in-command, had a lot of contact with all shift foremen.

Both the Steel Stock foremen and the C Alloy shift controller held rather unique positions; both were of shift foreman rank in actual practice if not in formal terms, and had control of important sub-sections, one at the very beginning of the production process, the other at the end before Inspection took over. To a large extent, their problems and attitudes were the same as those of the shift and day foremen with, of course, some individual differences.

CASE C: A LARGE ENGINEERING COMPANY[3]

Background

A large Swedish industrial corporation has launched a supervisory project to guarantee an effective supervisory staff for the future.

The general purpose of this project is framed as follows:

1. To analyse the role and work of the supervisors by studying their tasks and factors influencing these tasks.
2. To use that analysis—
    (i) to give a basis for the assessment of future requirements on supervisors;
   (ii) to lay down the broad outlines for future selection and training of supervisors;
   (iii) to work out guide-lines for the allocation of supervisory resources within various production areas.

The assignment of the external consultant team was to carry out a type of critical incident study in order to establish a basis for:

the assessment of present requirements for supervisors on the assembly lines;
the design of programmes for the selection and training of supervisors at the present time;
the evaluation of the effects of supervision on the production unit.

The report from the consultants was expected to give answers to the following questions :

From which personnel categories should supervisors be recruited, and how could these employees be made interested in applying for supervisory positions?
Which personal characteristics should these supervisors possess?
Which subjects are the most important ones in the training programme, and what changes should be made in the present programme of training?

Another expected output of the study concerns efficiency of the present supervisory organization and desirable changes of the organization, the allocation of responsibility, etc. in order to develop supervision and production.

Here follows a summary of the first part of the report presented by the external consultant team.

After introducing the project to the personnel groups involved and their union representatives the collection of critical incidents was made. Data were collected in group interviews, in the case of workers carried out by the consultants, and in the case of other employees by the administrative staff units of the company.

The following personnel have contributed with incidents:

> 16 assembly line supervisors (pilot study)
> 24 assembly line supervisors
> 20 workers (Swedish, Finnish, and Yugoslav)
> 10 work study men
> 3 supervisors from materials handling
> 4 supervisors from production control
> 3 supervisors from fitting department

Total 80 individuals interviewed

Data collected

Altogether 416 incidents have been collected. Some of these could be attributed to two incident categories in Table 7.15 and, therefore, the total number of incidents equals 504.

The assembly line supervisors were requested to estimate the duration and frequency of various incidents and the data collected appear in Table 7.16.

Analysis of incidents collected

Shortage of personnel

The great number of incidents under this heading refer to abnormal absence due to, for instance, 'Friday illness', fine or bad weather, and, to some extent, influenza. A shortage of personnel occurs once or twice a month. Usually these incidents appear at the start of a shift.

A shortage of personnel causes the supervisor to try to borrow personnel from other areas like preceding stations, other parts of the same line, utility men and fitters. Borrowed personnel do not normally know the operations they are placed to handle and this in turn leads to lower quality and requires more supervision and instruction by the supervisor, who consequently will be strictly tied to the line.

Overtime work might be necessary both at the department that borrows personnel and the department that supplies personnel.

In this situation a large number of contacts with peers and superiors are necessary.

Shortage of personnel causes lower speed on the line, minor stoppages and in many cases extra work for the fitting department.

Personnel work

The incidents under this heading have various origins: counselling, 20 per cent; relations between workers and supervisors and among workers themselves,

TABLE 7.15

Distribution of incidents

Type of incident	Assembly line super-visors		Workers	Produc-tion control super-visors	Materials handling super-visors	Fitting super-visors	Work study per-sonnel	Total
	No.	%						
Personnel	70	23·5	34	3	—	—	—	107
shortage	23		3	—	—	—	—	26
personnel work	16		20	—	—	—	—	36
health	9		7	—	—	—	—	16
language problems	9		2	—	—	—	—	11
discipline	13		2	3	—	—	—	18
Materials	61	20·5	3	9	11	2	2	88
shortage	16		—	1	5	—	—	22
defects	32		3	7	6	2	2	52
fit	13		—	1	—	—	—	14
Equipment – tools	47	15·8	7	5	—	—	4	63
shortage	14		4	1	—	—	1	20
defects – rejection	33		3	4	—	—	3	43
Methods – balance	31	10·4	3	1	1	1	22	59
Information – consultation	33	11·1	8	3	—	3	40	87
superior	4		—	—	—	—	2	6
subordinate	5		7	1	—	3	6	22
peer	1		—	—	—	—	1	2
other departments	23		1	2	—	—	31	57
Erroneous work	24	8·1	—	4	—	7	9	44
Process control	15	5·0	3	—	—	—	—	18
Force majeure	9	3·0	—	—	—	1	—	10
Design of the work place – safety	6	2·0	18	—	—	—	—	24
Design	2	0·7	1	1	—	—	—	4
	298	100·1	77	26	12	14	77	504

TABLE 7.16

Supervisors' estimates of duration and frequency of incidents

Type of incident	FREQUENCY per week	per month	occa- sional	Duration per incident (hours)	Time per week (hours)	Time distribution among categories
Personnel						
shortage	1·0			1·0		
personnel work			x	8·0		
health			x	1·0	} 3·7	25%
language problems	4·0			0·2		
discipline			x	6·0		
Materials						
shortage	1·5			0·7		
defects	1·5			1·0	} 3·5	23%
fit	3·0			0·3		
Equipment – tools						
shortage	3·0			0·5		
defects –					} 2·7	18%
rejection	3·0			0·4		
Methods – balance		1·5		2·1	0·8	5%
Information – consultation						
superior			x	1·0		
subordinate		0·6		1·0	} 1·3	9%
peer		—		—		
other departments		2·0		2·0		
Erroneous work	5·0			0·3	1·5	10%
Process control	2·0			0·5	1·0	7%
Force majeure		1·0		1·0	0·1	1%
Design of the work place – safety				—	—	—
Design			x	4·0	0·5	3%
					15·1*	100%

* 15 hours per week amounts to about 35% of total working hours.

40 per cent; personnel not being able to carry out their work due to physical or mental limitations, 25 per cent.

The supervisor voluntarily takes on most of this work himself instead of sending employees to the specialist departments concerned, e.g. Personnel Department. A reason for that is obviously the shortage of personnel and the extra work necessary to handle further absenteeism.

A great portion of supervisory time is occupied by personnel relations, matters of placement, etc.

There is a risk of bad quality of work, defective work, and rising labour turnover.

Health

Seventy per cent of the incidents refer to acute cases of illness at work and occupational diseases. Other incidents express workers' discontent with the company's health service.

Similar consequences here as under the heading 'Shortage of personnel'. Personnel shortage, but not so serious.

Language problems

The incidents describe situations in which misunderstandings, erroneous work, etc., could be attributed to language problems.

Erroneous work results in lower quality and adjustments. Interpreters have to be called in to convey instructions, information, etc.

The members of the various language groups tend to stick together and the social distances between the groups increase.

Discipline

The origins of the incidents are as follows:

Absence without permission, 50 per cent.
Resistance to changes manifesting itself as obstruction.
Unrealistic demands.
Late arrival.
Other reasons like drunkenness, abuse of signals, violation of rules.

Absence without permission makes it difficult for the supervisor to allocate resources and could undermine his authority.

Resistance to changes makes it difficult for the supervisor to change the membership of teams, for instance, and takes more of his time.

Materials – shortage

Shortage of various components is often reported. This applies particularly to one complex unit with a small buffer, and that means that also minor deficiencies of the unit cause stoppages of the line. Very often the suppliers do not deliver components in time or they deliver faulty components (50 per cent of the cases).

F

A shortage could also be due to the fact that materials handling has failed to order components or furnish the line with components and parts in due time.

In extreme cases, the shortage causes a stoppage of the line, but usually delays arise and supplementary operations become necessary. These supplementary operations are carried out by a utility man, in most cases also requiring action by the supervisor. In a few cases it becomes necessary to put aside unit assemblies for completion later on, mostly as overtime work. Often the final fitting is involved, too.

Materials – defects

Here the causes could be both internal and external. Eighty per cent of the cases are due to supplier failure and 80 per cent could be remedied at the line jointly by supervisor – utility man – inspection – fitting. Twenty per cent of all defects in materials are passed on to final adjustment. Defects in materials appear daily.

When defects appear, new materials have to be procured. In the meantime delays occur and in some cases the line stops and additional personnel, utility men, etc., have to be put in. It also happens that new materials have to be ordered from the supplier, which generally causes a delay.

Materials – fitting

Eighty per cent of the incidents belonging to this category are fitting problems in connection with parts which keep within the tolerance range. That results in extra work of some kind in 80 per cent of the cases.

When fitting problems arise, i.e. when the part lies just within the tolerance limits, the supervisor usually takes the following measures:

1. He gets in touch with quality control, and that department mostly finds that the part complies with the tolerance requirements.
2. He gets in touch with the methods department to call their attention to the fact that the balancing might be wrong. After investigation the methods department usually answers that they have considered variations of fitting in doing the balancing.

Several consecutive narrow fits (just within the tolerance range) undoubtedly lead to difficulties for the operator to carry out his operations within the time allowance. This is a fact known by the methods department which takes corrective steps in 50 per cent of the cases. The remaining 50 per cent cause irritation between the parties involved, and often extra personnel has to step in and assist the operator. The co-operation between the methods department – the supervisor – the operator is often hampered when no factual information about the reasons for non-action is given.

Equipment – tools, shortage and defects

The reason for shortage is in all cases the fact that tools break down and no serviceable tools are in reserve.

In 10 per cent of the cases spare tools are available, but out of order and useless. In at least 25 per cent of the cases production engineering failed to supply extra tools.

In 65 per cent of the cases defects in equipment and tools are due to normal wear; 15 per cent are due to erroneous design, and slightly more than 10 per cent are due to breaks in the supply of electric power and water. Occasionally, the tool is wrongly set.

In the first place, the supervisor tries to borrow an equivalent tool from another department, but is successful in doing that only in 10 per cent of the cases. In the remaining cases he has to make an emergency repair himself or arrange for a repair at the machine shop.

Consequently, he has to spend much time on tool problems. Tools break down twice or three times a week on the average, which influences quality and causes difficulties for the operator to keep up with the balance. The utility man often has to step in and assist the operator.

Methods – balance

The critical incidents here mainly consist of balancing problems taken up in discussions between the supervisors and the methods department. At the introduction of new balances the supervisor has well-founded ideas leading to a change of balance in 80 per cent of the cases. As far as changes of existing balances are concerned, production engineering and the supervisor contribute to about the same extent.

The data show that in those cases where there has been no open flow of information between the parties concerned, disturbances will arise in connection with the introduction of new balances and change of old balances. Sometimes the supervisor is not fully acquainted with his balances, resulting in erroneous work performance.

If the supervisor does not have good relations with his workers, he gets into an intermediate position between production engineering and the workers.

(*See also:* Materials – fitting.)

Information – consultation, with superiors

Nearly all incidents are due to the fact that the supervisor has not received any information from the superintendent about production changes necessary to carry out work.

Lack of information of that kind might lead to production of too many or too few components in those cases where the supervisor is responsible for sub-assembly operations off the main line. Acute disturbances of production will occur and scrapping and stoppages will follow.

Information – consultation, subordinates

Most incidents are due to insufficient information or instruction. In some cases this could be explained by the fact that the supervisor is not available when a worker needs instruction. Moreover, some workers need more information/ instruction than is normal.

Consequences here are erroneous assembly and poor quality.

Problems arise in succeeding operations and sometimes fitting or rejection are necessary.

Information – consultation, other departments

Eighty per cent of all cases of communication are between the supervisor and the methods department. Forty per cent of those contacts are regarded as useful consultation. Twenty per cent are experienced as negative consultation resulting in a solution only after very time-consuming discussions. In the remaining 20 per cent of the cases consultation has taken place but has not led to any result.

Twenty per cent of the incidents here refer to sporadic communication with other departments, mainly production control, materials control and design.

In all those instances where communication and consultation take place, the problems are solved in a way satisfactory to all parties concerned. In the other cases, the supervisor usually gets into a difficult situation, being squeezed between production engineering and the workers.

The incidents related also show that the supervisor in some situations is inactive. He might only act as conveyor of information and consequently does not contribute to a quick handling of disturbances.

Insufficient information might also result in bad relations between production engineering and the supervisor with possible effects on workers.

Erroneous work

Under this heading are reported incidents where the worker does erroneous work so that adjustment has to be made at the same or a succeeding station.
The following reasons could be distinguished:

Carelessness on the part of the worker, 35 per cent.
Bad instruction by the supervisor, 15 per cent.
Given balances are not followed.

The incidents occur daily.

Adjustments have to be made which might cause scrapping of material, etc. Utility men have to be called upon to correct the errors.

Poor quality, complaints by customers and delayed deliveries are the result.

Process control

Most incidents refer to daily errors caused by wrong assembly specifications given by the production control department. It sometimes happens that specifications for special assemblies are given, only when the unit has already passed stations were special operations should be carried out.

There are also incidents showing that the strict control and the high speed of production make it difficult for the employees to go to the rest room, for instance.

With the limited number of utility men, an employee might have to wait for a long time before he can leave the line.

Another type of incident is caused by faults in the line, for example, electric or mechanical disturbances.

When wrong specifications of assembly units are given, extra personnel has to be used to correct errors. Delays might occur as well as stoppages of production.

The mechanical and electric disturbances might be caused by excessive utilization of the production resources and might result in damage to assembly units and equipment as well as in delays and stoppages.

Another consequence is bad motivation to work.

Force majeure

Most incidents appear at bad weather (cold, snow, etc.), influenza, traffic changes, theft, faults in equipment and tools which are not foreseeable.

Incidents outside the company often cause shortage of personnel at the start of a shift which makes it necessary for the supervisor to reorganize his personnel or perhaps borrow personnel from other departments. Also the superintendent steps in on these occasions. The reorganization often leads to irregular work performance and many minor stoppages. This is due to lack of experience with the new tasks and lack of time for the supervisor to give instructions to everyone. All this often leads to overtime work by employees borrowed from preceding stations, when they have to catch up with their regular work.

Design of the work place – safety

Several incidents are caused by the fact that a work place is overcrowded. Another group of incidents has to do with the fact that the materials arrive directly to the work place from outside and therefore are cold in winter-time.

The design of the assembly lines, e.g. the driving, might cause assembly units to go off the line. The platforms at the line also get damaged by the trucks and therefore cause safety hazards. The truck drivers drive too fast.

The various types of incidents are equally frequent. Most of the incidents were reported by the workers.

Accidents might occur, such as crushing, spraining, etc. Colds, rheumatism, etc., could be caused by the conditions at the work place.

Assembly units can come off the line and cause stoppages, adjustments, scrapping and delays.

It often takes quite a long time to handle these disturbances and irritation easily spreads among the employees.

Notes and References

1 HAMBLIN, A. C., PINSCHOF, M. & THURLEY, K. E. (1962). Report on a study of supervisory jobs at — (Johnson) Footwear Ltd. London School of Economics and Political Science (mimeographed).

2 HENLEY, J. S., JONES, P. & PAPARAJU, B. (1966). *The production foreman in a*

tube works. (May). Student project report on the roles and training needs of foremen. Report of 31 pages plus 12 pages of tabulations. London School of Economics and Political Science. Personnel Management Diploma (mimeographed).

3 BERGSTEN, G., HAMMARSTRÖM, O. & ROSÉN, K. (1969). *Rapport från undersökning enligt critical incident-metoden av banarbetsledarna vid AB QZ-verken.* The report is 55 pages. Swedish Council for Personnel Administration, Gothenburg (mimeographed).

8. Design of Strategies

BASIC PROBLEMS

We move at this point to the problems of designing change strategies. The various areas of the conceptual model suggested for analysing the supervisory problem have now been discussed and illustrated. The practical questions remain and demand an answer.

Does a more sophisticated way of thinking about supervisors help to suggest ways of improving effectiveness or satisfaction?

In what situations, should managers or supervisors use which route?

Should one intervene to further existing change processes or to counter them?

What entry points to cycles of change are possible?

Can changes be planned in accordance with distinct strategies?

These are questions of great importance for consultants, trainers and change agents of various types. They are also relevant for managers and supervisors themselves, who may or may not wish to accept or promote change programmes. They are also important for researchers and those concerned with the study of supervision, if it is granted that undertaking a study of supervisory behaviour and supervisory systems is facilitated by studies of changes taking place. Whatever the perspective or objectives, all the parties involved in the supervisory situation would seem to be vitally affected by any suggested strategies for change.

There is an old (Irish) saying that if you want to know how to get somewhere, you should ask where you are first. Decisions on the route depend not only on the expected destination, but on the point of departure, the type of terrain to be crossed, and the type of transport available. The time of expected arrival is also clearly important.

One of the main difficulties raised in trying to locate the point of departure is that provided by the personal and social experience of continual change in which we are all caught up. It is an obvious fact that nothing is completely stable in society and that most apparently firm and dependable sets of expectations about our social structure are likely to be questioned in our own lifetime. Sets of changes, therefore, are in process of occurring as we consider our problem at the respective levels of the individual, the work groups, organizations, and society itself. We will be considering in some further detail the nature of these changes as they affect supervisory work behaviour in the next to last chapter of this book. For the moment, it will be enough to note the point that successful strategies of *planned* change are likely to be related to some of the broad undercurrents of change already taking place.

At the organizational level, the point of departure may be crucially affected by the way that supervisory 'problems' are perceived by the actors in a situation.

Take, for example, the contrast between two typical cases where 'supervisory change programmes' might be discussed.

In Case I, we can imagine a situation of a company with no formal supervisory training or selection programmes in which the management are aware of the type of deficiencies in their supervisory performance mentioned in Chapter 1. In this case one could say that the change might be initiated by the manager asking for outside assistance from consultants so that 'something can be done about our supervisors'.

In Case II, we can picture the situation of a large manufacturing or construction company in which training programmes have been organized for ten or fifteen years, in which formal selection procedures have been used for the recruitment of foremen, and in which the problem of supervision has been discussed among management (and especially in the personnel department) also for a number of years. In such a company, it is likely that at some stage of development, consultants will have been used, either for training or selection purposes. In this case, management may have decided with some disquiet that their sophisticated methods for improving supervisory performance have not really produced adequate results. They feel that something new is required and they are actively looking around for a new solution. New consultants are asked to look again at the problem.

In Case I, the first problem for the consultant would be to make an initial assessment of the supervisory system. This involves a study of any data available which would allow him to identify any of what would appear to be critical factors in the supervisory system. Such variables would be in all the boxes of our model. The type of investigation implied here would mean an interview programme and might well take several weeks. The information available would have to be collected either by discussions with managers and supervisors or from documents, records of production and personnel indices. The type of production system would have to be studied and some assessment made of such indefinite factors as leadership climate and the expectations of middle management about their supervisors' performance. Similarly workers' expectations would have to be assessed, as well as some indication of the most important type of individual characteristics. Age data, length of service and type of educational background of each person would, perhaps, be available freely from records but many of the other factors which have been discussed would be much more difficult to obtain. In a very short time, therefore, the consultant would have to make a crude model of the supervisory system getting what information he could. Only after a descriptive model of the supervisory system had been assembled, containing the numbers and types of supervisors, the type of production system, the views on leadership of middle management and so forth, could the consultant begin to answer his first two most important questions, i.e. (*a*) What at first glance *appear* to be the most crucial problems and defects of performance in the system? and (*b*) What types of *barriers* to change ('road-blocks') are likely to be erected in any programme of implementing new procedures and new ways of thinking?

In Case II, the consultant's problem is a more complex one. On the surface, he would find it much easier to build up a historical picture of the supervisory system. In such a company, the data would be more freely available. He might find available, for example, test scores of supervisors, information on their performance in potential supervisory training courses, information perhaps on their departmental performance in terms of productivity and personnel indices, labour turnover, and absenteeism. He also might find in such a company better-documented evidence on the type of norms and expectations which management have of supervision. For example, job descriptions and specifications taken together with procedures, minutes and memos issued by factory management might elaborate, fairly exactly, the objectives, targets and procedures that supervisors ought to be meeting. One problem in this case is that there is probably an accepted view of the supervisory situation which it will be difficult for the consultant to challenge. He might have very considerable difficulties in being able to test how far the management's view (or the personnel department's view) of its supervisory problem was valid or not. In this case, therefore, there would necessarily be much more importance in using shop floor observation and discussions with supervisors themselves, spending relatively more time in this activity than in the first case.

This preliminary investigation, for both Cases I and II, might appear, correctly, to be very similar to the type of investigation usually carried out by consultants in this field. It is, however, only the first stage of an analysis of a supervisory system. It can be seen as a type of inventory of factors for a particular supervisory system in which the consultant would use a checklist and attempt to get what data he could within a short time. The information collected might easily be misleading.

In both cases, described here, after the initial study, the management and consultants are then faced with their first major decisions. In terms of our model, there are six possible main routes or types of change which may affect supervisory actions and their effects. It may be that the consultant or investigator at this stage thinks there is enough evidence to show that many of the supposed deficiencies in supervisory performance are really due to *other* problems. In this case, it would be prudent to try to test this thoroughly before investing in any further resources in a programme of improving supervisory performance. This may, in reality, be a low priority in this particular company. If the consultant feels (from his preliminary investigation) that there is a *prima facie* case for possible improvements in supervisory performance, he has then (with the management) to decide if such supposed deficiencies would be likely to be affected by any move along our six routes of change. It may be that one particular route is more appropriate to the situation than another. In other cases, many needs may be apparent and one could start with, for example, *either* training *or* selection. In many cases, however, it is likely that any supposed deficiencies in performances could be affected by changes in *any* of the six routes. The problem then is whether to launch a *simultaneous* attack on the problem on six fronts or, if this is impractical, how to programme the approach.

An examination of each of the types of change, (*a*) organizational, (*b*) climate, (*c*) technical, (*d*) selection and placement, (*e*) training, (*f*) education, reveals that they are, in many aspects, interdependent. If, for example, a new training programme is introduced, there is much evidence, in for example the Sykes article,[1] to show that training may be frustrated in its intended effects if it takes place in a climate which is unfavourable. Similarly there are interrelationships between the type of climate for any organizational change which will take place. Formal organizational change, for example, the creation of new role specialisms within the supervisory system, may need attitudinal changes and changes in role expectations to make them effective. The items in job training programmes designed to produce a certain type of 'terminal behaviour' are likely to be related to certain attitudes and beliefs which may themselves be changed by educational experience. In all these ways, therefore, (and there are many more possible examples) the changes we are discussing seem to be likely to be interdependent.

Some differences exist, of course, between the situations postulated in Cases I and II. In Case I it is much easier to try a comprehensive approach when no previous attempt has been made. In the second case, programmes of selection and training already exist and any attempt to improve on these would have to take into account the established programmes and the beliefs of those running such programmes. In this latter situation it would be likely that the best strategy might well be to start with a recognized problem area. For instance, where formal training programmes have been carried on for many years but with little support from either supervisors or management it could be more effective to attempt an entirely new approach to training than to work by improving existing schemes.

This brief comparison of the two cases surely serves to underline the complexity of the problem of choice of strategy. We have already emphasized the importance of diagnosing (a) the main characteristics of the supervisory system in question, (b) the choice of *area* of change, (c) the problem of deciding between selective and general change. In reality, we have to add to this (d) the philosophy behind the approach, (e) the objectives of the change, (f) the problem of the most appropriate sequence of actions in a change cycle, and (g) the problem of maintenance of the change.

In diagrammatic form, the choice of strategy could be expressed as Figure 8.1.

Bearing in mind the numbers of variables involved, it is apparent that a prescriptive approach is ruled out as being too *simpliste*. We cannot, at the present stage of knowledge, prescribe particular remedies for particular needs. Nevertheless, it is possible to give sets of classifications for each of the sub-problems indicated in Figure 8.1, and, using an ideal type approach, it will be possible to indicate the type of strategy which can be hypothesized as likely to be most effective for a given (ideal type) supervisory situation. The systematic evaluation of experiments with such strategies should enable us gradually to refine our conclusions. Each sub-problem is therefore discussed in turn.

CHOICE OF BASIC APPROACH

We must start by examining some of the literature on planned change. The collection of material by Bennis, Benne and Chin in the second edition of their book

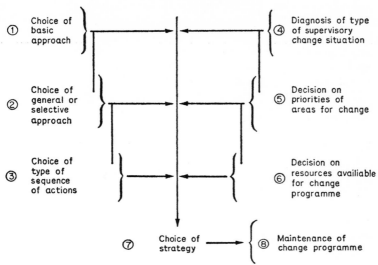

FIGURE 8.1 Choice of strategies for change

The planning of change,[2] is a very useful place to begin. Four classifications are given of strategies by different authors (Table 8.1).

None of these classifications are quite suitable for our purpose, as they tend to mix up the philosophy and techniques used. All of them use a 'systems' frame of reference and it is important to add the possibility of analysing change from a social action viewpoint (Weber,[8] Cicourel[9]). We can, however, use the general classification of Chin and Benne and adapt it to our purpose (Table 8.2).

As Table 8.2 shows, the problem of change is approached differently according to whether one looks at it as a question of power, or re-education, or new information, or the solution of problems. The examples illustrate the possible differences in the objectives of change strategies which follow from these broad approaches.

CHOICE OF GENERAL OR SELECTIVE APPROACH

This choice is also clearly affected by the prior decisions on approach. We are familiar with the contrast between the deductive logic of the eighteenth-century enlightment which leads to complete re-design of systems (and revolution) and the piecemeal reform of the empiricists. Clearly if one takes the line that *fundamental* or *structural* change is necessary to provide a lasting solution, one is driven to develop a general approach. An emphasis not on systems but on the understanding of how people actually think and behave will lead to emphasis on the particular and on limited changes. The latter approach, as seen in the action-centred school, will, of course, be likely to lead to a variety of suggested changes, covering different areas of change, but it will always be selective in its emphasis on the particular problem.

TABLE 8.1

Some classifications of change strategies

I. CHIN & BENNE[3]
1. *Empirical – rational*
   (a) Basic research and dissemination of knowledge
   (b) Personnel selection and replacement
   (c) Systems analysts as staff
   (d) Applied research and linkage systems
   (e) Utopian thinking as a strategy
   (f) Perceptual and conceptual reorganization through classification of language
2. *Normative – re-educative*
   (a) Improving problem-solving capabilities of a system (feedback)
   (b) Releasing and fostering growth in persons
3. *Power – coercive*
   (a) Non violence
   (b) Use of political institutions
   (c) Changing composition and manipulation of power elites

II. BENNIS[4]
1. Exposition and propagation
2. Elite corps
3. Human relations training
4. Staff programmes
5. Scholarly consultation
6. Circulation of ideas to elite
7. Development research
8. Action research
9. Planned organizational change
   (a) applied research
   (b) consulting
   (c) training

III. BENNIS[5] QUOTED BY BARNES[6]
1. Planned change (with change agent)
2. Indoctrination change
3. Coercive change
4. Technoratic change
5. Interactional change
6. Socialization change
7. Formulative change
8. Natural (accidental) change

IV. GREINER[7] QUOTED BY BARNES[6]
1. Decree approach
2. Replacement approach
3. Structure approach
4. Group decision approach
5. Data discussion approach
6. Group problem-solving approach
7. T-group approach

TABLE 8.2

Basic approaches to change

Name	Type of thinking and assumptions	Examples
A. *Power – coercive*	Change is the result of stimuli being applied (e.g. directives) backed by force or possible force	(a) Decision by old elite (b) Protest/challenge by emerging elite (c) Pressure or threat from external source, e.g. legislation (d) Collective bargaining
B. *Normative – re-educative*	Change is the result of individuals and groups adjusting their norms and attitudes so that they want to behave differently	(a) Programmes designed to 'develop' individuals (fostering growth) (b) Programmes designed to change attitudes and improve social 'skills' (human relations) (c) Programmes designed to reduce intergroup conflict and improve collaboration, e.g. management grid (d) Teaching new conceptual skills, e.g. Kepner & Tregoe[10] (e) Indoctrination of followers by elite (cultural revolution) (f) Emulation of cultural patterns in other organizations (management systems) (g) Establishing acceptance of new objectives (MBO)
C. *Empirical – rational*	Change is the result of new understanding reached by making available new data on the variables affecting performance. It comes from the acquisition of knowledge of all types and leads to design of new systems	(a) Redefinition of roles after study (b) Use of performance appraisal schemes (c) Organization data feedback discussions (d) Operation research studies (e) Educational courses in social sciences (f) Use of staff experts' reports
D. *Action – centred*	Change is the normal result of the shifting inter-play of individuals and groups with different objectives and different perceptions of significance around specific decisions and problems. Change can be stimulated by focusing attention on such problems	(a) Group discussions of common problems and possible remedial action (vertical training) (b) Use of working parties and committees (c) Case study simulations followed by problem solving meetings

CHOICE OF TYPE OF SEQUENCE OF ACTIONS

We have already seen that there are five problems to be tackled in any change programme:

(a) Analysis and diagnosis of the nature of the situation.
(b) The setting of objectives.
(c) The design of the change(s).
(d) The carrying through of changes.
(e) The evaluation of the results of changes.

These problems have been shown as stages of a learning cycle (Figure 2.1). We can show this again as in Figure 8.2.

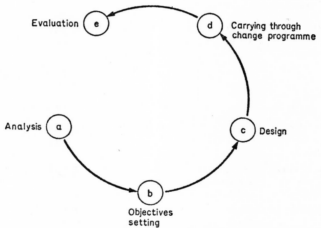

FIGURE 8.2   Stages or sub-problems of a programme of change

The choice of *sequence* involves decisions about :

(a) The best entry point to the cycle.
(b) The sub-problem which receives the greatest emphasis.
(c) The *way* in which it is planned to develop one stage into the next.

Figure 8.3 can be used to indicate some 'ideal type' strategies which can be linked to our previous classification.

This is not meant to indicate that the first two strategies never cover all the stages of a learning cycle, only that the typical strategy does not do so. The differences between the emphasis in III and IV are clearly important in that the classical method presupposes that it is possible to jump from (a) to (b) (where it may be very difficult); whereas the fourth strategy implies it is possible to go from (*e*) to (*a*), which again may not be easy, particularly if frustrations have been exposed at the stage (*d*) (Figure 8.4).

This Figure illustrates the differences in complexity between the four 'ideal type' strategies and the differences in the emphasis placed in the change cycle. It also indicates something of the advantages and disadvantages of each strategy

Basic approach	General/selective	Ideal–type strategy	Sequence
A. Power–coercive	Tends to be selective but could aim at general change	Directed change or bargaining I	(b) ⟶ (d)
B. Normative–re-educative	Tends to be general	Method based II	(c) ⟶ (d) (e)
C. Empirical–rational	Biased towards a selective approach	Work analysis III	(a) ⟶ (b) (c) ⟶ (d) ⟶ (e)
D. Action centred	Always selective in character	Problem solution IV	(d) ⟶ (e) (a) ⟶ (b) ⟶ (c)

FIGURE 8.3   Four 'ideal-type' strategies of change

and the problems each one has to deal with, but discussion of this will be expanded in the next chapter.

DIAGNOSIS OF TYPE OF SUPERVISORY CHANGE SITUATION

We turn now from the strategies themselves to the situations to which they might be applied. In Chapter 3, Figure 3.1, we suggested a fourfold classification of supervisory systems :

(*a*) Traditional supervisory role systems.
(*b*) Bureaucratized systems.
(*c*) Joint Management/Supervisory control systems.
(*d*) Sophisticated organic self-regulating production systems.

Using the same dimensions, we can add two 'half-way' positions or types, namely:

(*e*) Mass-production, management-structured systems (where strong management control co-exists with the experience of a large number of crises and unexpected contingencies, stimulating unofficial supervisory action).[11]

I Directed change or bargaining   II Method based

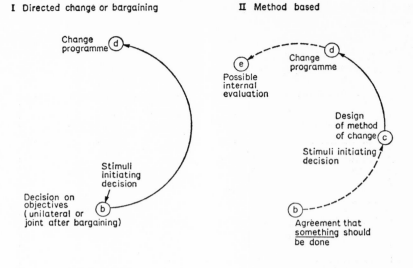

III Work analysis   IV Problem solution

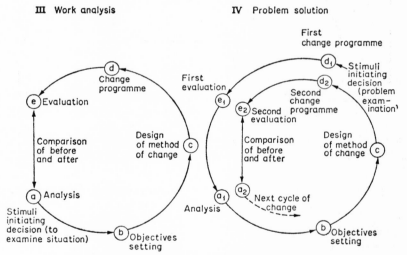

FIGURE 8.4   Pictorial representation of the four strategies

(f) Traditional craft foreman systems (where autonomy exists together with the need to solve many non-programmed decisions).

Traditional construction site management would be typical here.[12]
Figure 3.1 can then be reproduced as Figure 8.5.

These six cases are, however, not sufficient to provide us with an overall classification of the situations in which change programmes are likely to be applied. The reason for this is that the model so far is an entirely static one. If manage-

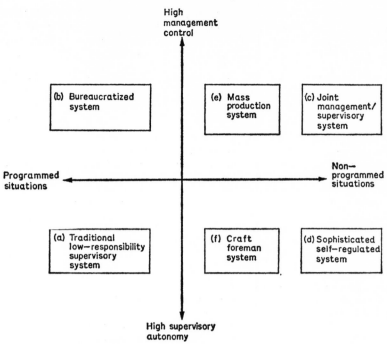

FIGURE 8.5   Types of supervisory system

ment, unions, superiors themselves are stimulated to change this situation, it means that someone, perhaps all, are dissatisfied with the existing conditions and results and that they believe that something can be done about it. The dissatisfaction is clearly linked with the problems experienced with that particular type of system in a certain environment. We cannot attempt a list of all the problems which might be experienced in all possible situations; the possible combinations are immense. At the risk of over-simplification, however, it is possible to use the positions on Figure 8.5 and postulate possible directions of change which may appear to be desirable. These are given in Table 8.3, together with some problems experienced and the objectives of change.

TABLE 8.3

Supervisory systems, problems, and probable directions of change

Initial position	Example	Main problems experienced	Results	Probable direction of change
(a) The traditional low-responsibility supervisory system	Working chargehand ganger, sub-contractor	Allocation of labour. Practical assistance to subordinates	Management criticism of low labour productivity	(A) Enforcement of 'rational' management controls over supervision (Bureaucratization)

Initial position	*Example*	*Main problems experienced*	*Results*	*Probable direction of change*
			Management criticism of supervisory conservative/ authoritarian attitudes	(B) Job enlargement and creating new organizational climate and structure (New climate)
(*b*) Bureaucraticized supervisory system	Office supervision (pre-automation)	Controlling subordinates and enforcing rules	Following automation, management sees need to shift supervisors' attention to contingency handling	(C) De-bureaucratization. Encouraging a more flexible and responsible approach (De-bureaucratization)
(*e*) Mass-production management-structured system	Assembly-line foremen	Dealing with crises under intense management pressure for standardization	Low morale for supervisors and workers. Inflexible and irresponsible attitudes by supervisors perceived by management	(D) Attempts to develop problem solving skills and enlarge job (Job enlargement)
(*f*) Traditional craft foremen (high responsibility) systems	Meister, craft foremen in construction industry	Technical decisions and quality control	Management desire to integrate control systems through computers. Fear of inconsistency in local decisions	(E) Absorption of craft supervision into rational management system (Rationalization)
			Management desire to improve decision-making process, but see need to keep local decisions	(F) Agreement between management and supervision to develop professionalized supervisory team to strengthen local control (Professionalization)

Initial position	Example	Main problems experienced	Results	Probable direction of change
(c) Joint management/ supervisory systems	Process industry plant super- vision	Integration of skills or out- looks, technical decisions, problem solving strategies	Management see need to develop teams and improve communications	(G) Attempts to develop individuals and grow effective teams (Team management)
(d) Sophisticated autonomous self- regulated supervisory system	Profession- alized project management team	Technical knowledge, relations with management and organiza- tions, problem solving strategies	Supervisors demand assist- ance with problems. Management see need to improve decision-making	(H) Attempts to develop individual judgement group prob- lem-solving strategies and improve external rela- tions (Autonomous supervision)

The movements shown are all away from traditional practices, but this seems to be very plausible. We can show the eight types of direction of change on the same two-dimensional map as in Figure 8.5.

Figure 8.6, therefore, gives a crude but useful classification of eight types of change situation, all of which clearly require a separate approach.

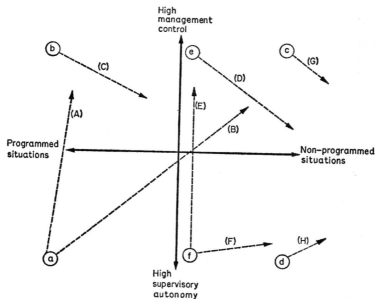

FIGURE 8.6   Pictorial representation of eight types of change

DECISION ON PRIORITIES OF AREAS FOR CHANGE

We have indicated already that we face the choice between six 'routes' of change:

Organizational change.
Climate change.
Technological environment change.
Selection and promotion change.
Training change.
Educational change.

It will be clear from examples quoted and the basic model itself, that these routes are interdependent. Sometimes changes on one route will be neutralized by changes in other routes. For things never stay still. There are constant changes occurring on all routes in most situations and the only choice open is whether to plan additional changes. We should not be misled into thinking that these routes form a natural hierarchy from fundamental to superficial change. It is *not* necessarily valid to postpone action in bringing in new educational and training programmes until the organizational situation 'has been put right'. This is often alleged, but it presumes that organization can be designed to be entirely functional and acceptable to all parties. This is not likely to be achieved. The most that organizational reform may achieve is a new equilibrium position dependent on current beliefs, objectives and the power of the various groups within the organization. It may not achieve even that. To delay training until organization is requisite is likely to delay it a long time indeed.

It follows that any plans of change have not only to decide on the greatest area of need, but also on what is likely to be acceptable and what *combination* of changes are probably going to be most successful in the short and long run. As we will see, the choice of basic approach and strategy also limits the *areas* which are most suitable for change.

DECISION ON RESOURCES AVAILABLE FOR CHANGE PROGRAMME

We will follow current practice and call the person concerned with 'easing', directing, planning and controlling the change a *change agent*. This role can be distinguished from that of the *client* on the one hand and that of a *researcher* on the other. The latter's objectives are usually to study the process of change and to test the appropriateness of change strategies, to gain understanding of the dynamics of change and the nature of supervisory action. In this capacity, a researcher may be more interested in an illuminating failure than a smooth-running success story. The change agent, on the other hand, will be judged by the success or failure of *his* proposed or suggested strategy. The client is clearly

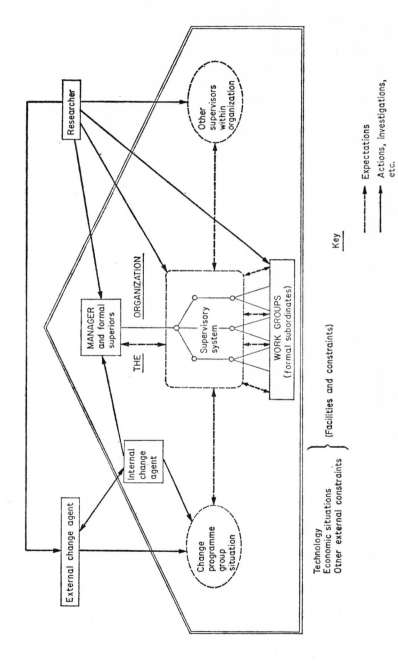

FIGURE 8.7   The parties concerned in a supervisory system change

likely to be only interested in success and cost. Conflict of objectives is therefore endemic in this threefold relationship.

We need to distinguish further between change agents external to the organization and those internal to the organization. Similarly, there are clearly likely to be differences of objectives in change situations between supervisors, subordinates, managers and these agents and researchers concerned only with the process of change. Figure 8.7, therefore, shows the parties which usually need to be distinguished in change situations.

We can see here that the normal relations and expectations of action within the line of authority and between supervisors themselves are greatly confused by the arrival of change agents and a researcher. Evaluation of changes taking place needs to take account of the perceptions of all the parties concerned. It is very difficult for the change agent himself or the managers or supervisors to collect relatively objective information about such perceptions. Nobody can see the whole picture. The researcher is shown as being in a key position for the collection of data which might be useful for evaluation. He may only be able to interpret it, however, if he collaborates and discusses with the change agents and the various groups within the client. This collaboration, however, may be difficult for the reason discussed above. There are also many opportunities for confusion of role between researcher and change agent.

The resources required depend on the size of the project, the complexity of the situation and the strategy adopted. We can indicate roughly the stages of the various strategies and the type of roles required (Figure 8.8).

Generally speaking, for all the three lower strategies, it is probably more effective to use a double change agent role, the external agent initiating and gradually handing over to the internal agent. The researcher takes no role in the first strategy (although he could, of course) but is *essential* to the success of the final strategy. This is because the strategy depends on finding relevant problems and making an impact on this solution and the evaluation stage is essential if this is to be successful.

CHOICE OF STRATEGY

We can now put the various pieces of our jigsaw together. Figure 8.9 summarizes the argument so far.

From Figure 8.9 we can see that the crucial decisions are :

(*a*) over the appropriateness of our four ideal type strategies to the eight directions of change;
(*b*) over the most appropriate areas for change, given the strategy.

There seem to be four general hypotheses which can guide our choice in this matter :

1. It can be postulated that when autonomy in supervisory systems is being reduced, then power has to be used (Directive strategy I.)

	ANALYSIS	OBJECTIVES	DESIGN	CHANGE PROGRAMME	EVALUATION	ANALYSIS	OBJECTIVES
Directive or bargaining		Bargainer/ manager is also change agent. No researcher		Supervisors			
Method based		Change agent (internal and external) Managers supervisors	Change agents necessary (internal and external). No researcher	Change agents and supervisors			
Work analysis	Researcher necessary		Change agents and researcher	Change agents and supervisors	Researcher necessary		
Problem solution				Researcher, change agents, and supervisors necessary	Researcher necessary	Researcher necessary	Change agent, supervisors, researcher

FIGURE 8.8   Resources required for each strategy

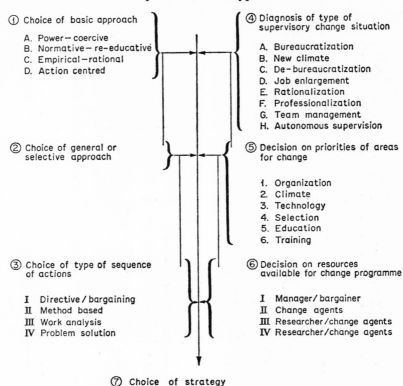

① Choice of basic approach

A. Power—coercive
B. Normative—re-educative
C. Empirical—rational
D. Action centred

④ Diagnosis of type of supervisory change situation

A. Bureaucratization
B. New climate
C. De-bureaucratization
D. Job enlargement
E. Rationalization
F. Professionalization
G. Team management
H. Autonomous supervision

② Choice of general or selective approach

⑤ Decision on priorities of areas for change

1. Organization
2. Climate
3. Technology
4. Selection
5. Education
6. Training

③ Choice of type of sequence of actions

I Directive/bargaining
II Method based
III Work analysis
IV Problem solution

⑥ Decision on resources available for change programme

I Manager/bargainer
II Change agents
III Researcher/change agents
IV Researcher/change agents

⑦ Choice of strategy

FIGURE 8.9 Strategies available for various situations

2. It can be hypothesized that when social systems are being deliberately de-structured, so that roles are enlarged and become more ambiguous, it is necessary to provide an overall view of the situation to those within the system. (This allows them to see their relations with one another in a new light and gives some security for the change.) (Work Analysis III.)

3. It can be asserted that when it is necessary to change whole sets of attitudes and perceptions in a previously prescribed direction, then a method based strategy is appropriate. (II.)

4. It can be hypothesized that where improved task performance is desired and where considerable supervisory system autonomy exists, then a problem solution strategy is appropriate. (IV.)

These propositions would lead to the following suggestions, *see* Table 8.4.

TABLE 8.4
Appropriate strategies for various situations

I Directive/Bargaining	A. Bureaucratization	E. Rationalization
II Method based	B. New climate	G. Team management
III Work analysis	D. Job enlargement	C. De-bureaucratization
IV Problem solution	F. Professionalization	H. Autonomous supervision

It should be recognized that these are logical choices given on hypotheses which may not be true and assessing other factors not to be important (which they are). *This is therefore only a rough guide.*

Our second question can now be fairly easily answered by another matrix (Table 8.5).

TABLE 8.5

Strategies appropriate for particular areas of change
(three major priority areas shown)

Strategies		Organization	Climate	Technology	Selection	Education	Training
Directive/ bargaining	I	A E	—	—	A E	—	A E
Method based	II	B	B G	—	—	G	B G
Work analysis	III	C D	C D	C	—	—	D
Problem solution	IV	F	H	—	F	H	H F

Again, these conclusions should not be taken as final and exclusive judgements. It seems *probable* that these strategies applied to these situations would use the routes indicated. How much weight would be placed on one route rather than another, of course, depends on many other factors, particularly the precise objectives of the chosen programme.

MAINTENANCE OF CHANGE PROGRAMME

Finally, we must consider the problem of maintaining any planned change or sets of changes. In the literature[13] the usual distinction is made between the stages of : (a) unfreezing; (b) movement towards equilibrium; (c) refreezing.

This, however, is clearly only appropriate to certain situations, particularly D and C. A more fundamental approval should connect the maintenance with the strategy used (Table 8.6).

The question of maintaining change successfully depends on how far the initial decision on the direction and strategy of change was a wise and relevant decision. It depends also on how successful the change agent is in mobilizing support around the supervisory system to confirm the wisdom of the change. This may depend on the level of involvement of the related parties. It also is dependent on how successful the changes are in meeting the stresses and strains experienced by supervisors in their daily work. The probable results indicated in Table 8.6 suggest that the first two strategies may create considerable problems for the maintenance of change.

SUMMARY OF ARGUMENT

We are concerned here with the problem of the design of change strategies which are relevant for supervision. The approach followed has been to break down the

TABLE 8.6

Maintaining change programmes

Strategies	Reasons for approval: initial stimuli	Maintenance of change	Probable results
Directive/bargaining I	Pain/problem experiment by power elite	Institutionalize change. Use formal controls	Unofficial resistance
Method based II	Perception of need for change by functional management	Use follow-ups and replace by further programmes	Varied response. Backsliding
Work analysis III	Scientific bias and communication problems	Structured audit/ evaluation over time	No change in short term, only long term
Problem solution IV	Conflict between local and HQ management. Withdrawal symptoms	Cyclical, continual and gradual change programme	Possible changes in behaviour maintained

question of broad strategies into a number of specific problems for discussion (*see* Figure 8.1). It was argued that those concerned with supervisory changes should not expect to find a set of detailed prescriptions for such changes. They should rather work through a set of questions as follows:

1. What type of supervisory situation are they dealing with?
2. What is the direction of change required or needed?
3. What are the assumptions of the approach planned?
4. Do they need to consider a general or selective approach?
5. What priorities exist over areas of change?
6. What resources are available?
7. What strategy type is most appropriate?
8. What methods are most relevant to the strategy used?
9. How can change be maintained?

For all these questions, there is *some* indication of the choice open and the literature quoted can be used to give *some* indication of problems likely to be encountered. We should admit, however, that the 'maps' given are indeed rough-and-ready charts and as yet should be treated as general guides and not substitutes for hard judgement.

Notes and References

1 SYKES, A. J. M. (1962). The effect of a supervisory training course in changing supervisory perceptions and experience of the role of management. *Human Relations* (August), pp. 227–43.

2 BENNIS, W. G. *et al.* (1969). *The planning of change.* Holt, Rinehart & Winston, New York.

3 CHIN, R. & BENNE, K. D. (1969). General strategies for effecting change in human systems. In W. G. BENNIS *et al.* ibid.

4 BENNIS, W. G. (1969). Theory and method in applying behavioural science to planned organisational change. op. cit. pp. 62–79.

5 BENNIS, W. G. (1966). *Changing organisations.* McGraw-Hill, New York.

6 BARNES, L. B. (1969). Approaches to organisational change. In W. G. BENNIS *et al.* op. cit.

7 GREINER, L. E. (1965). *Organisational change and development.* Harvard University, Cambridge, Mass. (Ph.D. thesis).

8 WEBER, M. (1957). *Essays in sociology.* Translated and with introduction by H. H. Gerth and C. W. Mills. Routledge and Kegan Paul, London.

9 CICOUREL, A. V. (1964). *Method and measurement in sociology.* The Free Press of Glencoe, New York.

10 KEPNER, C. H. & TREGOE, B. B. (1965). *The rational manager.* McGraw-Hill Book Company, New York.

11 WALKER, C. R. *et al.* (1956). *The foreman on the assembly line.* op. cit.

12 DEEKS, J. *et al.* (1967). *Problem solving behaviour in construction management.* Anglo-Swedish Conference on 'Human factors in the construction process' (September) (mimeographed).

13 BECKHARD, R. (1969). *Organisational development. Strategy and models.* Addison-Wesley, New York.

9. Action: Carrying Out a Change Programme

The previous discussion attempted to define the various issues which require decision in the design of a relevant strategy of change. If these decisions are taken and the design is formulated, the next step, logically, is the carrying out of the programme. The action phase is then concerned with three types of activities:

(a) The collection and allocation of resources.
(b) The co-ordination and management of various activities.
(c) The control over these activities to ensure that previous plans are actually carried out.

The prime difficulty here is that the use of such conventional management terms – 'control', 'resource allocation', 'co-ordination' and so forth – hides considerable difference in meaning, situation by situation, strategy by strategy.

Let us take as two examples, the contrast between supervision in a small or medium-sized firm in a craft-based industry, probably family-owned, and supervision in a large, formally structured enterprise, in a mass-production engineering industry. Our argument to date implies that successful changes depend not only on accurate diagnosis; they depend on skilful introduction of changes, the allocation of sufficient resources to support such changes, and the capacity to sustain the new situation against erosion by many opposing factors. Social change implies social power, which may be explicit or hidden. Social power can be seen as 'coercive', 'remunerative' and 'normative' in the language of Etzioni;[1] that is, capacity to change people and social situations can be based on force, agreement or bargains about mutual benefits and acceptance of the legitimacy of the actions either because of the position of the 'actor' or the acceptability of the content of the action. In the case of the small family firm, it is probable that changes in the situation, characteristics or behaviour of supervisors will be accepted because of 'normative' power. Most managerial theory of the classical school[2] assumes this normative base for managerial power. It allows management to be seen as a 'scientific' or technical[3] set of functions, such as operating various control systems.

Our second case may not be as simple as this. In large organizations with formalized structures and some degree of bureaucracy, it is probable that there are a number of status levels, occupations, departments and locations in which members perceive differences of 'interest' and objective.[4, 5] Change, in this situation, might be based on coercive power, remunerative power as well as normative power. If supervisors identify together as a group separate from workers and managers, then successful change clearly depends on the perception by the various parties to the situation as to who is initiating the change, who will benefit from it, and who will lose most from it. Change might be accepted because it is preferable to the destruction of the organization under severe external pressure. It might be accepted because the legitimacy of the action taken is accepted as prior to misgivings about the outcomes. It might be accepted because it is seen as enhancing the power of supervisors. Whatever the motivation, we have to consider action in a potential conflict situation. Action cannot be restricted to questions of operating systems; it is bound up with persuasion, bargaining, the use of threat, and possibly actual force.

For each of our ideal type strategies, there is a clear distinction in the meaning of 'action'.

For *Strategy I*, Directed Change or Bargaining, action involves the giving and acceptance of orders, and the negotiation process. It may be, as we have seen, a simple process; it may involve a complex power game.

For *Strategy II*, Method Based, action involves the administration of a standardized plan or programme.

For *Strategy III*, Work Analysis, action involves the implementation of particular changes, based on factual evidence of need available to all parties concerned. It thus means both instruction and argument and could lead to a complex discussion process.

For *Strategy IV*, Problem Solution, action involves the discussion of difficulties and contingencies and the debate about causes and solutions. We have seen that action may take place here firstly on an experimental basis, to be tested by results. The action phase is likely to be repeated therefore a number of times and to be interspersed by periods of criticism.

Because of this difference of meaning, it is difficult to make standard rules for the advice of change agents and others. Guide-lines can only be worked out for particular strategies as given in the example at the end of this chapter. It seems better to give references to a number of examples of supervisory change strategies (Table 9.1) and to bring out the need to build up a library of comparative cases of change.

A number of conclusions can be drawn from the examples given in Table 9.1 :

1. The absence of examples of problem solution strategies contrasts with the many cases cited of the other strategies. This may be misleading. It is probable that many examples of the fourth strategy may exist, but as they were not perceived as distinct from everyday managerial consultation and action, they have not been examined or recorded. We can conclude therefore merely that the fourth strategy is rarely perceived as a distinct approach to supervisory problems. An example of such a strategy was given by one of the authors in a previous publication[42] and is summarized in the notes below.

TABLE 9.1

Examples of supervisory change strategies in certain areas of change

Strategy type	Organizational change	Climate change	Technical environment change	Selection change	Education change	Training change
I	Local Authority housing maintenance supervisors affected by new work study and gang system. Chargehands had to learn to drive and change method of work control[6]	Swedish Foremen's Union exerted pressure on Employers Association to persuade managers to attend supervisory training courses[7]	Introduction of conveyor system for shoe uppers sewing shop[8]	Introduction of a pool system for potential supervisors[9]	Sending supervisors on external course to change attitudes (after policy innovation by Pers. Mgr.)[10]	Arranging human relations training course[11][12]
II	Californian aircraft plant supervisory job enlargement experiment.[13] Japanese supervisory re-organization in steel plant (new roles and exam.)[14]	Use of ERGOM exercises.[15] Management Grid course.[16] Likert's System 4[17]	Standardized office provided for foremen[17]	Application of PA Council selection system[18] Use of qualification system for foremen[14]	Use of NEBSS programme.[19] Univ of Purdue programme.[20] ALI programme[21] ISM programme[22]	Use of TWI.[23] JIVTA training programme.[24] Kepner-Tregoe programme.[25] Lab training for foremen[26]
III	Analysis of critical incidents followed by recommendations of support for foremen.[27] EITB recommendations.[28] Study of housing maintenance[29]	ITS Orange Book approach,[30] Philips organization change approach.[31]	Critical incident study of disturbances[27]	Building industry foremen study and recommendations[32]	Nursing and hospital administrators study and experiment.[33] Site management Educational Experiment[34]	ITS Orange Book.[30] Paper Mill Study.[35] Ford Training programme.[36] Shoe training project[37]
IV	Swedish Development Council project[41]	Port Foremen projects[38][40]		Swedish Development Council project[41]		Steel-works project.[39] Port foremen project[40]

2. The *direction* of changes planned in the cases cited may be quite different and indeed contradictory. The directed changes, for example, could be towards greater managerial control. Equally, they might be used by a powerful supervisory union to put pressure on management to change their expectations of supervision. Similarly, the third strategy of work analysis has been used to produce a formalized, bureaucratized system of supervision.[36] More typically, it has been used for precisely the opposite objective: to de-bureaucratize a formal supervisory system.

3. It appears to have been more popular in the past to try to 'improve' supervision by educational and training measures than it has been to try to change selection criteria or the technological environment. Why is this so?

   The most obvious reason is that it is comparatively easy to organize training and educational courses, compared with other areas or routes of change. The ease of starting such courses, however, has often been a trap which has prevented a more fundamental approach from taking place. Much of the frustration previously referred to in this book has arisen from the mistaken judgement that training or education was the easiest way to change supervision.

   A secondary reason for this state of affairs is that managers often try to reshape supervision according to *a priori* judgements (as we discussed in Chapter 1). Such judgements have concerned the personal traits and abilities of supervisors and have been less concerned with their roles. Selection has been seen as a vital strategy for getting younger more qualified men into supervision, but this has often been vitiated by the unwillingness of management to consider any changes in status, promotion or reward systems for supervision. In this respect, Japan contrasts with European cases, as there are several Japanese examples available of radical restructuring of supervisory roles and promotion routes.

4. It seems clear that we urgently required documented evidence of a variety of case histories of various strategies tried in different situations. It has been difficult to draw conclusions from cases when there has been no overall framework to allow comparison. It is hoped that within the suggested framework, such comparisons are now possible, and indeed essential for any real progress in our knowledge.

The following is an example of problem solution (training) approach,[42] containing guide-lines for action.

Seven point plan for a new approach to supervisory training

1. It is important to start from job problems or potential job problems; discussion of training needs or of the direction of training prgrammes is best started at a concrete level. This is by far the most acceptable way in to launching a new training programme and should also give many useful clues as to the perception of training priorities.

2. The training programme should involve supervisors (at various levels) *and* those managers, whether in the line or staff departments, whose role brings them into direct contact and involvement with shop floor problems. Supervisory training cannot be restricted to supervisors alone if it is to be effective. It is probably as important to try to influence the views and perceptions of such managers (particularly those immediately above the supervisory system) as it is to alter or influence supervisory attitudes or behaviour. A fully effective programme, therefore, would include training measures for managers, staff and supervisors, though not necessarily together.

3. There is a basic need for the managers and supervisors involved in the programme to feel that they are fully consulted in the definition of the training. This implies attention to feedback on the course to the trainers and some systematic method of evaluation.

4. The methods used in the approach to training are likely to include a mixture of (*a*) on-the-job discussions about problems between managers and supervisors, (*b*) off-the-job group discussions about work problems, and (*c*) studies of job problems by third parties, to discover some objective information about job situations, which can then be fed back to the group for discussion. The objective of these discussions is to allow reflection on the work experience of supervisors, so that strategies can be made explicit and previous mistakes in judgement can be seen more objectively.

5. This type of programme needs to be started by training officers who act as catalysts in the situation, trying to get the process under way and under its own steam, and helping occasionally to service it.

6. Training of this type is not to be seen as a once-for-all exercise, but as a normal and continuous activity for dealing with work problems. If successful, it should probably not be seen as training at all, but as part of normal consultation on the job among interested parties.

7. Training needs cannot be met all at the same time. It is necessary to proceed step by step, starting with the most urgent priorities. A lengthy period of supervisory work analysis by 'experts' is therefore probably not a good way to launch such a programme. It is better to start with immediate problems, carrying on the discussions about needs at the same time as taking action to start training, or making changes in organization, as appropriate.

Notes and References

1 Etzioni, A. (1961). *A comparative analysis of complex organisations*. The Free Press of Glencoe, New York.

2 Lee, J. (1928). *Dictionary of industrial administration*. Pitman, London.

3 Urwick, L. (1933). Organisation as a technical problem. In *Papers on the Science of Administration*, edited by L. Gulick and L. Urwick. Columbia University Press, New York. (1937), pp. 49–88.

4 March, J. G. & Simon, H. A. (1958). *Organisations*. John Wiley & Sons, New York.

5 CROZIER, M. (1964). *The bureaucratic phenomenon.* University of Chicago Press, Chicago and London.

6 THURLEY, K. E. *et al.* (1969). *First interim report on structure and operation of selected maintenance organisations in the public and private sectors.* Building Management Research Unit, London School of Economics and Political Science (mimeographed). *See* Section 2.

7 Swedish Employers' Association and Swedish Foremen's Union (1969). *Arbetsledare, nutid-framtid.* Stockholm.

8 THURLEY, K. E. & HAMBLIN, A. C. (1962). Report to company under research project 'Systems of supervision' discussed this case (mimeographed).

9 LAWRENCE, K. C. (1962). The next five years in supervisory training. *Personnel Management and Methods*, (June), pp. 22–4.

10 British Productivity Council Film (released in 1961). *The man in the middle.* The story relates how a decision to send supervisors on an external course misfired and creates false expectations of change.

11 GOLDTHORPE, J. H. (1961). La conception des conflits du travail dans l'Enseignement des Relations Humaines. *Sociologie du Travail*, No. 3.

12 SYKES, A. J. M. (1962). The effect of a supervisory training course in changing supervisory perceptions and experience of the role of management. *Human Relations*, (August), pp. 227–43.

13 DAVIS, L. E. & VALFER, E. S. (1966). Studies in supervisory job design. *Human Relations*, Vol. 19, pp. 339–52.

14 OKAMOTO, H. & MORI, G. (1964). op. cit.

15 BASS, B. M. (1961). *Experimenting with manufacturing organisations* (mimeographed).

16 BLAKE, R. (1969). *Grid organisational development.* Addison Wesley, New York.

17 LIKERT, R. (1967). *The human organization.* McGraw-Hill, New York.

18 WIRDENIUS, H. & LÖNNSJÖ, S. (1964). op. cit.

19 THURLEY, K. E. & HAMBLIN, A. C. (1967). *The basis of supervisory training policy.* Pergamon, Oxford. (Also article in *Industrial Training International*, Vol. 2, No. 2, Feb. 1967.) *See also:* HENSON, B. (1967). N.E.B.S.S. A progress report. *Industrial training international*, Vol 2, No. 10 (October).

20 BELMAN, H. S. & HULL, T. F. (1958). Industrial supervisory training at Purdue University. *Training Directors Journal* (October), pp. 37–41.

21 Svenska Arbetsgivareföreningen (1969). General principles of supervisory training (mimeographed in English). (Available from the Swedish Employers' Confederation, Stockholm.)

22 See publicity in *The Supervisor* (now *Supervisory Management*). Institute of Supervisory Management, Lichfield (monthly).

23 There is surprisingly little independent comment available on TWI programmes which are still important in many countries. Descriptions of programmes are available; for example see :

MANGRULKER, G. Y. (1962). Staff training in TISCO (Tata). *Indian Management*, New Delhi, Vol. 1, No. 5 (May–June), pp. 31–2.

WARMAN, P. A. (1962). Supervisory and clerical training in the port industry. *Kenya TWI Topics*, Nairobi, No. 11 (July), pp. 3, 8.
See also for an attempt at evaluation :
CASTLE, P. F. C. (1952). The evaluation of human relations training for supervisors. *Occupational Psychology*, No. 26, pp. 191–205.

24 THURLEY, K. E. & TAWARA, J. (1967). Industrial supervision in Japan and Europe. A research report. *Sangyo Kunren Zasshi* (Industrial Training), Vol. 13, Nos. 5 & 6. Japan Industrial and Vocational Training Association (in Japanese). Programmes are occasionally published by this body in English. They cover a large proportion of external supervisory training courses in Japan. *See also:* THURLEY, K. E. (1967). Industrial training in Japan. *Industrial Training International*, Vol. 2, No. 3 (March), pp. 90–4.

25 EYRE, J. (1969). Training in problem analysis and decision making at Rootes Motors in Coventry. *The Supervisor*, Vol. 20, No. 10 (October), pp. 226–7.

26 BENNIS, W. G. (1966). op. cit. Chapter 8. Also GAUCHET, F., MEIGNIEZ, R. & NODIOT, S. (1961). *Projet d'evaluation des résultats d'une formation appliquée à la maîtrise* (mimeographed). AFAP, Paris.

27 BERGSTEN, G., HAMMARSTRÖM, O. & ROSÉN, K. (1969). *Rapport från undersökning enligt critical incident-metoden av banarbetsledarna vid AB QZ-verken.* Swedish Council for Personnel Administration, Gothenburg (mimeographed).

28 Engineering Industry Training Board (1966). *The training of supervisors.* See also: THURLEY, K. E. & HAMBLIN, A. C. (1967). op. cit.

29 THURLEY, K. E. (1969). *Planned change in bureaucratic organisations.* Paper delivered to Joint Conference on OR, and the Behavioural Sciences (ORS, BPS, BSA, ERA) December. Bedford College, London.

30 MEADE, J. P. de C. & GREIG, E. W. (1966). *Supervisory training – a new approach for management.* HMSO, London. *See also:* JONES, A. (1969). Supervisory training – A critical evaluation of the experiences of the industrial training service. *Industrial Training International*, Vol. 4, No. 2 (February), pp. 66–8.

31 HESSELING, P. (1966). *Strategy of evaluation research.* Van Gorcum, Assen, Netherlands. Chapter 4. *See also:* Personnel and Industrial Relations Division & Technical Efficiency and Organisation Department publication (1969): *Work structuring; a summary of experiments at Philips – 1963 to 1968.* N. V. Philips' Gloeilampenfabrieken, Eindhoven.

32 WIRDENIUS, H. & LÖNNSJÖ, S. (1964). *Functions of supervisors in the building industry.* Stockholm: The National Swedish Council for Building Research, (Foreign Language Series No. 2).

33 GOULD, A. & THORNLEY, P. (1970). Partners in management training. *Industrial Training International*, Vol. 5 (December), pp. 504–10.

34 This is a current experiment (1971–72) being carried out by the Institute of Builders (Site Management Section) in London at a Technical College. Sixteen site management staff are collaborating in a course which is largely

tailor-made from case studies and exercises designed from data collected from the group.

35 WIRDENIUS, H. (1961). *Förmän i arbete*. Swedish Council for Personnel Administration, Stockholm, pp. 76–81.

36 Ford Motor Company (1966). *The professional supervisor*. Course booklet. (The first statement of supervisory agreed responsibilities was published by Ford (U.K.) in 1963.)

37 NIGHTINGALE, M. B. L. (1963). Unpublished report from Clarks Ltd., Street, Somerset, U.K.

38 EAGLE, F. (1970). Group discussions as a contribution to organisational effectiveness. *The Management Teacher*, Vol. 2, No. 3 (September).

39 SACK, J. G. (1961). *Arbetsledarnas ställning i organisationen, arbetsuppgifter, befogenheter, utbildningsbehov m.m.* SKF, Hofors Bruk, Hofors. (Unpublished report.)

40 WELLENS, J. & THOMPSON, M. (1968). The Olson project. *Industrial Training International*, Vol. 3, No. 10, (October), pp. 456–63. *See also:* JACKSON, P. (1970). Ph.D. thesis. University of London. (Example in Chapter 10 of the present volume is taken from this study.)

41 WIRDENIUS, H. (1970). *Experiments with a participation process for the development of the supervisory function in a company. Project outline for the Development Council.* Swedish Council for Personnel Administration, Stockholm (mimeographed).

42 THURLEY, K. E. & HAMBLIN, A. C. (1967). *The basis of supervisory training policy.* Pergamon, Oxford. Chapter 3. (Also found in *Industrial Training International*, Vol. 2, No. 4, April.)

10. *Evaluation of Change*

THE CONCEPT OF EVALUATION

The problem of evaluation is at present under much discussion. In European countries, this interest can be dated by the stimulus given by Project 7/07 of the OECD in 1961, which was reported by Robert Meigniez.[1] That report reviewed the literature and laid down the basis for a common conceptual frame. The literature at that time was largely American, but the work set in motion in 1961 and the relationships established between research workers in different countries have done much to redress the balance. The approach discussed here is closely related to the OECD studies and their aftermath, not least in its underlying philosophy.

The major publication in this field since 1961 is undoubtedly still that of Pjotr Hesseling[2] in 1966 (with the title *Strategy of evaluation research*). It has been discussed by one of the authors;[3] the argument has been put in simpler form for trainers in a CIRF publication;[4] it has been elaborated by Hesseling in a more recent paper[5] and used for a practical guide to training officers.[6] The main Hesseling concept and approach, however, is the basis for most of this discussion. It can be summarized by these propositions:

(a) It is necessary to look at the whole process of change (usually seen as training), as the meaning of 'evaluation' depends on the stage reached and of main interest.

(b) Evaluation can be seen to mean different questions and different criteria and measures according to *who* is evaluating and *for whom* the evaluation is taking place.[7]

(c) There are a large number of techniques available, all have many limitations and have specific rather than general uses.

(d) The idea that one can *prove* the value of a certain type of change is a false one and misleads the efforts of evaluators.

(e) Evaluation should be rather understood as the study of strategy both of research and of planned change, with the objective of building in to the strategy enough data collection to ensure that direction can be controlled and problems immediately recognized.

We have already noted that evaluation of change depends on the strategy used. In particular, it is only with the 'full learning cycle strategies' (III and IV) that evaluation becomes really significant.

In the context of the problem of supervisory change, there are four questions of importance for discussion:

1. Bearing in mind everything written to this point about the complexity and unpredictability of planning change, is it really worth considering? Could one not leave it all to natural evolution?
2. Assuming that intervention is decided upon, how can one check the validity of judgements about the choice of direction?
3. How can the decision on the choice of strategy used be evaluated?
4. How is it possible to decide on a reasonable level of expenditure of resources for the purpose of supervisory change?

Each of these aspects of evaluation will be discussed.

THE CASE FOR INTERVENTION

It is certainly important that the case for changing supervisory systems should not be overstated. In many situations, particularly in the craft industries, supervisors in European industry have learnt their job as an extension of their experience at work. In Britain, for example, a study published by the Institute of Supervisory Management, *Essential facts on the British foreman*,[8] found that:

(a) 42 per cent of shop floor supervisors had been promoted from the same department where they were now holding office;

(b) 43 per cent of the shop floor supervisors said that they had no training provided by the company, i.e. internal training, whilst in their present job.

In a similar survey in Sweden in 1961,[9] it was discovered that:

(a) 78 per cent of shop floor supervisors in the engineering industry had been promoted from the same department and 76 per cent in the steel industry;

(b) 77 per cent of engineering shop floor supervisors said that they had no training in connection with their promotion and 56 per cent in the steel industry.

Is it of *net* benefit to change this situation? How far can we say that systematic selection schemes and comprehensive training programmes improve the performance of supervisors and those supervised?

Arguments for both these policies have usually come from personnel specialists and little concrete evidence has been produced to support their faith. Let us take the example of human relations training again in its European context. Much of the experience in the design of 'human relations courses' in supervisory training has come from the United States. In Europe, certain firms have taken up such courses with great enthusiasm. The typical pattern has been the use of a method-based strategy. A new type of American training technique such as the incident process method or sensitivity training has been introduced with much fervour but this often tails off into lack of support. It can be argued that very often line managers have not really been convinced of the importance of such supervisory training. Within a traditional and stable production system, it may indeed be very reasonable for managers to argue that human relations training is really an optional extra. Similarly, the question of worker discipline and the methods used for grievance could perhaps be left to the common sense and experience of those who have worked together for many years. Some of the evidence from *The supervisor and his job*,[10] carried out in the early part of the 1960s seems to indicate that human relations problems were not important for the supervisors studied.

Nevertheless this argument has some defects. Firstly, if we return to our classification of supervisory situations (Figure 3.1) and consider the tasks of supervisors in *traditional* industry, it becomes apparent that there are considerable differences between the needs of such supervisors in terms of the personnel control which has to be exercised. Whereas it may be true in craft industries that skilled workers need not be supervised closely, it is also true that where there are gangs of unskilled labourers, for example in the docks or in warehouses, few supervisors would argue that they could afford to leave such groups completely to supervise themselves. Argyris[11] found that workers were rejecting any close supervision by foremen and seemed quite satisfied themselves with an impersonal relationship with their supervisors. There are, however, a number of studies which indicate that work groups may reject managerial norms of performance and reject responsibility for dealing with product difficulties if they occur.[12] Supervision is therefore under some pressure to exercise controls over work group behaviour. The work of the Tavistock Institute for Human Relations[13] and of Dr Thorsrud[14] argues for the adoption of *autonomous* work groups, but recognizes that the form these take depends on the technology and that they may have to be deliberately created through the use of, among other methods, training procedures. Training, therefore, may be necessary even if (which is doubtful) all work groups can be made autonomous.

Secondly, there is a considerable problem in mass production industry with the relationship between supervisors and the specialists and staff of functional departments. The organizational problems created by the vast number of components and integrated procedures which are necessary for large mass production often meet a critical threshold in the relationship between supervisors and such specialists. This relationship is certainly affected by the different cultural and educational backgrounds of the personnel concerned. Thus, in Japan one author reports considerable conflict in relationships between management and supervision, but conflict greatly affected by the ages of supervisors and their education.[15] Human relations training in the mass production situation, therefore, might be of value in improving relationships.

A third point comes from the problem of the great power of trade unions in a full employment economy. This has often and rightly been shown to provide many difficulties for supervisors trying to exercise disciplinary powers over the timekeeping of workers and the allocation of tasks and trying to control quality standards. Human relations training might be regarded as useful at least in modifying authoritarian behaviour which may only produce greater conflict.

There is also a growing tendency among companies to promote supervisors at an earlier age. This was shown in *Essential facts on the British foreman*, where the data show that in the preceding five or six years in Britain, supervisors were being increasingly selected in their late twenties or early thirties and introduced to their job through potential supervisory training. This training typically takes the form of courses giving information about the various departments of the company, instruction on the legal responsibility of the supervisor, and guidance on the practical methods of undertaking supervisory work. Such training would appear to help the young supervisor at a very vulnerable period of his induction into his job.

Even more important than this, however, is the realization that until recently a very narrow concept of supervisory training has been accepted by managers,[16] namely that of grafting certain types of supervisory skill on to existing manual skills. Increasing competition between firms has emphasized the necessity for supervisors, even in technical change, to improve the work performance of operatives and plant.

Managers may also consider that supervisors need to be taught how to assess the work load of their subordinates, how to plan and programme the tasks which their sections are carrying out and how to avoid unnecessary waste of effort, plant and operative time, materials, etc. A strong managerial argument could be made, therefore, even within traditional industry, for a deliberate attempt to change detailed tactical behaviour of supervisors on the job. It is very easy to assume that, because a supervisor has previous experience in the job as a worker, he therefore knows how to deal with work crises and to settle work problems on his own section. The very reverse is probably true. The very familiarity with the situation which goes with experience may make such a man conservative in attitudes and may prevent any new critical approach to the task of raising productivity. It is therefore difficult to maintain that new types of supervisory organization and a more critical approach to work problems among foremen *cannot* produce striking changes, even where the situation is one of stability and tradition. Obviously, this type of traditional situation is becoming less and less typical. In most industries in Western Europe technological changes are now being introduced at a very fast rate. Traditional industries, such as the boot and shoe industry, have changed beyond recognition, in the last ten years. There is no need to go to the dramatic examples of electronics or the chemical industry to find situations in which supervisors are having to deal with radically new types of machinery, completely new staff relationships and new types of pay systems, such as that of measured day rate schemes.

These arguments, therefore, lead to the conclusion that the reassessment of traditional supervisory systems is likely to be forced on managements in many, if not all, industries. Something has to be and will be done to and for supervision. If this is seen as unimportant compared with changes in industrial relations and managerial performance, this seems likely to be because of the lack of ideological significance of such changes, apart from the declining importance of the 'supportive' philosophy of Likert and Ann Arbor. In reality, such changes could be of profound importance for European society, in determining the possibilities for the extension of democratic controls and personal freedom in many industrial situations.

Little has been said in the discussion to date about the integration of an approach to changing supervision with other broader objectives of management, such as management development and manpower planning. It can be argued that supervisors receive attention because of their relative weakness in internal and national political power. It is an easy place for staff departments and training boards to start their training plans. The effect of this, however, could be to 'overdevelop' supervision in the sense that foremen may come to expect special treatment and aspire to unrealistic promotion possibilities, given the aspirations and power of other occupational groups. Isn't it possible, therefore, that this approach, if carried out, could lead to serious organizational conflict?

In considering this objection, it has to be admitted that there *is* a danger, as with all approaches, of concern and emphasis moving to obsession and fixation. It is certainly true that it is dangerous for managements to concentrate on supervisory development, without considering the implications for the status and career development of other groups of employees. It is also true that changes in the effectiveness and cohesiveness of supervisory systems will have effects on the power balance of the various groups within a work organization and certainly could lead to new conflicts. None of these problems, however, amount to any real evidence against the policy of trying to bring about changes in supervisory role behaviour and attitudes. They are implications of the policy and not arguments against it.

The reasons for this lie in the naïvety of the concept of 'over-development' for supervisors. This idea is based on the acceptance of the traditional routes of promotion to supervision from the shop floor or junior technical staff positions. These promotion routes have been limited in that the assumed 'ceiling' has been that of a senior foreman or, more rarely, a line position in middle management. It seems clear that the other side of the familiar complaint of foremen that they 'are not really members of management' is the usually unexpressed view of managers that foremen may be quite satisfactory for limited responsibilities but are unlikely to be capable of higher things. Supervisory training for the present job can be encouraged, and for this purpose, the job specifications of supervisors and their training needs have to be agreed between each supervisor and his boss.[17] The introduction of any systematic method of promotion and selection for supervisors, however, which includes some formal test of abilities or uses formal qualifications, is already a threat to tradition, in that aspiration levels of candidates who have been successful are already likely to have been raised by the experience. In reality, one suspects (although no conclusive evidence is available yet) that supervisors, industrial and commercial, are particularly likely to be among those who have adjusted their aspiration level upwards since the Second World War.[18]

It is therefore naïve to imagine that young supervisors of the present will be content with a career restricted to a few rungs of the supervisory ladder.

At the moment in many European countries, some firms are experimenting with the use of university and other technically qualified graduates in the roles of supervisors. The American experience in this matter has been examined and discussed by Ken Hopper.[19] The overall proportion of such supervisors is still small, but the trend is likely to be upwards. It is clearly highly convenient to provide for shop-floor experience for future senior managers in this way. The implications for the supervisory role, if this ever becomes the standard practice, is in the direction of programming the supervisory role. Graduates with little experience can hardly be expected or trusted to take many decisions which at the moment, perhaps by default, are still taken by shop-floor supervision. This point is less valid for technical decisions, and is strongest in the organizational sphere. If it is desired to keep a number of crucial decisions within the supervisory system, then there may be some conflict between the use of the supervisory role as a training ground for higher management and the requirements for supervisors with capacity for such decisions.

The points raised in this objection, therefore, lead us to an emphasis on the importance of planning supervisory development schemes within an overall policy governing management development, appraisal and salary matters.

An opposite argument may, however, also be expressed. The 1960s have seen an increased tendency for supervisors to be organized by trade unions, along with other white-collar workers. Where supervisors are already strongly unionized, as in Scandinavian countries, the unions may resist an approach which in several ways will threaten the traditional role and status of meister and foremen. Where manual worker unions or white-collar unions are engaged in a struggle for the organization of supervisors, as in the steel industry in the United Kingdom,[20] there would seem to be little chance of obtaining collaboration in a more 'rational' and comprehensive set of changes.

There are two tendencies which tend to be confused in this problem:

(*a*) The development of 'white-collar' trade unionism.
(*b*) The development of supervision as a 'professional' role.

In the first case, one can inquire as to the causes of the growth in trade union membership among supervisors in recent years in Britain and other European countries. It is, of course, true that in Sweden and other Scandinavian countries supervisory unions have existed for many years. In Britain, craft unions have normally kept supervisors within membership after promotion to foremen. However, full employment and technical change have both combined together in situations where foremen have previously been unorganized to threaten the traditional attitude of neutrality. Many complaints have been made since the Second World War about the problem of the relative decline in supervisory pay differentials compared with workers' earnings. The growth of company schemes for fringe benefits for workers has threatened other relative advantages for a man who has achieved a supervisory position. Lastly, in cases of redundancy, it may be true that many of the workers have had more consideration from management, because of their trade union membership, than their supervisors. In such a situation, supervisors can easily feel that they are rather unprotected without union membership.

The growing tendency to see supervisory roles as a special type of job with unique characteristics can be traced to the effect of several different factors. Primarily, there seems to be an emerging consciousness among supervisors of common difficulties and problems; agreement that supervisors nearly everywhere are in an unsatisfactory position in a firm. The young supervisor taking up the job after promotion from being a manual worker after a few years' work experience often perceives the role in a manner quite distinct from that of a person who is promoted after twenty to thirty years' service. The former sees the job as the first rank of the promotion ladder to management. As we have seen, systematic and formal supervisory selection schemes tend to have the effect of marking out supervisory roles as a distinct type of job, distinguishing them from those of both workers and other types of management. This leads to some demand for 'professional' recognition, either in industry as a whole (the Institute of Supervisory Management) or in particular trades. (The various associations within local government in the UK are good examples.) The results of the growth of the 'professional' concept of supervision and of the 'trade union' concept tend to go in the same direction – towards organization of supervisors in specific interest groups. Although the total numbers in British industry of supervisors organized in trade unions or professional associations probably do not make up more than 30–40 per cent at the outside, this percentage appears to be rapidly on the increase.

If the introduction of change is to be successful, these facts cannot be ignored. It is impossible to train supervisors adequately if there are fears as to security of employment or severe lack of satisfaction as to relative pay. There seems to be no necessary problem for managers in accepting the fact that in many situations in future supervisors will be organized collectively and will negotiate collectively for conditions of employment, pay increases and job rights. Security of employment, adequate salaries and good career prospects for supervisors may all have to be accepted by managers before any planned changes for supervision can stand any chance of success. Conversely, there may be little value in attempting to negotiate with supervisory trade unions if supervisors are remaining within their traditional roles and if there is no attempt to help and train supervisors to carry out their jobs more successfully.

In Sweden, where the SALF (Foremen's Union) has a record of acceptance of schemes of training and systematic selection, there is now some evidence of radical rethinking of supervisory organizational role systems needed by new technologies.[21]

If we wish to redesign salary scales of supervisors, there is some need to carry out systematic job analyses of the supervisory role at each level. Job analyses, of course, do not answer the problem by themselves. Decisions have to be made as to the relative merits and importance of different aspects of the various tasks. Appraisal of the individual approach of each supervisor to his job and his performance in meeting job targets may also be necessary. It seems logical that any new pay structure, if it is to be successful, should be related to career routes and training programmes which may develop.

A further point which may be raised by managers, and which is connected with the question of unionization, is the problem of supervisory loyalty. Many writers on management and training practitioners have argued that the crucial problem for supervisors is to detach them from identification with workers and to inculcate in them a new loyalty to management. This is a far too simple view. In the future, there seems a strong case for arguing that an efficient management system will be seen to be pluralist rather than authoritarian in structure. This means that there will be room within management for many groups who hold at least two types of obligation, first to their professional reference group and secondly to their organization. The professional consciousness may include some wider social responsibilities. It seems much more likely that supervisors will be persuaded to drop conservative attitudes and to be more positive in their response to technical and organizational change if they are encouraged by management *to have pride in their own role and to see themselves as a special group organizationally and collectively.* The tendency to try to bind supervisors to loyalty to a particular management may only serve to cover up the development of considerable informal 'underground resistance' to the purposes and policies of senior management.

In sum, from several points of view, it appears that intervention in the supervisory question is likely to became more and more necessary. It should be clear that supervision, however, is very far from being a purely managerial problem. On the contrary, it affects a large number of groups and interests in industry and commerce.

EVALUATING THE CHOICE OF DIRECTION

We have argued two propositions which are crucial to this problem. First, it was said that motivation to change comes from the perception of a gap between the actual situation and the potential situation. This means that motivation rests on a set of selective perceptions, clearly dependent on values and beliefs. The second point is that strategies and points of entry to change rest on the power situation and the culture of the organization and society in question. It follows that decisions on the choice of direction of change must be also greatly affected by the perceptions, values and relative power of those taking the decision. In organizations where social distance is minimal, where consensus values exist, where 'communications' are seen as good, and where conflict is seen as limited to the personal level, it can be hypothesized that the choice of direction is easily determined. The question here is more one of stimuli to move at all, as discussed in our last section. The pressure to move may well be mainly from external sources. In the opposite case, of 'bureaucratic' organization,[22] with large areas of potential conflict between perceived interest groups, there is much difficulty in diagnosing the 'best' direction of change. No group has access to all the necessary information; all are prisoners of their own perceptual sets. Evaluation here means providing for continuous review of decisions to move in particular directions. It means both the design of relevant data collection and the provision for discussion. Three examples may be of use here.

In the first case, quoted by Warr, Bird and Rackham,[23] the managers of a chemical company wanted to find out the likely effects on supervision of proposed changes in work procedures. Discussions had been held on the changes with all personnel concerned, but supervisors and managers were both asked, by a short questionnaire, to name the areas of work where they thought that changes would have to take place and where training for supervisors was necessary. There were considerable differences between managers and supervisors in the replies, showing differences in priorities and perceptions of reality. Thus another problem was added to the one perceived by management as the salient one in the first instance.

The second case is a research example. A study of the effects of supervisory leadership by Rosen[24] led to a decision to switch supervisors between sections according to work group preferences detected in an earlier phase of the study. This was done by management edict (against some opposition from foremen), supposedly quite separately from the research project, i.e. as a normal management decision. Data were collected on productivity, workers' preferences on groups, their judgements on the foremen (by scale ratings) and their criteria for such judgements. Major shifts in these measures, before and after the experiment, were detected. In examining the significance of these data, however, Rosen was forced to widen his study to deal with situation factors. He fell back on a 'system equilibrium' model to explain the changes, although he claims the part played by supervisory leadership to be important. It appears to be a successful case of using strategy I, but alternative directions of change are not considered (presumably because the research objectives were priorities).

Our third example is given in detail, partly because it is a fairly rare case of Strategy IV which has been documented, partly because it illustrates the type of evaluation possible in such situations. The summary has been written by the research worker in question, Dr P. Jackson.[25]

THE OLSEN STUDY

F. Olsen Lines Ltd. is a major international shipping organization. That part of the organization with which we shall be concerned is essentially the Port Terminal Berths based at Millwall Docks, London. The shipping lines using these berths at Millwall are primarily engaged in short-sea traffic, the most important line carrying perishable food cargo and passengers between the Canary Islands and Millwall. The other lines using Millwall are the North Sea Services and the Mediterranean Services.

During the winter of 1966–7 the organization, which is heavily committed to a unit load concept of through transportation (i.e. all cargo palletized) decided to build a new berth ('P' Berth) at Millwall Docks to be ready for the summer of 1967. The unit load system also necessitated, apart from a new berth, new ships with side-port loading and discharge, requiring totally different cargo-handling techniques.

As far as London is concerned then, the organization now controlled two berths, Canary Wharf and 'P' Berth, both situated in Millwall Docks with a distance of approximately half a mile between them.

It was clear to Olsens from the start that the traditional precedent-bound labour force with its maximum protective practices, casual system and fluctuating wages would not permit fully effective time-saving in the way that a unit load system could optimally give. For this reason senior management in London decided that the quickest way to overcome these labour problems was to 'buy the book'. The existing labour force, 250 strong, was then decasualized, in the sense that every man was offered a Terminal Agreement Contract which ensured a salary of £29 10s. per week plus overtime. The average take-home pay for a dock worker, including piecework, bonuses and overtime, before September 1967 was £25 10s. In September 1967, decasualization became operative for the Port transport industry as a whole.

The organizational structure on the Berths at that time was as follows:

Senior Management

Superintendent	Superintendent
Canary Wharf	'P' Berth
5 Supervisors	5 Supervisors

250 Dock Labour Force

It was precisely at the point of the Work Force Terminal Agreement described above being signed that the senior manager at Olsens contacted the Training Division of the National Ports Council.

The major problems as defined by senior management at that time were as follows:

1. The supervisors were working as individuals rather than as a team.
2. The supervisors would not accept that they were an integral part of the management hierarchy.
3. The intergroup rivalry between the two berths (Canary Wharf and 'P' Berth), which was a result of previous status differences, was having a detrimental effect on the work output.

The negotiations

Having been given the apparent problem areas as seen by senior management, the major problem for the training consultant and the research worker, after negotiating the project design, was to produce some form of quantifiable, factual evidence on the performance of the individual supervisors and, indeed, of the management team as a whole. The objective of this preliminary data-gathering exercise was essentially twofold. Firstly, to try to obtain a 'neutral' picture of what was going wrong in the organization and the possible causes of any weaknesses found, and, secondly, to attempt to provide data for feedback purposes to the management group on their job performance.

It was agreed initially that in order to achieve these objectives the training consultant and the research worker should meet the supervisory team as soon as possible. At this first meeting (with no member of senior management present) the training consultant explained to the team that senior management felt that the performance of the management team could be improved. He further stated that senior management recognized the inherent difficulties of the supervisory team in terms of the technological changes that were currently taking place and had cited the lack of experience within the operational personnel in the new methods being utilized as a possible cause. Certain specific difficulties were then pointed out that were apparently arising through individual supervisory inconsistencies regarding the working of the new agreement, and finally the consultant explained that he had been called in to attempt to define and overcome some of these organizational problems as defined.

Initially it was obvious, the consultant argued, that objective data were required on the performance of the supervisors, in order to put the management view into perspective. To establish the scope of this particular part of the study and determine the types of information needed, a list of objectives was drawn up at this meeting which delineated the specific, immediate results desired.

These objectives were essentially as follows:

1. To develop a practical concept of the supervisor's role in the management structure.
2. To assist in the development of job specifications for the supervisory jobs.
3. To establish criteria for the evaluation of performance of supervisors.

The analysis also showed that, in addition to the original problem areas that management recognized, supervisors were also expected to cope with a number of factors over which they had limited control. These could be summarized as :

1. Organizational difficulties:
   (*a*) uncertainty about actual duties and responsibilities;
   (*b*) poorly defined lines of communication;
   (*c*) lack of clearly defined and acceptable organizational objectives.
2. Work difficulties:
   (*a*) equipment shortages and inadequacies;
   (*b*) problems caused by other organizations over which there was no direct control (customs, merchants, etc.).
3. Labour problems:

(a) lack of responsibility shown by work force;

(b) lack of skill on the part of the work force in basic handling techniques;

(c) the change from a piecework incentive system to a high timework one required much more direction of labour.

Once having obtained this data, the problem now was to decide the priority on objectives for change and the means by which these objectives could be attained. The defining of the change objectives was made after a complex series of 'give and take' meetings between senior management, the trainer and the researcher. The major point to be made within these objectives is that only those changes envisaged which could be measured and which were defined in terms of their measurement were accepted by the research worker as meaningful change objectives. The result was the following list:

Change objectives

(a) To demonstrate an increase in the openness of communications between supervisors and senior management. This to be measured in terms of a questionnaire rating.

(b) To demonstrate a reduction in (i) the number of critical incidents arising between senior management and the supervisory team; (ii) the percentage of differences in perception of these critical incidents between senior management and supervisory team. This objective to be measured in terms of observation and interview.

(c) To demonstrate a change in the attitude of the supervisors to work and to subordinates. This to be measured through both attitudes questionnaire and interview.

(d) To demonstrate a change in the supervisors' perception of job requirements. This to be measured through rating scales.

(e) To demonstrate a change in the work force attitude to work at the new berth. This to be measured by a random sample of structured questionnaire individually supervised.

(f) To demonstrate a change in the perception of the work force in terms of the quality of supervision in the organization. This to be measured through a structured questionnaire individually supervised.

(g) To demonstrate an increased effectiveness in group decision-making and pre-planning. This to be measured in terms of the amount of information brought to meetings, the efficiency of the process of decision-making and the acceptance of the implications of decisions by those concerned, measured three months after the decision had been taken.

(h) To demonstrate a decrease in manning costs as a result of the above. This to be measured in terms of an increase in tons per man per hour loaded and discharged at the two berths. The analysis should be made separately for each of the lines using London Millwall in order to show specific output trends.

Training methods

The question remaining now was how the change objectives as stated might be most effectively achieved. It seems clear from the research evidence available that the concept of internal, vertical organization work groups employed on problem-solving discussions similar to that described and developed by Thurley and Hamblin in their seven-point plan for supervisory training was likely to be most useful. It was intended that by using this training method the supervisors at Olsens could discuss and decide on 'optional strategies' in dealing with their problems.

Following on this decision a second meeting between the supervisory team, the training consultant and the research worker was arranged. The process of investigation being envisaged for tackling particular supervisory difficulties was then discussed and agreed to be essentially threefold. Firstly, the objective information collection on individual job performance had to be continued. Secondly, the information thus collected should then be fed back to the supervisory team alone at weekly meetings in as meaningful and complete a way as possible. Thirdly, the supervisory team function would then be to discuss and work through the information given to them in order to determine possible solutions to major areas of difficulty, with the help of the consultant. Full confidentiality of any information given to the research worker was agreed and the consultant explained that any discussions or decisions taken at the meetings would not be reported to management without their consent.

It was emphatically stressed at this point, that any learning, development or changes that might result from these meetings would be totally the responsibility of the supervisory team. The training consultant would not be making recommendations for change, he would simply be steering the information available to the team for decision-making purposes. The purposes of the meetings would be:

(a) To identify problems facing the work group system and the reasons for their existence.
(b) To invent possible solutions to the problems in the form of needed system changes.
(c) To plan implementations of these solutions through regular, and newly constructed channels.

Results

After three months, the supervisors asked the senior management to be present at the meetings.

The weekly meetings have now (1969) been in existence for fifteen months. Apart from these weekly meetings, the whole management team have spent two week-ends on the south coast to give themselves more time for discussion of particular problems. Some twenty-five major policy decisions in terms of methods of work have been made. So far as the original change objectives are concerned, the results are approximately as follows:

Openness of communications

Significant positive difference between group mean scores taken after one month and after six months. No statistical difference between the measures taken after six months and after twelve months.

Conflict incidents

(a) Management/Supervisor. Significant decrease in both the number of incidents and the percentage of disagreement on their effects.

(b) Supervisor/Supervisor. An initial increase in both the number and difference in perception followed by a significant decrease in both these measures.

(c) Supervisor/Work Force. An increase in both the number and the percentage of disagreement between the two occupational levels.

Attitudes

Significant changes in attitudes towards the senior management have taken place. No apparent differences in attitudes towards subordinates or the work itself.

Job perception

In the first measure taken the supervisors said that technical skills (e.g. rigging a ship) were most important in their job followed by social skills (i.e. ability to motivate the labour) followed by conceptual skills (i.e. decision-making or solving problems). The same measures taken after nine months showed that technical skills were still seen as the most critical requirement – followed by conceptual skills and finally social skills.

Work force attitudes

The work force attitudes to work on the new Berth have changed positively. Attitudes to the Work Units have not changed significantly and attitudes towards styles of supervision have changed to some small degree (*see* objective F).

Work force perception of supervisors

No significant differences. However, changes have been seen, to some extent, in the area of 'initiating structure' as opposed to 'consideration', i.e. best supervision was seen as 'handling emergencies well' or 'planning the work method well' as opposed to 'spending more time with the 'work force'.

Decision-making

The essential difference as measured with a technique described by P. Hesseling[26] was an apparent increase in effectiveness of the time spent on decision-making for the first twelve months. There has now followed a gradual *decrease* on the effectiveness measure over a period of three months.

Output

Perhaps the critical one. Two of the five lines have had an increase in output of approximately 0·2 tons per man hour (approximately 12 per cent) over the fifteen months. One line had an increase of 0·15 tons per man hour and on the other two lines positive changes between 0·05 and 0·1 tons per man hour.

Comment

In all cases the problem for the person or group steering the change is to decide *when* the feedback information is decisive (so that a change of direction is merited) and, necessarily with this, *how* the validity of the feedback data could be tested. This clearly underlines the virtue of using several different forms of data collection.

EVALUATING THE CHOICE OF STRATEGY

We should face, at this juncture, the problem raised by the abstract concepts used in discussing our various strategies. Is it really practical?

There may indeed be a reaction which can be expressed by the argument that few trainers or consultants, in the real world, could afford to indulge themselves in such elaborate academic concepts and strategies. Supervisors, as we have noted, tend to live with immediate problems and in the midst of urgent crises. Action often has to be taken quickly and results have to be achieved. Anybody, it could be argued, can draw up ideal strategies for ideal situations. The problems of training and selecting supervisors require more precise guide-lines: programmes spelt out in detail, with practical manuals, to assist at every stage. Such programmes should be presented with the evidence that they do and can produce demonstrable payoffs in terms of improved supervisory performance.

This objection, therefore, can be summarized by saying that a general approach, with the emphasis on choice and judgement, is both unrealistic and academic. Detailed prescriptions are necessary before the vast bulk of managers and consultants will take the approach seriously. Clearly, this is a fundamental objection and has to be answered if the approach outlined is to be accepted.

The case against reliance on detailed prescriptions (which are clearly easier to handle and sell to customers) rests on the nature of supervisory work actions and the factors affecting it. It has been argued above that there is an enormous amount of variety in the nature of supervisory tasks and behaviour, i.e. between societies, industries, companies, factories and work groups. This variety is caused by the large number of variables which may affect behaviour, perceptions, effects flowing from supervisory action and criteria applied to that action. This variety of situation makes it difficult to rely on a universal set of prescriptions for the solution of problems.

There is, however, a further point which strongly reinforces this conclusion. If variety was the only problem, then after a lot of research it might be possible to determine a set of situations in which detailed prescriptions could be made. This was indeed one of the assumptions behind earlier drafts of this book. It now appears, however, that we are generally underestimating the lack of predictability about supervisory action and its effects as well as its variety. This unpredictability is based on two main factors:

(*a*) The considerable lack of any adequate social science theory to use for the purpose of making detailed predictions for particular situations.
(*b*) The essentially subjective nature of the data involved in any exercise in diagnosis.

We have tried to show that supervisory action depends, in the last resort, on the perceptions of individuals on their objectives, on the threats to those objectives by those around them, on their estimates of what they can and should do in each set of events. In a word, it depends on their reading of the situation. Anybody attempting to predict such readings, will have to rely on their judgement, based on the 'local' experience of such men and women in previous situations. We have every reason to believe that it is difficult to develop objective measures of judgement on the part of those directly involved with events.

This unpredictability is further supported by recent discussions of decision theory in which a number of situations in which future action is fundamentally indeterminate have been cited.[27] We are left therefore with the knowledge that we have to deal with a large variety of fairly unpredictable supervisory situations. To apply detailed prescriptions to these would itself be highly unrealistic. A detailed prescription implies that there is a reasonable chance of knowing the effects of the medicine used. As we do not have this knowledge, our only practical course of action is to help those who have to exercise judgement by showing them a series of crude 'maps', with possible routes across the difficult terrain. This is precisely the purpose of our so-called general approach, with the use of diagrams, lists of possible variables, and ideal-type strategies.

The choice of strategy is likely to be made in terms of the expectations and training of those concerned with innovation. It is important to emphasize that even if the 'cookbook' approach is rejected, it is not necessary to go to the other extreme and accept that *any* strategy is as good as another for a given situation. On the contrary, it is likely that there are considerable payoffs available from the use of one strategy rather than another. Care is necessary in taking a decision about the use of a strategy so that, if possible, there should be a systematic comparison of the costs and benefits of each approach. This takes us to our fourth question, namely, systematic evaluation of strategies: how can one decide on appropriate resources for use in such change strategies?

We can first discuss the possibility of making some type of cost/benefit analysis for each strategy.

COSTS/BENEFITS OF VARIOUS CHANGE STRATEGIES

It is necessary to distinguish between various types of costs and negative and positive effects of any given set of changes. (Figure 10.1.)

We are reminded in Figure 10.1 that the evaluation of costs and benefits depends on the personal criteria used. We can compare the different viewpoints on the benefits following change directly with the four major types of criteria shown in Figure 6.2. It follows that the effects of change could be evaluated positively from one viewpoint and negatively from another. It is also possible

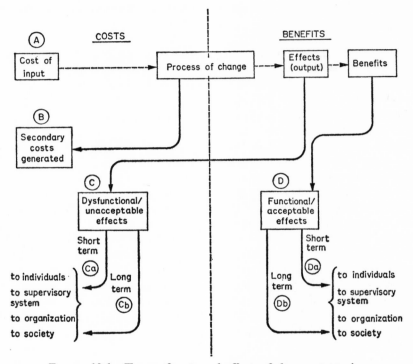

FIGURE 10.1   Types of costs and effects of change strategies

that the effects could be seen as positive in the short run and negative in the long run, and vice versa. These points show that the cost/benefit equation is not a simple question of measurement and addition. The results will vary according to the person or group making the equation.

If we are considering how one might try to set up such cost/benefit equations in practice, it is fruitful to try out the method first on the ideal-type strategies discussed above. Figure 10.2 shows the types of costs and benefits which may accompany a use of each of the four ideal strategies. This diagram illustrates very clearly the different characteristics of each of the strategies.

We could summarize these characteristics as in Table 10.1.

It will be noted that a rational decision on the use of the four strategies can only be made if certain information is known about the situation to which it is to be applied, namely:

	(A) COST OF INPUT	(B) SECONDARY COSTS	(Ca) SHORT TERM DYSFUNCTIONAL EFFECTS	(Cb) LONG TERM DYSFUNCTIONAL EFFECTS	(Da) SHORT TERM FUNCTIONAL EFFECTS	(Db) LONG TERM FUNCTIONAL EFFECTS
Directive or bargaining	Minimal	In case of bargaining could demand management/union time and resources	Resistance possible / Also power struggle → / Withdrawal / Misplaced goals	High risk of lack of maintenance of change / Action may be inappropriate	Speedy action to meet perceived problem / Demonstration effect (of power)	Minimal
Method based	Predictable large or small payments to external organization	Some consumption of staff (functional management time) / Otherwise low	Risk of inappropriate action / Probably low overall effects	Backlash after perceived failure / Withdrawal / Intrench hostilities	Quick stimulant → / Could be individual learning situation	If successful multiplier effect
Work analysis	High investment of time and resources difficult to predict	High consumption of supervisory and management time	Possible irritation at investigation / Frustration with lack of understanding of strategy	Delays between investigation and action	Scientific appeal / Low risk of disappointment as aspiration level low	Possibility of genuine long term change relevant to situation Learning possible
Problem centred	Small investment in supervisory and management time (controllable)	Gradually increasing consumption of management/ supervisory time / Unpredictable effects	Risk of frustration if partially successful / Increase in open conflict possible	Possibility of partial change strategy omitting crucial areas	Relevant action perceived / Motivation may be stimulated	Possibility of genuine long term change in difficult conflict-ridden situations

Key: ⟶ Effect carried over from short to long term period

FIGURE 10.2 Costs/benefits of four ideal type strategies

TABLE 10.1

Contrasting characteristics of each strategy

	Cost/benefit comparison	*Appropriate situation*
Directive or bargaining	Low input costs; pay-off according to power situation	Where power is acceptable (management or union)
Method based	Moderate input costs; high risk of negative pay-off, but some chance of considerable benefits	Where risk can be absorbed e.g. large company
Work analysis	High input costs; low chance of short run effects (positive or negative), moderate chance of high long term pay-off	Where resources are available for long term investment in change
Problem solution	Small initial input costs, rising gradually over time; some immediate positive pay-off possible, chance of considerable negative and positive pay-off in long run	Where immediate resources are limited, but changes are very necessary

(*a*) The importance of change *vis-à-vis* the *status quo*, as perceived by the various parties in the situation.

(*b*) The perceived urgency of achieving benefits in the short or long run.

(*c*) The capacity of one party to impose its solution on the others (or for a coalition).

(*d*) The relative size of resources available, in the short or long run.

To repeat, it is not possible to decide on the use or non-use of any of these strategies by examining the strategy itself. The crucial problem is to *relate* a strategy to a diagnosis of a supervisory situation.

It follows that we cannot be sure that any strategy of change (in Simon's language[28]) will be an optimal or even a satisfying solution. Our previous discussion of costs and benefits showed the type of factors to look at and the different characteristics of each of the various strategies. There is no guarantee that it pays to introduce changes – for any of the parties concerned. One can only emphasize the type of calculations that have to be made at the beginning of any strategy of change and the importance of using a strategy which has a built-in strategy of evaluation. Bearing in mind the problem of unpredictability, it would seem to be more important to proceed with a strategy in which periodically the costs and benefits are compared than with a strategy in which such calculations are carried out *only* prior to the change taking place.

PROBLEMS OF THE SMALL COMPANIES AND ISOLATED SUPERVISORS

It may seem an objection to the above argument that, realistically, it is impossible to expect small personnel departments to carry out any large-scale programme of analysis and training. Many companies with less than a thousand personnel can only afford one or two members for a personnel department and possibly the same number of work study officers. Small companies cannot afford, in many cases, to have any specialists of this type. Are we therefore arguing that this is an approach that can only be used by a large company? If so, this would seem to mark a severe limit to its usefulness.

If we return to Table 10.1, it will remind us that one answer to our problem lies with the type of strategy used. The small organization would find the first or fourth strategy more suitable than the second or third, because the latter require resources beyond their command. In traditional industrial situations, it may be that the first is the simplest and easiest approach to use. The fourth strategy recommends itself where changes are urgently required but are unlikely to appear from the existing power structure and patterns of thinking. It is really with this method that we have to be concerned about the supply of internal and external change agents. There might appear to be three main sources:

(*a*) The training of line managers to carry out supervisory work analysis.
(*b*) The use of consultants from private organizations, training boards, the Industrial Training Service, the Swedish P.A. Council, etc.
(*c*) The use of independent staff experts from other companies (including group training schemes).

Line managers could be trained, undoubtedly, to carry out certain of the techniques which have been outlined above. Accurate measurements of perception and behaviour are necessary, and judgement of work requirements, say, even for a person who is extremely familiar with the work of his subordinates, can easily be biased. Evidence from the Swedish studies shows that estimates and observation undertaken by superiors of supervisors' performance was highly inaccurate.[29]

It seems necessary in the small and medium-sized company, if change agents are to be employed (to lead discussions and evaluate data), that some independent person should be used. It is possible that peer group perceptions and self-recorded data by supervisors themselves could be used as a basis for discussion, provided an independent person used such data and assessed the relative bias of the information given. Such an independent person could be a training or work-study officer from another branch of a large company; a consultant from a commercial consultant organization; a training officer from a training board; or 'a professional job analyst'. He might also be on the local technical college staff or employed on a group basis by a number of companies. His task would be similar to that of any person, say from the training department in the larger company, whose job essentially is to act as a *catalyst* for the various processes to take place. His function would consist of convincing management and supervisors concerned that a systematic and objective analysis of the situation was worth while; that it was important to investigate and measure behaviour objectively; that mutual discussions could take place comparing jobs and roles within the assumptions of policy and organizational procedures as laid down in company policy. It would also be the role of the independent person to persuade supervisors and managers by mutual agreement to set performance targets and to analyse the training needs which seemed to be required if these targets were to be met. Professional advice might also be necessary to demonstrate ways of dealing with the training or other needs exposed by this analysis.

In short, therefore, the same change routes as are applicable to the large organization could be applied to the smaller one even if there were only one or two supervisors to be considered. The relative freedom of action of the change agent might be seen in the smaller company to be more restricted, but this is not necessarily so. Supervisory, operative and managerial roles might also have to be considered together.

THE PROBLEM OF THE AVAILABILITY OF CHANGE AGENTS

The adoption of strategies III and IV (work analysis and problem solution) by many organizations at the same time could clearly lead to a great shortage of change agents. It is already true in the United Kingdom that many of the policies defined under the Industrial Training Act of 1964 are still-born due to shortage of competent training staff. Organizational change programmes in the large companies in the United Kingdom are also running into acute shortage of consultants and are throwing up needs for training programmes for consultants. Are we forced to advocate a large programme for developing change agents on these lines?

The crux of this problem lies in the nature of skills and knowledge required by change agents in the processes of work analysis and decision-making implied by the various strategies outlined. It is clear that the model used in this volume presupposes a social science frame of reference and a scientific methodology. It also presupposes that appropriate changes may take place if the power holders are convinced of the necessity to make changes. We have seen above that even the small organization may require the outsider to help this situation develop. The large bureaucratic organization certainly breeds many defensive attitudes which make the outside view even more of a necessity. This outside view is particularly a 'detached' although necessarily also a biased view, like others in the situation. The ideal change agent, therefore, will combine the approach of a social scientist with the capacity of an engineer to appreciate hard technical facts and constraints, together with the social skills of a group therapist. Such a paragon seems unlikely to exist in the short or even long run.

If we recoil from the foolishness of idealizing the change agent – a favourite habit of social scientists, who may see themselves in the role – we can look at the problem in the same way that we have learned to look at supervision, after the collapse of theories of individual supervisory leadership. We are discussing processes of change and the roles which develop, temporarily, within that process. These roles are interconnected and can be seen as a type of system, again even though this may be a temporary phenomenon. The change agent does not need to be seen as some type of new professional and occupational group, although there are already dangers that this may be perceived as necessary and desirable. Instead, we can envisage the multitude of change situations (under various strategies) throwing up needs for members of that organization to act as innovators and catalysts and evaluators at different times. It is also likely that there will be needs for such inside 'change agents' to act with the help of various outside specialists, trainers and consultants. The prime condition of this happening would appear to be the existence of networks of personal relationships and good communications between those wrestling with the problem inside the organization and the various agencies in the wider society. If such networks exist, then there are many possibilities of finding resources by asking individuals to undertake short-term assignments and to adapt their normal work role. The shortage of change agents does not disappear, but it becomes possible to utilize much existing talent and skill so that some action can be undertaken.

Our problem now seems to lead to three policy implications. There is first a need to develop much better links, personal and organizational, between universities, consultants, companies and public organizations so that more projects can be handled and results compared and evaluated. There are clashes in objectives between these parties but their needs can be demonstrated to be largely complementary.

There is also a need to discuss the problems of supervisory change strategies within a given frame of reference. This book is an attempt to provide such a frame, as well as can be expected with existing theory and levels of knowledge. With the current rate of change in the social sciences, the authors would be the first to accept that this attempt will probably need radical revision within five to ten years. Nevertheless, unless some frame is provided, it becomes difficult to compare cases and draw conclusions from experience, and it is certainly difficult to develop a group of competent and sophisticated change agents who are aware of the variety of approaches possible and the steps in diagnosis which are desirable.

The third implication of the argument is that evaluation must be linked with the approach to change being attempted. In a word, in all cases there should be a conscious attempt to integrate change strategies with evaluation strategies. The type of data collected determines the range of criteria possible for evaluation. The design of the strategy chosen limits the type of data which could be available. The evaluation procedures and conclusions have further effects on the change strategy itself. If failures are recorded and discussed among participants of a change situation, it may have crucial effects on the motivations of those present. Evaluation is *not* a discrete problem. The assumption that it is has undoubtedly been at the root of much abortive discussion on the problem in recent years.

Notes and References

1 Meigniez, R. *et al.* (1963). *Evaluation of supervisory and management training methods.* OECD, Paris.

2 HESSELING, P. (1966). *Strategy of evaluation research.* van Gorcum, Assen.

3 THURLEY, K. E. (1967). Evaluating supervisory and management training. *A.T.M. Bulletin* (December).

4 CIRF (1965). *Training for progress*, No. 4. ILO, Geneva. (Compiled by Hesseling, de Sitter, Meigniez, Nodiot, Gustavsson, Wirdenius and Thurley.)

5 HESSELING, P. (1970). *Evaluation of management training in some European countries.* TEO, N. V. Philips' Gloeilampenfabrieken, Eindhoven (mimeographed).

6 WARR, P., BIRD, M. & RACKHAM, N. (1970). *Evaluation of management training.* Gower Press, London.

7 HESSELING, P. (1966). *Strategy of evaluation research*, p. 67. van Gorcum, Assen.

8 HAMBLIN, A. C. et al. (1963). *Essential facts on the British foreman.* ISM, Lichfield.

9 *Arbetsledarnas rekrytering och utbildning* (Survey of Foremen) (1963). Swedish Council for Personnel Administration and SALF (Swedish Supervisors' Union), Stockholm.

10 THURLEY, K. E. & HAMBLIN, A. C. (1963). *The supervisor and his job.* DSIR, London.

11 ARGYRIS, C. (1960). *Understanding organizational behaviour.* Dorsey Press, Homewood, Illinois.

12 BUCKLOW, M. (1966). A new role for the work group. *Administrative Science Quarterly*, June, pp. 59–78.

13 TRIST, E. L. et al. (1963). *Organisational choice.* Tavistock, London.

14 EMERY, F. E. & THORSRUD, E. (1969). *Form and content in industrial democracy; a study of workers' representation at board level.* Tavistock, London.

15 OKAMOTO, H. & MORI, G. (1964). Nihon no Genba Kantoksha (Workshop supervision in Japan). *Sango Kunren Shriyo*, No. 57 (October).

16 WELLENS, J. (1967). We need to broaden the horizon of supervisory training. *Industrial Training International*, Vol. 2, No. 9 (September).

17 MEADE, J. P. de C. & GREIG, E. W. (1966). *Supervisory training – a new approach for management.* HMSO, London.

18 RUNCIMAN, W. G. (1966). *Relative deprivation and social justice.* Routledge and Kegan Paul, London.

19 HOPPER, K. (1967). The growing use of college graduates in production. *Management of Personnel*, Summer, pp. 2–12.

20 Court of Enquiry (1968). *Report of the Court of Enquiry under Lord Pearson into the dispute between the British Steel Corporation and certain of their employees.* Cmd. 3754, HMSO, London.

21 Swedish Employers' Confederation and Swedish Foremen's Union (1969). *Arbetsledare nutid-framtid*, Stockholm.

22 CROZIER, M. (1964). *The bureaucratic phenomenon*, pp. 61–142. University of Chicago, Chicago and London.

23 WARR, P., BIRD, M. & RACKHAM, N. (1970). *Evaluation of management training*, pp. 33–5. Gower Press, London.

24 ROSEN, N. A. (1970). *Leadership change and work group dynamics: An experiment*. Staples, London.

25 JACKSON, P. (1970). *Organisational change and supervisory effectiveness*. Ph.D. thesis. University of London (unpublished).

26 HESSELING, P. (1966). *Strategy of evaluation research*. van Gorcum, Assen. Chapter 11.

27 AUDLEY, R. J. *et al*. (1967). *Decision making*. BBC, London.

28 SIMON, H. A. (1958). *Administrative behaviour*. 2nd edition. Macmillan, New York.

29 WIRDENIUS, H. (1958). *Supervisors at work*. Swedish Council for Personnel Administration, Stockholm.

11. *The Future of Supervision*

PREDICTING THE FUTURE

Many discussions of the effects of automation refer to the possibilities of radical changes occurring to supervisory roles. Ten years or so ago, Professor Crossman mentioned the changes which he saw as likely to affect supervision in process automation:

> 'The foreman's position tends to become equivocal. If he possesses sufficient technical skill and knowledge, he may act as a roving technical adviser; and if he has also the necessary personal qualities, he may become the accepted leader of an integrated team. But however good he is at managing men, unless he has extensive technical knowledge and experience, he is apt to find himself a fish out of water, merely keeping records and arranging rotas. Where there is a qualified engineer on each shift, it is doubtful whether there is a place for him at all.'[1]

Leavitt and Whisler argued in their study of management in the 1980s[2] that middle management would, in organizations affected by computerized control systems, tend to be replaced by overall co-ordinators, systems analysts and programmers. They forecast a growth in centralized decision-making and in the amount of programmed decision procedures and actions undertaken at lower levels of management. This implies that the traditional autonomy of foremen will finally disappear. This argument finds some support from a case study of the introduction of a computer-controlled production system in an English factory:[3]

> 'For example, the foreman has now no responsibilities or worries concerning the planning of the work in his section for weeks ahead; neither is he responsible for ensuring that the materials, tools, blueprints, etc., are physically available before he issues the work to a specific operative; nor to see that the sections responsible for prior operations are, in fact, keeping up to schedule, in order not to invalidate his own programme. All these facets are now part of the total scheme and no work authorities are issued to him unless all these pre-requisites are satisfied.'

There is also, however, the contrary argument of Professor Zalewski that certain functions of supervision will become more important under automation:[4]

'Co-ordination of specialized tasks will become the prime function of the supervisor, while subordinates will be expected not only to supply information and report progress, but to identify problems and initiate proposals for their solution. Apart from giving orders, the supervisor will supply the general information that enables subordinates to direct their specialized activities towards the fulfilment of organizational objectives.'

Zalewski sees some need for upholding the authority of a supervisor, 'for it is his function of co-ordinating diverse efforts towards a common goal that entitles him to make responsible decisions at a policy level.[5] Zalewski apparently sees this co-ordination role as becoming more critical in automated systems of production because of the greater interdependence of individual operations and decisions.

Can such diverse views be reconciled? Is there any hard evidence either way? The short answer would seem to be that there is not. Individual case studies of automation cannot prove the matter one way or the other. Most such studies are not only not under controlled conditions; they do not compare like with like. If one uses any of the suggested scales or criteria of automation, such as the one proposed by Professor Crossman,[6] it is evident that there may be highly critical differences in the design of certain operations between plans which appear on the surface to be quite comparable. Crossman himself, in this paper, notes that certain changes in supervisory roles might be taking place in process technology with or without automation:

'Consequent on the disappearance from the scene or reduction in numbers of semi-skilled operators, the plant operating team becomes more cohesive, members are more individually responsible, and the role of supervision changes from discipline to technical leadership. However, this is seen in a process plant without automation.'

One might indeed conclude from such examples that the case for associating automation with radical changes in supervisory roles is not proven.

In discussing the future, it is important to accept two basic points which are, in fact, at the heart of the position adopted in this book:

1. Fundamentally, the long-term future is unpredictable, for the reasons set out by Karl Popper[7] and summarized by J. W. N. Watkins:

'The first thesis says that human decisions collectively shape historical events; the second thesis says that it is sometimes impossible for a decision-maker to calculate an optimum solution for his decision problem, and the third thesis says that, where this is the case, it will normally be impossible for a would-be predictor to predict the decision – there may be occasional exceptions to this, but the exceptions cannot become the rule. Hence at least some of the factors which shape future events are unpredictable; hence the future history of mankind is unpredictable. (A stronger argument, due to Popper, relies on the unpredictability of the future growth of human knowledge.)'[8]

2. The effects of previous and current decision-making can, however, be distinguished and these yield trends, i.e. over the immediate and short-term future. These trends may be interrelated, but they may also be contradictory. We will see that the implications for supervision of current technical and social trends are, indeed, contradictory.

Our approach to discussions of the future of supervision must be a realistic one, therefore, and not a collapse into prophecy. It is obvious to all of us that changes are taking place in most areas of society, and supervision is certainly included in this. It is important, therefore, to try to set out some conceptual scheme which can act as a set of guide-posts for those changes. The only logical way to do this would appear to be to use the concepts and 'maps' developed in this book to survey the types of changes taking place in European society and to try to isolate the possible major directions of change for supervisory systems.

SOCIAL CHANGE RELEVANT TO SUPERVISION

We have already noted, in Chapter 1, the development of modern types of supervisory system, through sub-contracting labour groups, towards more bureaucratized systems. We argued there that certain aspects of traditionally perceived foreman roles were still extant and important for understanding supervisory behaviour. The growth of centralized personnel departments and of functional management generally, however, is tending to eat away at the traditional autonomy of foremen. The deliberate moulding of foreman behaviour is being attempted by organizational role definitions, by formal selection and promotion systems, by educational and training programmes. Managements, sometimes governments, begin to adopt conscious policies for changing supervision. Such deliberate programmes, however, do not always reach to objectives perceived by management. Indeed, the actual changes taking place are a compound of deliberate changes, unanticipated consequences of such changes, and unexpected effects from other changes, often outside the control of managers altogether. In particular, there are shifts in values and beliefs and in perceptions of the significance of supervisory roles by supervisors and congruent actors in the work situation, all of which may throw managerial policies out of gear and off target. This can be illustrated by looking again at Figure 2.6 on page 22.

That diagram emphasizes the choice and interrelatedness of the various routes of change for supervisory systems. It shares with all 'systems' models the emphasis on the feedback loops within the system. This is, of course, an important distortion of reality in that it underplays the exchanges across the 'boundaries' of the system and the 'other influences' shown bearing down on the system at the top. The latter represent all types of changes from outside the situation which might affect variables within it. It should be clear that *all* variables and *all* areas are open to change. The primary variables in the situational and individual characteristics boxes are obviously likely to be affected by environmental changes. The dependent variables in the other boxes in the central area are also, however, open to change in that the process of determining effects and behaviour might be subject to general change. The same is true of the routes for intended change. Finally, it is clear that the potential 'boxes' might also be subject to general change from outside the system. If supervisors' perception and values are changing in society at large, then these boxes and the size and gap between the actual and potential might also change.

Without hoping to make a comprehensive list of possible changes, it should be useful to illustrate some of the types of changes which may take place and which may be important for the future of supervision.

In Table 11.1 we list the principal variables in the situation box and show some possible trends.

TABLE 11.1

Possible changes for work situation variables

Variables	*Possible trends*
1. Number and type of subordinates	Reduction in span of control. More female labour. Greater variety in ethnic and nationality groups. Higher educational attainments. Greater mobility of labour.
2. Behaviour of workers	Greater autonomy for work groups demanded. Less acceptance of supervisory authority. More strategic bargaining. Growing preference for leisure.
3. Rewards and sanctions for workers	Smaller number of individual PBR schemes. Common fringe benefits for all staff. Smaller differentials between workers and management. Formalized disciplinary procedures grow in importance.
4. Type of production system	Development of mechanization. Growth in various types of automation (Figure 11.1). Greater risk from mistakes in production decisions. More formalized and structured decisions process. Greater number of shift systems.
5. Rate of technical change	Faster rate of innovations. Greater tendency to bunch changes at different times.
6. Type of supervisory system	Growing number of technician roles. Reduction in number of status levels. Growth in role specialization.
7. Number and type of prescribed supervisory tasks	Two opposing trends – greater rationalization and more effective control systems lead to more programmed tasks, more complex technology *and* pursuit of more ambitious management goals can mean a less programmed role.
8. Rewards and sanctions	Lower differentials with rewards of workers. Job enrichment programmes. Growth in possibility of job mobility as supervisor, so less dependence on organization.

Variables	*Possible trends*
9. Type of management administration system	Further development of specialist management departments. Growth of MBO programmes. Growth of computer based control systems. More printed out data available for supervisors (costs, programme, etc.).
10. Behaviour of superiors	Continued existence of various management styles – possibly greater variety and more role conflict.
11. Values of other supervisors (peers)	Greater variety found in style. Greater role conflict.
12. Trade Union organization	Formalized bargaining procedures more important. Greater recognition of worker representatives role. Greater unionization of supervisors.
13. Level of labour market	Continual labour shortage and continual economy in use of manpower. Greater mobility means constant turnover.
14. Level of demand	Fluctuations continue as international markets become more important.
15. Community restraints	Growing number of legal constraints for supervisory action. Race relations and conservation important areas.

AUTOMATION

A simple reading of this list of possible trends shows the contradictory nature of social change. There is not much indeterminacy, but there are also contradictory trends. Automation is a good example, as it is one in which many writers have assumed that there are social consequences in a given direction. The effects of computers on supervisors have been examined in detail elsewhere,[9] but here we can note that, in Simon's terminology, there is a crucial difference between decision tasks which can be easily programmed and those which are operating with so many unknowns that programmes are impossible to construct. We can indeed assume that computer-based technologies will be able to expand in the variety of tasks which can be attacked in a systematic way. This means that unprogrammed decisions today will perhaps be programmed tomorrow. What has to be remembered, however, is that the frontier of managerial problems travels constantly and that fresh uncharted problems are continually arising. The space programme is a good example of this. As trips to the Moon become commonplace, so other space ventures occupy the time and energy of space managers. It is not possible, therefore, to predict that automation will result in more and more programmed decision systems and in less unprogrammed decision activity. Figure 11.1 shows four types of automation, all of which might affect supervision in different ways.

Popular attention has focused on Situation I, where supervision might be seen as likely to be reduced to monitoring results and carrying out routine procedures. In all the other situations, however, supervisors might play a much more active and responsible role. In Situation II, process supervisors can contribute to the development programme by assisting with plant experiments and observing effects and behaviour of plant; and, by using their detailed knowledge of operative skills and capacity, help in the interpretation of failures and breakdowns. In Situation III, supervisors may well have to carry out precise recording of data in order to feed it back to the computer. Crises and unexpected events cannot be

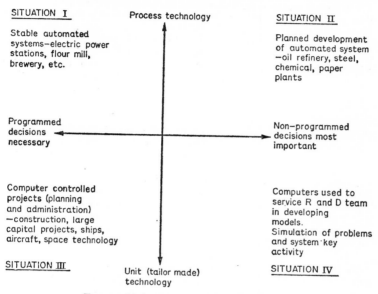

SITUATION I — Process technology

Stable automated systems—electric power stations, flour mill, brewery, etc.

SITUATION II

Planned development of automated system —oil refinery, steel, chemical, paper plants

Programmed decisions necessary ← → Non-programmed decisions most important

Computer controlled projects (planning and administration) —construction, large capital projects, ships, aircraft, space technology

Computers used to service R and D team in developing models. Simulation of problems and system key activity

SITUATION III — Unit (tailor made) technology

SITUATION IV

FIGURE 11.1 Four types of automation

avoided, however, and new skills are required for supervisors to be able to draw the additional data available from the computer for the solution of such problems. It is increasingly recognized that the computerization of planning in construction projects, for example, may increase the responsibilities of supervisors and not diminish them.

Situation IV is obviously in an unprogrammed area and here it is necessary only to assert that supervisory experience may in future be an essential component of such teams, in order to avoid the otherwise inevitable gaps between theoretical reasoning and actual performance. In R & D, one needs a critical awareness of relevant variables and problems, and an ideal team would balance theoretical knowledge and skills with long-term experience and 'grass roots' knowledge.

Our point here is therefore merely to clarify the meaning of the term 'automation' and to restrain any simple deductions from technical change to supervisory behaviour. Further advances of automation are likely to involve all four types of situation. Further, the actual effect on supervision is a product of the way the technical requirements of each situation are perceived and of the way that supervisory roles are perceived and valued. It follows that automation might result in a variety of 'mixes' of different effects for supervisors.

H

THE EFFECT ON INDIVIDUAL SUPERVISORS

In a similar fashion (Table 11.1) we can show in Table 11.2 the possible effects or changes to variables in the 'individual characteristics' box of our main model.

TABLE 11.2

Possible changes for 'individual characteristics' variables

Variables	Possible trends
1. Age and sex	Younger initial promotion to foremen. Growing proportion of female supervisors.
2. Family background	Higher proportion from middle class families with more introverted personalities, greater sensitivity? Wife at work may mean greater domestic responsibilities.
3. Social background and occupational history	Growing variety of career routes. Less first-hand knowledge of worker culture. Less identification with work force. More experience of supervisory roles in other industries.
4. Education and brain knowledge	Greater length of full-time education. More paper qualifications. More experience of adult courses. Greater theoretical knowledge.
5. Technical knowledge	Less first hand practical experience. Greater theoretical knowledge.
6. Skills	Less manual skills. Higher conceptual skills. Possibly more inadequate social skills.
7. Opinions, attitudes, perceptions and expectations on work roles	Less clear-cut expectations. Greater aspirations for promotion. Possible professional role perceived, possibly role is quite unclear.
8. Requirements for work satisfaction	Increased demand for job enrichment. Increased emphasis on technical functions. Greater risk of personal frustration.
9. Ideology and values	Greater variety of values, i.e. range from radical to conservative views. Greater chance of ideological opposition to management.
10. Intellectual capacity	Contradictory trends – low status supervisory roles can only attract drop-outs. Sophisticated organizations may use high calibre supervisors.
11. Personal traits	Indeterminate. Companies could select reliable company men, good as janitors for plant, but could be quite the reverse.
12. Interests	Possible decrease in work as central life interest. Professional role leads to opposite conclusion.
13. Drives and motivation	Increase in significance of role for promotion. Decrease in need for task satisfaction. Increase in need for achievement.
14. Physiological capacity and health	Increased need for stress tolerance. Lower physical demands.

Such hypotheses about the direction of change are clearly dependent on a whole host of other variables, such as the selection policy and practice of the firm, the state of the labour market, the relative attractiveness of the wages and inducements offered by the firm or organization in question, the cultural values and beliefs inherent in the workers' trade groups from which supervisors have been selected, the type of family system, educational system of the society in which the firm operates, etc., etc. We can only make such hypotheses therefore as a guide to possible trends.

CHANGES IN CRITERIA OF EFFECTIVENESS

In Chapter 6, we explored the types of criteria which could be used for determining the effects and performance level of supervisors. Table 5.17 showed a range of such criteria. Table 11.3 reminds us that long-term changes might also be taking place in the relative importance of criteria used to judge effectiveness.

TABLE 11.3

Changes in criteria of effectiveness

Criteria	*Changes*
1. Extra-organizational goals.	Possible growing competitiveness among businesses and less toleration of broken delivery dates may make keeping to production programmes more important for supervisors. Growing trade union power may increase the dysfunctional effects of disputes sparked off by trade union response to supervisory action. In general, this area could be increasing in importance.
2. Organizational goals.	Growing number of managerial control systems might reduce the relative importance of supervisory performance here.
3. Supervisory system objectives.	As seen above, this area could increase or decrease in importance, according to the design of supervisory systems and the degree of autonomy and discretionary tasks preserved.
4. Personal needs and objectives.	This area may well increase in importance significantly on the evidence of current debate and emerging values. (Increased emphasis on personal work needs fulfilment.[10])

It is clearly only possible to make highly tentative hypotheses about such changes, but nevertheless we are concerned here with a vital part of the frame of reference used to view supervision. This book has recorded, in many parts, the inadequacies of the current mode for considering supervision in terms of leadership characteristics, i.e. judging performance by the contribution made to organizational goals. In European society, the survival of traditional occupational norms and perspectives has prevented the total isolation of and concentration on the organizational implications of supervisory performance, as appears to be more common in the United States. If the social and personal effects flowing from supervisory action are becoming more demonstrable at the same time as it becomes easier to see that supervisors can have only limited effects on total organizational group performance, then can we not expect a radical new orientation among supervisors about their role? Could we not expect traditional perspectives based on occupational skill groups and organizational perspectives equally to merge into a new and wider orientation, i.e. one in which supervisors view their role in terms of its significance for society at large and for the personal needs of those interacting with them?

The answer surely is that the opportunity exists but we cannot predict with any certainty that it might be taken up. In terms of Zollschan and Perucci's theory of institutionalization,[11] we have to view the likelihood of social change taking place from an analysis of the processes of socialization, as it is here that 'horizons of expectations and horizons of justification are formed in individuals'.[12] 'Any new articulation of needs and their associated goals as it were "filters through" or, more correctly stated, has to be consistent with individual horizons of expectations and justifications.'[13] These will change if individuals are placed in situations where their experience contradicts their expectations, where they experience subjective dissatisfactions and where problems of cognitive dissonance and normative dissonance are created.

Going back to our own conceptual model, we are again in the area of the definition of *potential* behaviour and performance as discussed in Chapter 6. It was argued there that the possibilities of social change rested with the perception of a 'gap' between actuality and potentiality and with the understanding and acceptance of some strategy of change. We discussed Management by Objectives schemes as managerial attempts to consciously mould and direct such perceptions. The effects of such attempts may not always be as originally planned. We arrived, therefore, in Chapter 8 at the position where four basic strategies were discussed and their appropriateness to various situations. The relevance of such strategies to each situation depends very much on the understanding of the nature of 'individual horizons of expectations and justifications' and on the presence and type of frustration and dissatisfaction experienced by supervisors. Our approach implies starting with the realities of the actual situation, with all its contradictions and dissonance, and then trying to stimulate change by utilizing social science methods to show new 'images' of the actual and the potential to those within the situation.[14] Although we have emphasized a macro and case-by-case approach, and have distrusted simple generalizations about all supervisors, there is no doubt that managers and supervisors, when presented with 'facts' about their own situation, will sooner or later demand some type of world view or overall 'map' in order to place their particular case and in order to determine their required direction of change. However inadequate, some type of measure of choice of direction is necessary.

MAJOR CHOICES OF DIRECTION

There are certainly many dimensions and many choices possible when we consider the range of factors discussed. Two of these, however, stand out as of particular importance. The first has been used several times previously in this book: the degree to which supervisory role systems are structured or programmed. At one end of this continuum, we find a great deal of predictability and a high percentage of routinized discretionary tasks. At the other end, the lack of structure implies low predictability and a high percentage of non-programmed decisions, in which reactions to the perceived pressures of the environment are seen as unique and ever changing. In their discussion of models of organizations, Burns and Stalker[15] used this continuum to distinguish 'mechanistic' and 'organismic' types of system.

The second crucial dimension has not previously been discussed here and that is the degree of *involvement in the work role* actually perceived and experienced by supervisors themselves. A recent study of John G. Maurer's,[16] developed from his thesis prepared at Michigan State University, tries to define this concept and measure the degree of work role involvement for 315 first, second and third level supervisors in eighteen companies. He defines work role involvement

'as the degree to which an individual's work role is important in itself, as well as the extent to which it forms the basis of self-definition, self-evaluation, and success-definition. It is a term used to denote an individual's orientation to the pattern of activities and social interactions in which he engages by virtue of his specific employment position in an economic organization.

'The self-definition aspect of work role involvement refers to the degree to which an individual defines or conceptualizes himself as a person primarily in terms of his work role, as well as the degree to which he wishes others to so define him. Self-evaluation refers to the extent to which an individual evaluates or ranks himself as a person in terms of his work role, as well as the extent of his desire for others to so rank him as a person. Definition of success refers to the degree to which an individual defines success in terms of work role success. Perception of work role as important in itself refers to the degree to which an individual considers his work role as important in its own right, rather than the evaluation of it primarily as a means to the future enactment of more important non-work roles.[17]

Maurer has developed a Likert-type questionnaire for measurement of his concept. His study shows a low but definite correlation between the degree of work role involvement and a number of job characteristics: importance and required amount of esteem, autonomy and self-actualization. He failed to find correlations between a number of job satisfaction variables and the level of work role involvement. The study, in its approach, is open to criticisms, similar to those expressed in Table 4.1, about older questionnaire studies. The concepts developed, on the other hand, appear to be most useful. It combines the approach of Argyris, with his emphasis on the organizational barriers to meaningful work[18] and those of Dubin[19] and Faunce[20] who look for occupational and social-structural reasons for lack of involvement.

Figure 11.2 brings the two dimensions mentioned together to make four

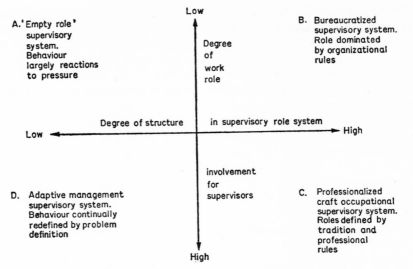

FIGURE 11.2   Four main types of supervisory situation

ideal-type choices for supervisory systems. Logically, we can discuss movement from one type to another and this yields twelve possible choices of direction of change for supervisors.

Of the four positions shown, position B and C are clear enough. They were already shown on a previous diagram, Figure 3.1. Position A is, however, a useful construct, as it describes the situation where there is no structuring of roles by occupations or organizations and where supervisors are simply accepting their roles as sent to them by their role set. Conflict is met here by constant adaption or by 'double-talk'.[21] Situation D implies that supervisors are heavily involved with their work which is constantly changing in its demands and complexities.

Figure 11.3 simply lists possible directions of change for the future.

Starting points		Main direction
A ⎯⎯⎯▶ C ⎯⎯⎯▶ D ⎯⎯⎯▶	B	Bureaucratization. Absorption of supervision into organization role
A ⎯⎯⎯▶ B ⎯⎯⎯▶ D ⎯⎯⎯▶	C	Professionalization. Creation of self-regulating occupational groups
B ⎯⎯⎯▶ C ⎯⎯⎯▶ D ⎯⎯⎯▶	A	Abolition of role content. Gradual loss of distinctive meaning in supervisory role
A ⎯⎯⎯▶ B ⎯⎯⎯▶ C ⎯⎯⎯▶	D	Creation of adaptive problem solving teams. Supervision remains defined by capacity for task completion

FIGURE 11.3   Whither supervision?

We can now briefly review the hypotheses given earlier in the chapter on directions of change in the light of this conceptual scheme. Table 11.4 summarizes this evidence.

TABLE 11.4

Implications of some general changes on the direction of change for supervisors

	Direction of change		
	Possible		Unlikely
1. *Technological*			
Automation. Moves to I	B. A.		C. D. A.
II	A. D.		B. C.
III	C. B.		A. B. C.
IV	D.		A. B . C.
Faster speed of change	A. D.		B. C.
2. *Organizational*			
Greater rationalization (controls)	B. A.		C. D.
Pursuit of more ambitious goals	C. D.		B. A.
Growth in specialization	A. B. C.		D.
MBO systems	Open according to interpretation		
3. *Economic*			
Internationalization of firms	B. A. D.		C.
Growing dependence on govt. planning (unpredictabilities)	A. D.		B. C.
Wider labour markets	C. A.		D. B.
Lower reward differentials	A.		B. C. D.
4. *Social*			
Democratization of rules and practices	A. B. C.		D.
Greater participation of women in labour force	A. B. C.		D.
Growing professionalization of labour force	C. B.		A. D.
Greater educational experience	C. D. A.		B.
Greater importance of leisure	A. B.		A. D. C.
5. *Political*			
Growing trade union power	A. B. C.		D.
Growing inter-dependence of economic on political structure	B. A.		D. C.
Greater shop floor autonomy demanded	A. B. C.		D.
More formalized industrial relations	A. B.		C. D.
6. *Psychological/value systems*			
Greater role stress perceived	A. B.		C. D.
Greater awareness of need for needs fulfilment	C. D.		A. B.
Greater significance placed in promotion	B. A.		C. D.
Less manual/trade skills	B. A.		C. D.
Greater variety of styles	A. C. D.		B.
Totals	A. B. C. D.		A. B. C. D.
	20 16 12 9		6 10 14 17

The scoring is crude and the predictions extremely rough, but on this evidence *the most likely direction of change is towards a situation where supervisors may tend to withdraw from their work roles,* either under the pressure of conflicting colleagues or because of the development of a bureaucratic situation. As we argued above, this is no inevitable trend of history – only the implications of the effects of a number of possible future trends. It merely highlights the importance of viewing the question of supervision as a problem area.

The reappraisal of supervision discussed in this volume is best seen as an attempt to give a new conceptual 'image' to supervisors and their problem. We have tried to widen the usual dimensions of thinking on this subject, whether practical or academic. We have tried to sketch out ways of approaching the study of supervisory problems and show that in attempts to change things, each situation needs diagnosing before following a particular strategy. As academics with practical leanings, we have a number of biases which will be clear to the reader by now. One bias can be admitted to without embarrassment, after a long exposure to contact with supervisors in their work situations: it is difficult not to care about the way that supervisors will be treated and dealt with in the emerging society of the 1970s and 1980s. In this respect, our approach has been twofold – to focus attention on some pessimistic trends (from the viewpoint of supervisors) and secondly, to sketch out ways of trying to bring about changes, both short and long term. In view of the type of trends reviewed, there seems to be some importance in emphasizing that strategies for change should be not only realistically based; they should be genuinely radical in their long-term implications. In a word, much supervisory activity at the moment is defensive. If this type of role is to be given any long-term coherence and significance, then it is extremely important for those concerned with the supervisory problem, to plan for a *major set of changes* to meet personal and social as well as organizational goals. If this book is successful in stimulating firms, employers' associations, unions and professional groups to set out on such a path, then the amount of evidence accumulated within the next five to ten years will no doubt require constant modification of our approach and argument. This seems to be the best criterion for measuring success in this particular endeavour.

Notes and References

1 CROSSMAN, E. R. F. W. (1960). Automation and skill. *Problems of progress in industry*, No. 9, DSIR, HMSO, London.
2 LEAVITT, H. J. & WHISLER, T. L. (1958). Management in the 80's. *Harvard Business Review*, No. 6, pp. 41–8.
3 GRANT, J. W. (1961). Production control system for Letchworth factory. *The Electronic Data Processing Symposium, 1961*, p. 43. Pitman, London.
4, ZALEWSKI, A. (1966). The influence of automation on management. In J.
5 Stieber (Ed.) *Employment problems of automation and advanced technology*. Macmillan, New York.
6 CROSSMAN, E. R. F. W. (1966). Taxonomy of automation: State of the art and prospects. Manpower aspects of automation and technical change. *Final report. European Conference Supplement*, p. 75. OECD, Paris.

7 POPPER, K. R. (1960). *The poverty of historicism.* 2nd ed. Routledge and Kegan Paul, London.

8 WATKINS, J. W. N. (1967). Decision and belief. In R. J. AUDLEY *et al. Decision making.* BBC, London.

9 THURLEY, K. E. (1968). Implications of the use of electronic computers for the future roles and behaviour of industrial and construction supervisors. Computers and Non-Manual Workers Conference. Bimetal. Report.

10 *See* the Herzberg debate. HERZBERG, F. (1966). *Work and the nature of man.* World Pub. Co., Cleveland.

11 ZOLLSCHAN, G. K. & PERUCCI, R. (1964). Social stability and social process. An initial presentation of relevant categories. In ZOLLSCHAN & HIRSCH (eds.), *Explorations in social change,* p. 99. Routledge and Kegan Paul, London.

12 ZOLLSCHAN, G. K. & PERUCCI, R. op. cit., p. 114.

13 ZOLLSCHAN, G. K. & PERUCCI, R. op. cit., p. 115.

14 BOULDING, K. E. (1961). The place of the image in the dynamics of society. In ZOLLSCHAN & HIRSCH (eds.), *Explorations in social change,* p. 5. Routledge and Kegan Paul, London.

15 BURNS, T. & STALKER, G. M. (1961). *The management of innovation.* Tavistock, London.

16 MAURER, J. G. (1969). *Work role involvement of industrial supervisors.* Bureau of Business and Economic Research, Michigan State University, East Lansing.

17 MAURER, J. G. (1969). op cit., p. 26.

18 ARGYRIS, C. (1957). *Personality and organization.* Harper & Row, New York.

19 DUBIN, R. (1963). Industrial workers' world: A study of the 'central' life interests of industrial workers. In E. Smigel (ed.), *Work and leisure.* College and University Press, New Haven, Connecticut, pp. 53–72.

20 FAUNCE, W. A. (1958). Automation and the automobile worker. *Social Problems,* Vol. 6, No. 1.

21 ROETHLISBERGER, F. J. (1945). The foreman: master and victim of double talk. *Harvard Business Review,* Vol. 23, pp. 283–98.

12. *Summary and Conclusion*

WHY IS SUPERVISION A PROBLEM?

In the first chapter of this book we gave a number of examples why managers and training specialists have considered supervision to be a problem requiring action. It was argued that, above all, managers have tended to regard foremen as their representatives on the shop floor. The consequence of this is that when innovations were introduced by specialist and functional management and accepted by senior line management, then foremen were expected to carry them into operation and convince workers of the importance and necessity of such changes. Innovations in personnel management, for example, payment systems, appraisal systems or, more generally, moves towards a more 'democratic' style of management, have followed the same route. The 'problem' for management has been the suspicion and fear that foremen were not actively behind such changes, were not competent to carry them through, and perhaps were passively sabotaging the change programme. The charge that foremen were of 'poor quality' stems directly from this concept of supervision as management representatives.

For academics, the 'problem' of supervision has tended to be seen a little differently. The great majority of studies have been dominated by two concepts, that of (a) leadership and (b) the link role (foremen between management and men). In the first category, many studies have attempted to relate leadership style to work group performance in production terms or job satisfaction indices. In the second category, studies have focused on the marginal nature of the foreman's role. The concept here of the role is not too dissimilar to that of management's. The analysis built on to it tends to emphasize the reasons for role conflict. Both sets of studies have influenced policy towards supervision. The leadership studies provided the framework and justification for supervisory training in many countries, not least in Western Europe. Supervisory training might well have been carried out, however, even if the academic research had not taken place. The actual research studies, and particularly those from the Institute of Social Research at Ann Arbor, Michigan, in the United States, were extremely acceptable to personnel managers and trainers. The studies were useful in that they demonstrated that it made good production and commercial sense to engage in training supervision in more 'democratic' ways of handling personnel, a course of action they already believed in as a first principle. The link role studies on the other hand, have been utilized to explain supervisory behaviour in industrial disputes and the problem of role stress for supervisors. In both cases, studies were focused on the vertical relationships between operatives, supervisors, and management. The 'problem' of supervision arose from the need to determine the most appropriate relationships and behaviour among supervisors so as to provide an optimum amount of job satisfaction (for the workers) and production (in quality or quantity) for the management. Supervision was judged by its effects. If academic research could establish principles to guide supervisory behaviour, then this would be shown in those effects.

For supervisors, themselves, the 'problem' has always been seen in another way altogether. The literature is full of complaints by supervisors that they were not treated as 'members of management'. The charge is persistently made that supervisors were prevented from having sufficient authority or relevant information which would enable them to meet their targets and deal with their problems. If management would only recognize their lack of status and authority and try to equalize their responsibilities and authority then supervision would cease to be a 'problem'. Some younger supervisors might have added that career prospects should also be improved, but the essential complaint was still the question of status. It is only recently in Britain, at least, that supervisors have found that job security also needed to be protected and have increasingly turned to white collar unions to help with this protection.

The main argument in this book started with questioning such concepts of supervision. There were three main reasons for doing this: firstly, the evidence from studies of supervisory roles pointed to the fact that the most critical aspects of such roles were the responses made to contingencies or unanticipated events. The degree to which supervisors had to cope with such contingencies varied greatly. At one extreme, there were programmed situations where tasks could be specified and planned in advance. At the other extreme, supervisors lived in constant crises and handled each problem as it arose. The importance of possessing an adequate supervisory system, however, seemed to be correlated directly with the occurrence of contingencies.

Secondly, the major threat to supervision could be seen as coming not from role pressures set by management and workers, so much as from a threatened collapse of the role as a specific and identifiable set of functions and relationships. The clue to this comes in the way that the terms 'foreman' and 'supervisor' have been used interchangeably in this volume. The traditional term 'foreman' is an occupational title of a role which was largely self-defined according to experience and belief among foremen in the particular trades concerned. The term 'supervisor' is a general organizational title indicating a role defined by that organization. In many industries, this has been a purely negative type of definition, with more and more functions reserved for qualified specialists. The supervisor retains certain functions, for example, the allocation of overtime or the testing of products, but for how long? The spread of the term 'supervisor' indicates the decline of trade consciousness; it does not necessarily mean the development of any new role consciousness. The very identity of supervision is threatened by the many technological, economic, and organizational changes now taking place, which prevent role stability and thus identification.

The third point relates to the reaction of supervisors to this situation. We have noted the demands for higher status, for better promotion prospects and for trade union protection. More important, perhaps, is the reaction in terms of defensive behaviour, the resistance to innovation and the possibilities of withdrawing from involvement in the role. It is surely demonstrable that an active response to contingency and crisis demands a considerable degree of involvement in the role. Problem solving, search processes, the playing for time, the 'cooling' of difficult situations all require self-confidence, adequate skills, and a sense of detachment from pressures which can only be built on role security. If supervisors do not know who they are and what they are doing then it is difficult for them to deal with the unexpected. Demands for job descriptions and definitions mirror anxieties about role identities; if granted, they are unlikely to eliminate such anxieties. This is because if it is extremely difficult to predict the types and nature of supervisory contingencies, then it is also difficult to define roles narrowly in a way that will match perceived reality. The result is that role withdrawal may be the only strategy left which will protect the individual supervisor. Role withdrawal itself can underly the 'symptoms' of the problem which are so often perceived as described above.

The implication of this argument is that supervision, indeed, needs a reappraisal because it has been conceptualized in ways that are highly misleading. Symptoms have been taken for the disease itself. The various perceptions of the 'problem' of supervision are, at best, signs of the emerging crisis of supervision. If our diagnosis is at all correct, then it is necessary to take some action to deal with the possibility that the capacity of organizations to deal with a continual flow of unexpected events may be diminishing, due to decay in supervisory problem-solving activities. There are two general strategies which suggest themselves for this situation: the first is that supervision is reappraised, reformulated, and redeveloped. The second is that existing supervisory systems are allowed to wither away, and problem-solving is either delegated to autonomous work groups or to project teams within the organization. The latter two approaches are certainly theoretical possibilities, but each have their disadvantages. If work-group autonomy is pursued, it follows that a great deal rests on the skills and capacity of workers. Considerable difficulties arise with the integration of decisions taken within the various work groups. The project-team concept has great attractions for contract management, but also requires highly developed skills to integrate the knowledge and views of the specialists within the team. Our approach here is to suggest that the reappraisal of supervision is, at the very least, an alternative which should be seriously considered. The difficulties should not be underestimated, but the possibilities of doing this are clear enough. The various strategies for change described in the book are ways of approaching the task of reappraising and redeveloping supervision.

THE DEVELOPMENT OF SUPERVISION

The importance of the number and types of contingency occurring in supervisory roles has been emphasized. If the causes of such contingencies are explored they could be found in any of a large number of factors affecting the supervisory situation. That is, problems might arise from human error, misconceptions or hostilities; they might be related to failures in machine performance, design faults, variation in component quality; they might be caused by changes of suppliers or customers, economic depression, strikes, actions of competitors, etc. The combination of many factors such as these means that the 'task environment' of supervision is infinitely variable. To take any appropriate action therefore needs careful diagnosis. The process of diagnosis, however, is not a simple question of listing variables and checking their importance. This is because supervision is composed of human actors with beliefs, bias, attitudes, and a variety of individual characteristics. Individuals and groups act and react to situations in different ways. They may or may not be learning from experience so that typical actions may change over time. The results or effects of those actions are also variable according to the situation, the type of individuals concerned. Sometimes actions by supervisors may have critical results and 'cause' a long chain of events to take place. At other times, actions may have little or no effect as their importance is not perceived or the action is futile.

Diagnosis, therefore, requires the building up of a working model of supervisory actions, taking into account the task environment, individual characteristics, and the effects of actions on the work situation and on supervisors themselves.

The purpose of the diagnosis should not be forgotten in grappling with the complexities of creating a realistic model of supervisory action. If supervisory development is to take place, some type of change strategy is necessary. The usefulness of any model is related entirely to its part in and relevance to such a change strategy. Diagnosis is not an end in itself. It follows, therefore, that there are no standard prescriptions for carrying out a diagnosis of a supervisory system. We can list possible key variables; we can discuss the most useful methods for data collection and the most reliable methods of measurement, but this does not tell a manager or researcher how to develop a model of a supervisory system in a particular case. All that can be done here is to suggest the variables of measures which may have to be used and the decisions which may have to be taken.

The root problem of supervisory development is not the nature of the diagnosis needed but the choice of change strategy. Four logical alternatives are suggested in the text. If change is based on *power* imposed either unilaterally or by bargaining, then a typical change strategy involves only the determination of objectives and carrying out changes to achieve those objectives (Method 1). If change is based on a change of *norms*, then typically it is introduced by a set 'package' of methods which are accepted because of the inherent attraction of the design of the package itself. There could be educational or training packages or packages dealing with selection, organization or the 'climate' (sub-culture) of a particular set of groups. In all cases, the strategy begins with the package design and moves to carrying it out. There may or may not be an attempt to evaluate success, but it is usually difficult because objectives have not been specified (Method 2).

The classical analytical approach (Method 3) starts with diagnosis or analysis and moves to the setting of objectives, the design of the change programme, the carrying out of the programme, and the evaluation of results. Fundamentally, this strategy is based on the concept that the collection of new facts will change the various actors' perceptions of reality so that they become more willing to accept and suggest changes. It is therefore called an *empirical/rational* approach.

The last approach is action-centred (Method 4). In this strategy, the problems of supervision as perceived are taken as the starting point and changes are attempted immediately. The strategy is based on the concept that motivation for change requires immediate personal experience in a set of limited experimental changes. When the changes prove difficult and some failures are experienced, there is then a clear necessity perceived to study the situation in more depth. Analysis, therefore, will *follow* action and evaluation of that action. Analysis will then move to objective setting, the design of further changes, and then further action and evaluation. This approach leads to a number of cycles of change, each undergoing close evaluation.

It is comparatively easy to make such distinctions of basic strategy. What is much more difficult is to know when to use each strategy and to what ends. The main suggestion made here is that there are four major objectives for supervisory development and that each of the four approaches might be seen as being most appropriate to a single objective. The objectives can be summarized and described as:

(*a*) Reducing work role autonomy and introducing standard procedures, criteria for decisions and performance, controls over work methods.
(*b*) Reducing conflict between supervisors and specialist managers by building up an integrated management team including shop supervision.
(*c*) Enlarging supervisory roles and increasing the discretionary content of the role.
(*d*) Developing problem-solving capacity among supervision.

It can be argued that power-based strategies are appropriate to (*a*); normative (method-based) change to (*b*); work analysis (empirical/rational) to (*c*); and action-centred strategies to (*d*).

Three limiting conditions must be made to these hypotheses:

1. The objective is always related to the situation, as argued previously. This implies that there *may* be crucial differences in appropriate strategies, even when the direction of change is similar, when the pre-change supervisory systems are very different (for example, between traditional craft supervision and office supervision).
2. The types of strategy are ideal types based on simple criteria. Judging an actual situation will probably lead to combinations of different strategies.
3. There are six 'routes' of change discussed in the text (organization, climate, and technological change; selection, education, and training). Some

strategies are far more appropriate for certain 'routes' than others; for example, normative (method-based) change is especially appropriate to education, training, and climate changes.

PLANNING SUPERVISORY DEVELOPMENT IN A WIDER CONTEXT

Like everything else, it can be highly misleading to concentrate on one problem (supervisory development) and one type of role (supervision) and neglect changes in society and the environment at large. Supervision is undergoing changes as a direct and indirect result of a number of what may appear unmistakable social, economic, and technological trends. We have to recognize the impact on supervision of moves to automation; the growth of further rationalization and specialization; the widening of labour markets and the collapse of traditional differentials; the upsurge of demands for further equality, participation in decision-making for further education, and careers for all employees; the growth of dependence of enterprises on government planning, trade union collaboration, and international business; the increase in the perceived need for individuals to 'fulfil' themselves; and in the prevalence of feelings of anxiety and stress. These trends may appear obvious, but they are at the same time, extremely treacherous to discuss. For society is not homogeneous and the pace of change varies in different areas, classes, and occupations. There is also the fact that social trends are perceived reality and perceptions can and do vary widely. At any given time or place, one trend might appear to be more relevant than another as it touches on particular social experience. All such changes are also not blind forces of history acting on men, but the product of human decision and action, anticipated and unanticipated. This makes it dangerous to adopt the role of social prophet, as social change is neither simple nor self-evident.

Our dilemma here is that although we cannot ignore general social changes, can we be sure enough to identify them accurately? The only way out is to chart the broad choices open and to try to see these choices through the eyes of the various 'actors' in supervisory situations. We have explored traditional concepts and beliefs about supervision already in this chapter. When we come to the future and its possibilities a number of alternatives appear to be perceived. They could be summarized as follows:

1. That supervision will wither away and be replaced by a more 'democratic' economic order in which workers and operatives will be relatively autonomous.
2. That supervision will lose its specific and recognizable characteristics and be replaced by work organizations which are bureaucratic in structure throughout.
3. That supervision will be 'professionalized', forming an occupation with specific tasks which is recognized as competent to regulate its own affairs.
4. That supervision will be transformed into temporary problem-solving teams

which will preserve their 'production' function, but not the status of the members of the team.

The implication of the argument in this book is that although supervisors may aspire to following alternative 3, they are generally in a weak power position to attain this. It is also difficult to believe that the drive to greater participation can be restricted to workers and work groups and that supervision and junior levels of management will be prepared to tolerate it without setting up counter-demands. A probable trend is surely the growth of further unionization of supervision and the development of a much more formalized industrial relations system regulating levels and the content of jobs. This trend can be complementary to the growth of bureaucratic structures. Bureaucracy and the definition of rules regulating jobs and behaviour are, however, highly disfunctional in sharply changing environments. It is possible therefore to envisage 'cyclical' changes or an oscillation between the growth of bureaucratic rules defined by collective bargaining and the erosion and avoidance of rules by supervisors, work groups, and managers anxious to solve problems and get the work out. We come back therefore to our main theme which is the motivation of supervision in increasingly difficult circumstances. For the counter-action against bureaucracy will only occur if supervisors perceive their work role and situation to be significant and important to their life interest. If work-rule involvement decreases sharply due to latent frustrations and the supervisory 'identity crisis', then we could see a growing vicious circle of declining flexibility and adaptability in work organizations, allied with low job satisfaction, little role identification, and growing demarcation problems between white and blue collar unions.

THE IMPORTANCE OF PROCESS EVALUATION

Evaluation is often perceived as a goal for those 'hard' critics, who doubt the value of popular and acceptable solutions and who demand to see the evidence. Economists who study the costs and benefits of industrial training or education often appear to see evaluation in this way. Evaluation research has been discussed in this volume with several studies reported of the 'before and after' variety purporting to measure the effects of change. The philosophy behind such attempts at evaluation is positivist, and the typical results are negative in character.

It will be clear from many passages in this book that the over-riding problem with which we have to deal is the decline of traditional supervisory roles and the effects of this on supervisory motivation and behaviour. Strategies of supervisory development are conceived as attempts to counter this decline. Evaluation of such strategies is not an optional extra to provide legitimacy or a harmless academic game for Ph.D. students. On the contrary, there would appear to be little hope of any 'successful' approach to supervisory development (as measured by its capacity to maintain role identification) unless it is an approach in which evaluation is built into the strategy used. Evaluation in this sense is a continuous attempt to judge the appropriateness of actions. It has to be built on a philosophy in which changing the world is a key premise of understanding the world. Experiment is a rigorous test of actions designed to achieve results and provides an opportunity for reappraisal and further action. It also provides the experience and the understanding for the actors concerned, which is the basis for their work motivation and their role identification. Evaluation of the results of experiments in which all the relevant actors participate need not be a negative affair, even if the changes attempted have not succeeded. It can develop commitment rather than corrode it. It has always to aim at furthering understanding of social process, constraints, and problems.

In practice, this type of process evaluation has to be built on a number of essential ingredients:

1. There has to be an acceptance by all parties to a 'change experiment' that it is useful to identify and document objectives at various points in the experiment as they are perceived by different actors and as they change over time. Inconsistencies in objectives are normal and should not be hidden by rationalizations after the event.
2. There has to be an acceptance by all parties that some systematic data collection is necessary, again on a continuous basis, using a variety of methods. Major data collection exercises are rarely necessary or justifiable.
3. There has to be acceptance of comparison of results between different situations. This means that it is necessary to use some standardized measures (but not all) and that comparisons are facilitated by more open exchanges of information between companies, departments, organizations in general. Clearly, this presents problems, but inter-firm comparisons of accounting data through an external centre provide a model of how this might be done. Anonymity is often an essential condition here.
4. There have to be close working relationships between academics, consultants, managers, supervisors, workers, and trade union representatives if the full pay-off of comparative process evaluation is to be seen. This seems to require change programmes planned by working parties drawing in 'experts' when required and using third parties for investigations at frequent intervals.

If the conditions are met, evaluation of change experiments would mean a set of studies on the effects of various changes, always relating data on behaviour, situation, and effects to changing criteria on objectives. It will be seen that one effect of this approach would be the growth of 'libraries' of case studies of supervisory changes and second order commentaries on these cases by academic researchers. A direct result could be the demonstration that supervision is not a forgotten area and this in itself could stimulate more support for change programmes.

The reappraisal of supervision cannot in reality be completed by writing a book. If reappraisal means 'revaluing the situation' then it has to be done comprehensively, continuously, and in many different ways, by those actors directly concerned with supervision. All that is attempted here is to give a set of charts, suggested instruments, and routes for this reappraisal to take place in earnest.

Standard Interval Sampling with Continuous Observation

In the course of the LSE research project 'Systems of Supervision', undertaken in 1961–63, it was found necessary to develop a classification of supervisory behaviour which could be used by observers who took observations on a systematic basis whilst following after individual foremen. The observations were taken every two minutes on a 'snap reading' basis and they were coded on the spot by the observer. The idea was to provide a detailed analysis of supervisory behaviour patterns, which could be analysed *both* in terms of actual time taken for various functions and also sequentially over the day. The classification used eight dimensions as follows:

A. Place.
B. Main observable activity.
C. Status of contact.
D. Position of contact.
E. Type of communication.
F. Subject of function.
G. Cause of function.
H. Time reference of function.

Diagramatically these dimensions can be seen as linked (Figure A.1).

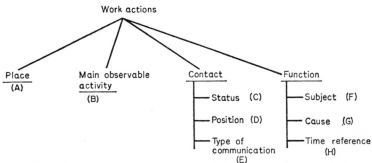

FIGURE A.1   SISCO Classification. Dimensions of supervisory behaviour

The classification is given in detail as it may be useful as a basic list of dimensions and categories. For any particular study extra dimensions may be added.

NOTES ON SISCO CLASSIFICATION

Dimension A: Place

0. *Not seen. Can't be found.* Only used when supervisor is known to be in the factory but can't be found. Followed by 'X' in all other dimensions.
1. *Own work area.* The whole area under the supervisor's direct control (or, in the case of a 'semi-supervisor', that of his immediate superior) except his office or desk.
2. *Own office or desk.* (Or, in the case of a 'semi-supervisor', that of his immediate superior.)
3. *Elsewhere in own department.* Only used when the supervisor is responsible only for part of a production department. Thus, if several charge-hands were responsible each for their own section, 3 would refer to 'other chargehands' sections' including their offices or desks.
4. *Other production departments,* including offices and desks.
5. *Functional departments* (not offices), e.g. stores, maintenance.
6. *Functional departments' offices.*
7. *Higher management offices* (not functional).
8. *Corridor, yard, etc.,* i.e. places of transit. Does not include corridors within production or other departments.
9. *Canteen, toilet, etc.,* includes locker-room, cloakroom, etc.

Dimension B: Main Observable Activity

The activity which the supervisor can be seen to be performing, irrespective of the reason for it.

XX. *Not seen* (after '0' in Dimension A).
YY. *Activity unidentified,* i.e., when the supervisor can be seen to be performing an activity, but it is impossible to tell what it is.
00. *No observable activity.* This includes 'doing nothing', 'thinking', etc. It can also include 'irrelevant' activities such as 'lights cigarette', or 'walks up and down to no purpose'.
01. *Talks* (direct, i.e. not on telephone). This can include 'gesturing' in order to pass on information. It also includes 'listening'. If the supervisor is at the same time performing another activity (inspection, physical work, paper-work) this is preferred to 01, as the details of the communication are in any case recorded in Dimension E. 01 does however take preference over 18 ('walks'), or over 19 ('personal') or 20 ('break') if the conversation is about work. (See 14 in Dimension E).

02. *Telephones.* This includes dialling and waiting for a reply on the telephone, and so does not necessarily imply communication.

03–06. *Paperwork.*

03. *Writes, draws.*

04. *Reads.* Does not include calculating or adding up figures.

05. *Deals with figures* (calculating, adding up, etc.).

06. *Other clerical activities*, e.g. sorting papers, searching in files, sharpening pencil, etc.

07. *Direct supervision*, i.e. standing over or beside a person and watching him work. General supervision of a group, or of a person from a distance, is classified as 00 or 18, though the function (e.g. discipline, welfare method of working) is recorded on Dimension F.

08–10. *Inspection.*

08. *Inspects product not on machine.*

09. *Inspects product under process*, e.g. automatic machine in operation. Used when product and machine are being watched together. To be distinguished from 07 where the operator and his actions are the object of attention.

10. *Inspects machine* (when not in operation), *plant, tools, building, etc.*

11–16. *Physical work.*

11. *Carry large object, pull or push trolley, etc.* Only to be used when physical effort is involved, i.e. not including carrying small components or tools, paper, etc., which is classified as 'walking'.

12. *Perform operation (not on machine).*

13. *Perform operation on machine.*

14. *Adjust or repair machine or tools.*

15. *Clean or tidy up* (apart from tidying papers, which is 06).

16. *Other types of physical work.*

17. *Handling or sorting small objects* when no physical effort is involved.

18. *Walks* or otherwise moves from one place to another. Any other activity (01–17) takes priority over 18.

19. *Personal*, i.e. goes to the toilet, washes hands, changes clothing, etc. This is used (with 9 in Dimension A and X in other Dimensions) if the supervisor has left the observer to go to toilet.

20. *Break.* This is used during official break-times (if these are recorded at all) and at any other time when the supervisor deliberately takes time off work to eat, drink, smoke, read newspapers, etc. Followed by X in Dimensions C–H.

21. *Talks to observer* or performs any other activity caused solely by the observer's presence. Followed by X in Dimensions C–H.

Note on Dimension C–D. Contact. These two Dimensions together refer to the position within the firm of the person or persons in contact with the supervisor. The definition of a contact is that a person is either in *communication with* the supervisor (directly or on the telephone) – in which case the type of communication must be recorded in Dimension E – or is engaged in a *joint activity* with him, e.g. inspecting the same article, repairing a machine, walking together. *Physical proximity does not constitute contact.* Thus if the supervisor is in a large group of people but is talking or listening to one of them alone, only that person is recorded. If, however, the supervisor is in contact equally with more than one person, then 2 or 3 (not more than 3) separate entries may be made in Dimensions C and D.

Dimension C: Status of Contact

The exact meaning of categories within this Dimension has to be worked out in terms of the individual firm. In the production departments under study, 1 is the operative level, and 2, 3, etc., are the next levels above this. Personnel in functional departments are given the same number as persons of the same status in production departments.

X. *Not seen, etc.* Used after 0 in Dimension A or 19, 20, 21 in Dimension B. Always followed by X in Dimensions D–H.
Y. *Not known.* Used when the contactee's status-level is not known, or when the concept is meaningless, i.e. visitors.
0. *No contact.* Always with 00 in Dimension D.
1. Operative level.
2. Operative with special responsibility (level D supervisor).
3. Semi-supervisor (level C supervisor).
4. First-line supervisor (level B supervisor).
5. Second-line supervisor (level B+ or A supervisor).
6. First-line manager (level A or A+ supervisor).
7. Second-line manager.
8. Third-line manager or above.
9. Director of Company.

Dimension D: Position of Contact

This records the horizontal position of the contact in relation to the supervisor, while Dimension C records the vertical position.

XX. As in Dimension C.
YY. If the contact's position is unknown.
00. *No contact.* Always with 0 in Dimension C.
01. *In direct line of command*, either directly above or directly below the supervisor himself (depending on the classification in Dimension C). Thus, for a supervisor at status-level 4, contacts with 'immediate superior' are recorded as 5–01, and contacts with 'immediate subordinate' as 3–01. An exception is clerical staff within the department, who are classified as 15.
2. *Other line in own department.* Only used when the supervisor is only in charge of part of the department (see 3 in Dimension A).

3. *Other production department* (corresponding to 4 in Dimension A).

04–15. *Functional departments.* The exact references of these categories will vary with the individual firm.

16. *Visitors* and other persons not employed by the Company.

17. *Union official* (e.g. shop steward) when contacted in that capacity rather than as operatives, etc.

Dimension E: Type of Communication

XX. As in Dimension C (and therefore including communications during break or personal time, or while talking to observer).

YY. If the type of communication is unidentified.

00. Not in communication, i.e. neither talking or listening.

01–03. *Linking,* i.e. passing on information, instructions or requests which have already been received from a third person.

01. *Linking upwards,* i.e. to superiors in the direct line of command.

02. *Linking downwards,* i.e. to subordinates in the direct line of command.

03. *Linking in other directions,* i.e. to someone who is not '01' in Dimension D.

04. *Teaching* (how to do something).

05. *Instructing, ordering or requesting* to do something (when this is not a 'link').

06. *Informing* that something has happened or will happen (when this is not a 'link').

07. *Is taught* (reverse to 04).

08. *Is instructed or requested* (reverse to 05).

09. *Is informed* (reverse to 06).

10. *Reprimands or praises.*

11. *Is reprimanded or praised.*

12. *Other shop conversations,* i.e. general discussion on shop matters, with no elements of linking, teaching, instructing or informing.

13. *Listening to others talking* (on shop matters). This does not include all listening (which may be categorized as 07, 08, 09, 11 or 12) but only cases when the supervisor is a 'third person' listening to others talking about matters relevant to the supervisor's own job. If the matter is not relevant to the supervisor's own job and he is not 'really listening', then he is 'not in communication' (00).

14. *Personal conversation.* This covers all communication, of whatever type, about matters not relevant to the supervisor's job or to the affairs of the Company. All other categories (01–13, 15) therefore refer only to 'shop' conversation.

15. *Requests information or instructions* (about work).

Note on Dimensions F–H: Function

These Dimensions are all aspects of the 'function' which the supervisor is performing. If there is 'no function' – that is, if the supervisor is inactive, or is acting for reasons unconnected with his work – then 0 or 00 is recorded on all three Dimensions. (This includes 'personal conversation' – 14 on Dimension E.) If however he is *waiting* to perform a function, *walking* in order to perform it, or *thinking* about a problem, then the details of the function should as far as possible be recorded. If it is impossible to tell what is uppermost in his mind, 'YY' should be used rather than '00'.

Dimension F: Subject of Function

XX. As in Dimension C.

YY. Subject unidentified.

00. No function (see above).

01. *Programming production* – the *order* of production and the *types* to be produced, rather than quantity (04 or 06).

02. *Allocation* of work to particular operatives or machines (both the planning and execution of this).

03. *Physical transfer* of work between operatives or machines (i.e. either actually transferring the product or arranging for its transfer).

04. *Quantity of raw materials or components,* i.e. the availability of the required amount of products or parts of products prior to entering the section or department.

05. *Quality of raw materials or components.* Includes inspecion of the product before the start of operations in the supervisor's section; also dealing with quality problems caused by variations in other departments or in the components entering the firm.

06. *Quantity of product produced – speed of work.* Includes all planning, programming or reporting of the *numbers* produced in a given time.

07. *Quality of product under process.* Inspection of product during or between operations; quality problems arising before the end of operations in the section.

08. *Quality of finished product.* Final inspection of product; quality problems arising after the end of operations in the department.

09. *Quantity of machines, plant, tools, etc.* Acquiring or planning for tools or machines; problems caused by shortages of these.

10. *Quality of machine, plant, tools, etc.* Dealing with the *behaviour* of machines, etc. (i.e. given the method, how well do they perform it?) rather than with the method of operation itself (12 or 13). Problems caused by machine breakdowns or variations.

11. *Quantity of labour force,* i.e. numbers of people, either at operative or at other levels. Recording of absentees, etc. Problems caused by shortage or excess of labour.

12. *Method of working a particular operation.* Changes or alterations in method. Supervising or inspecting in order to watch method. Problems caused by variations in method of working.

13. *Layout and overall method,* in the department or section as a whole.

Changes in this, problems caused by variations. General way in which department is run or organized. Housekeeping.

14. *Actual operation.* Only used when the supervisor is doing work which in his section would normally be done by an operative.

15. *Recording or reporting production in general,* i.e. recording or reporting of routine production for its own sake.

16. *Production costs.* Calculation of costs, or of any factor (e.g. amount of scrap) whose importance is rated in terms of cost to the Company. Discussion of costs.

17. *Filing and office procedures,* for their own sake. Not to be used when for example, the supervisor is getting out files in order to perform some other function.

18. *Formal consultation,* for its own sake, i.e. discussion of consultation procedure, or holding meetings for the sake of consultation rather than to discuss a specific problem.

19. *Selection and promotion* at all levels. Holding interviews, etc.; dealing with and discussion of procedures. Problems on selection and promotion.

20. *Training,* at all levels. Discussion of procedures; arranging for training courses; introducing new operative. (Training an operative on a specific operation would be coded rather as 12 (method) with 04 (teach) in Dimension E.).

21. *Welfare and working conditions.* Personnel matters not included in 11, 19, 20, 22, 23, and 24.

22. *Remuneration.* Wages, salaries, bonuses, piecework values, etc.

23. *Discipline,* in the widest sense, i.e. all matters concerned with the behaviour at work (apart from method of working) of all personnel at all levels.

24. *Safety: accidents.*

25. *Design and specification.* Dealing with, planning for or discussing the specification of a product as distinct from the method of operation. Discussion of or handling blueprints.

Dimension G: Cause of Function

X. As in Dimension C.

Y. Cause of function unidentified.

0. No function (as in F).

1. *Routine function,* i.e. a function which is regularly performed, or which had been planned for on this occasion – 'foreseen' behaviour.

2–9. *Contingencies,* i.e. behaviour caused by unforeseen events.

2. Problem handed to the supervisor 'from above', i.e. by his superior or by functional departments. (3–9 are mainly problems coming to the supervisor 'from below', i.e. from variations in the process itself or in operatives' behaviour.)

3. Problem caused by minor variation in behaviour of men, machines or materials, depending on the entry in Dimension F. For instance, 05–3

would mean variation in the quality or raw materials; 23–3 would mean minor disciplinary problems.

4. Problem caused by major variation resulting in 'stoppage', e.g. machine breakdown, cessation of a particular line of work, operative's absence from work.
5. Problems caused by shortage of men, machines or materials (when shortages or excesses rather than, for instance, machine breakdown is the main cause).
6. Problem caused by new methods, improvements, changes in layout, new lines or products, or other planned changes which result in unforeseen problems.
7. Problem caused by misunderstandings and failures in communication between personnel at any level.
8. Problem caused by shortage of time (when this rather than machine break-down, shortage of materials, absenteeism, etc., is the main cause).
9. Problem caused by dispute with union or operatives or between other personnel.

Dimension H: Time Reference of Function

The time reference does not remain static throughout the whole of a problem or function, and it should be recorded as far as possible by 'snap observations', i.e. the time reference which is uppermost at the particular moment.

X. As in Dimension C.
Y. Time reference unidentified.
0. No function (as in F).
1. *Investigation of or reporting on the past.*
2. *Dealing with present activity* without reference to future or past; or activity with no specific time reference, e.g. discussion of a permanent situation.
3–5 *Planning for the future.* The category which is used depends on the length of time over which the decisions being made will have effect.
3. *Planning for short-term future,* i.e. not more than one working day ahead.
4. *Planning for the mid-term future,* i.e. not more than one working week ahead.
5. *Planning for the long-term future,* i.e. more than one working week ahead.

Author Index

Subject Index

Page in *italics* indicates that the title-word is defined in that page.

Supervision : A Reappraisal

WITHDRAWN